Cultivating the Heart
of the Worship Leader

TO KNOW
YOU
MORE

ANDY PARK

IVP Books

An imprint of InterVarsity Press
Downers Grove, Illinois

InterVarsity Press
P.O. Box 1400, Downers Grove, IL 60515-1426
World Wide Web: www.ivpress.com
E-mail: email@ivpress.com

InterVarsity Press® is the book-publishing division of InterVarsity Christian Fellowship/USA® , a movement of students and faculty active on campus at hundreds of universities, colleges and schools of nursing in the United States of America, and a member movement of the International Fellowship of Evangelical Students. For information about local and regional activities, write Public Relations Dept., InterVarsity Christian Fellowship/ USA, 6400 Schroeder Rd., P.O. Box 7895, Madison, WI 53707-7895, or visit the IVCF website at <www.intervarsity.org>*.*

All Scripture quotations, unless otherwise indicated, are taken from the Holy Bible, New International Version®. NIV®. *Copyright* ©*1973, 1978, 1984 by International Bible Society. Used by permission of Zondervan Publishing House. All rights reserved.*

The excerpt from "Music's Surprising Power to Heal" is reprinted with permission from Reader's Digest, *August 1992. Copyright © 1992 by The Reader's Digest Assn., Inc.*

Permission granted for other excerpts can be found on page 266.

Cover design: UDG/Designworks
Photograph of hand: Stephen Gardner

ISBN 978-0-8308-3221-7 (paper ed.)

Printed in the United States of America ∞

Library of Congress Cataloging-in-Publication Data

Park, Andy, 1957-
 To know you more: cultivating the heart of the worship leader /
 Andy Park
  p. cm.
 Includes bibliographical references and index.
 ISBN 0-8308-2320-4 (hardcover: alk. paper)—ISBN 0-8308-3221-1
 (pbk.: alk paper)
 1. Public worship. I. Title
 BV15.P37 2004
 264—dc22

                                                                                    2004011524

P	19	18	17	16	15	14	13	12	11	10	9	8	7	6	5	4	3	2
Y	24	23	22	21	20	19	18	17	16	15	14	13	12	11	10	09		

*To worship leaders, pastors and others
who serve faithfully in the local church
year after year with a passion
to honor and love the Lord*

For more information on Andy Park
please visit <www.andypark.ca>

CONTENTS

Acknowledgments

This book is the product of many years of worshiping, leading and being a pastor. Along the way I've received lots of great teaching and read many good books that have inspired me and informed my journey of knowing God.

So, thanks to the different pastors under whom I've served—most notably, Kenn Gulliksen, John Wimber and Gary Best. Much of your teaching is woven into the fabric of my life, which in turn has provided much of the foundation for this book. There are so many other teachers and authors who have influenced me—thanks.

I am very grateful to my wife, Linda, for her insightful editorial comments and encouragement to go ahead with this project. And thanks for letting me sequester myself away to write amidst a very busy household.

Thanks to so many friends who have encouraged me along the way—especially Mac and Louise Jardine and John and Julie Bogart—for believing in me as a writer and encouraging me to go for it. Thanks to you who made it your project to pray for me along the way.

Finally, thanks to Cindy Bunch, my editor, for seeing the value of this book as a tool for equipping the church. Thanks for making it a better book by your editorial input.

Thank you, Lord, for the privilege of working for you in this way and for wisdom and grace. It's all a gift from you.

Introduction

God captured my heart when I was a seventeen-year-old freshman in university. Divine revelation crashed in on me. I saw that God was much bigger than I had imagined—he was much more holy, loving and *real* than I had imagined. As a child I had believed that God was out there . . . somewhere. I knew that Jesus once lived on earth and that his sacrifice was the basis of my salvation. But what difference did that make for daily life? Nobody had ever mentioned the possibility that I could be intimately acquainted with God. I thought he left us on earth to make good moral choices and pursue "the good life."

I remember the first time I attended a Vineyard worship service in 1976. It was in a Vineyard church pastored by Kenn Gulliksen in Reseda, California. Many of the young people in this church were converted through the Jesus movement of the 1960s and early 1970s. As the worship began, immediately I could see that people were *engaged* with God. It was more than songs, more than emotion. It was a group of people meeting with God; they were seeking him and *finding* him. The people weren't just looking into a hymnbook; they were looking into God's face. He was responding to them. He was *there*. I was captivated by this experience. I immediately began to explore this new form of worship. Little did I know that my life's work would be all about worship.

The spiritual renewal I received through these simple songs is an experience shared by many thousands of Christians the world over. There has been a reformation of church music in evangelical and charismatic churches around the world in the last thirty years. Beginning with the Jesus movement in the late 1960s, a genre of rock worship music has swept the world and become a common language for hundreds of denominations.

The English language and rock music are two international languages that have paved the way for this genre of worship music to be popular just about anywhere. All over the world, people sing worship songs that have sprung from this new stream of worship.

I've been leading worship for twenty-six years in churches that are part of the Vineyard Christian Fellowship—one of the many expressions of what God is doing in worship in the world today. I've had the privilege of leading worship in many countries and seeing times of renewal sweep across continents.

Worship is one of the most notable things about the Vineyard movement, which was born out of a desperate cry for more of Jesus. After years of being worn down by the rigors of church ministry, John and Carol Wimber began a simple prayer meeting in their home. For the first months, all they could do was worship and weep. God was drawing near to them with his tender love. Out of this visitation of God, a vision for worship was birthed, which spread like wildfire.

My intention in this book is not to exalt the Vineyard or to write exclusively to Vineyard people. I refer to many experiences in the Vineyard simply because it is the tribe to which I belong. God is moving powerfully through many other streams of worship in the world today. I am enriched by the great songs and passion for the Lord that I see in other worship movements. The strengths of other movements complement the strengths of Vineyard worship.

I am also a great fan of many of the classic hymns of the church. I often include a hymn in my worship sets—first, because there are so many powerful hymns that cause the heart to swell with worship. Second, it's a way of identifying with the historic church—many hymns dating as far back as the sixteenth-century Reformation are relevant for worshipers of all ages today. Classics such as "All Hail the Power of Jesus' Name" and "How Great Thou Art" stand on their own as great songs of worship.

I agree with the viewpoint of Eddie Gibbs, professor of church growth at Fuller Theological Seminary, who dislikes the term "contemporary worship." He argues that *any* genre of music that can stir the heart of a worshiper should be considered *contemporary*. Most of the chapters in this book apply to church musicians who favor *any kind of music,* whether classical, rock or somewhere between the two.

My purpose in writing this book is to give worship leaders advice that will enable them to survive and thrive in the long haul. Second, I think the book will be helpful to pastors and leaders who work with worship leaders. The guidelines, cautions and encouragement I share are the product of twenty-six years of worship leading. I have faced all kinds of challenges in being a worship leader, assistant pastor and senior pastor in seven different Vineyard churches. I have been involved in planting three different churches and have led worship at small, medium and large churches.

I've learned through the years that becoming a worship leader involves far more than developing a set of skills—it's all about developing a life in God. First and foremost, it's about loving God. The fire of worship, which is stoked by love for God, requires constant rekindling through a lifetime. Worship is also about loving your family, the church, and it's about serving the poor.

Worship is not about pursuing a successful career in worship leading, though a small percentage of worship leaders make a career of it. For the vast majority, worship leading is a volunteer pursuit done alongside of a secular job.

Because the phenomenon of the modern worship leader and worship band is a key element in churches today, worship leaders have a lot of influence and a lot of visibility. Inherent in this privilege is a set of challenges that every aspiring worship leader must wrestle with. We are not just music leaders; we are role models too. We influence the culture of our churches.

To address those issues, the first section of the book deals with the heart and lifestyle of worship. Through telling my own story—crucial turning points, mistakes I've made and hard lessons I've learned—I begin with the subject of integrity. Section one covers the essential issues of knowing God and developing godly character through the trials of life and ministry. A key theme in my life has been finding security in God's love rather than in human approval. This is a foundation stone for every worship leader.

The second section offers an understanding about how worship leaders fit into the big picture of the church. It's about the spiritual roles and gifts of a worship leader and the priority of working with people—band members, other worship leaders and pastors. To excel in worship leading requires an understanding of the church community and a willingness to be part of a team.

The third section is about the practical duties of the worship leader—leading worship sets, rehearsing a musical band, writing songs and developing other worship leaders.

I haven't set out to write a book that thoroughly lays out a systematic theology of worship, nor have I attempted to cover the gamut of artistic worship expressions such as dance, video and drama. My philosophy and theology of worship are expressed through the stories and practices that I espouse. But it is more than theology and theory; it comes out of my personal relationship with God and my practices of worship. Many essential biblical values of worship are woven into the stories and examples.

May God bless you as you pursue him and share your gifts of worship.

1

DIVING INTO WORSHIP MINISTRY

*I have seen you in your sanctuary and gazed upon your
power and glory. Your unfailing love is better to me
than life itself; how I praise you!*

PSALM 63:2-3

BECOMING A WORSHIP LEADER isn't about the pursuit of a ministry or a career; it's about the pursuit of a person. Out of knowing God, we make him known—we are first worshipers and then worship leaders. That kind of devotion is where my journey as a worshiper began. The most visible part of my worship is my songs. But the songs are simply a byproduct of a life-giving relationship with God. Worship music came out of me because I dove headlong into the wonderful, all-consuming pursuit of the greatest treasure in the universe—Jesus.

The Pursuit of a Person
When I was seventeen, Jesus surprised me with something I wasn't looking for—intimate knowledge of the most loving person in the uni-

verse—himself. A couple months before beginning my university studies, I hastily pulled a few books off the shelf as I was leaving for a family vacation. One of the books was about Jesus' Sermon on the Mount. As I read that book, God turned the lights on. I realized there was far more to the Christian experience than I had ever imagined—a person could know God, his personality and his direct influence in daily life.

As a high school student, I had attended church pretty regularly with my family. I knew the basic gospel story that Jesus died for my sins. I was in many ways a well-adjusted, responsible teenager. But I was restless and frustrated. I wasn't satisfied with my life. In high school, I was never among the "in" crowd. I hadn't made it big in sports, and I hadn't found the ideal girlfriend. In hindsight I can see that God didn't allow me to find fulfillment in the things of this world so that I would have a hunger for something deeper.

Then God did something miraculous. He revealed himself to me. He made his light shine in my heart to give me "the light of the knowledge of the glory of God in the face of Christ" (2 Cor 4:6). All of a sudden I was plugged in. For the first time, I *felt loved* by God.

Before this turning point, I only knew about Jesus as the virtuous God-man who shed his blood for me. I thought Christianity was about staying out of trouble and keeping the golden rule. Now I knew God as a real presence, a person who came into my bedroom to talk to me and breathe life into me. Now he was the object of my deepest passion.

As I began my freshman year at UCLA, I took a few stumbling steps toward Christian fellowship. Then the lights really started to turn on. As I got a taste of God, he gave me a hunger to know him more. The door was open a crack and a brilliant light was shining through.

I was bursting with zeal for God. Music was one way I expressed my love for God. I also got involved in other areas of ministry. In my first year of college I taught Sunday school, led worship in a small group and taught Bible studies for a youth group. But music was my strength, so I naturally followed that path.

I had taken many years of music lessons, but was mainly a bedroom guitarist. I majored in playing, not singing. As a little boy I dreaded the command performances in front of family and friends. By the time I was in high school, I ventured out to do a little singing in church, but it wasn't as a soloist.

I clearly remember the first time I sang one of my songs for the college class at Bel Air Presbyterian Church, where I attended for a year. I wasn't a natural performer—I was so nervous I could barely croak out the words, and I trembled as I struggled through the song. But as I sang and led worship in various church meetings, gradually my voice and confidence grew stronger.

Before my conversion, I had never written songs. After meeting the Lord, I began to write songs almost immediately. I could tell that God's blessing was on my songwriting—not because the songs were great, but because the fellowship of the Holy Spirit was often strongly with me. Those honeymoon days of knowing God were a sweet time in my life, where he graciously let me catch a glimpse of how wonderful he is.

Surrounded by other zealous Christians, mostly college students, we learned to worship together—in home groups, in informal gatherings and on Sundays. We were filled with a sense of awe for God; we were enthralled with him and excited about discovering this new jewel of knowing and worshiping God.

I started leading worship in a small group at the West Los Angeles Vineyard, a church pastored by Kenn Gulliksen, and from which the first handful of Vineyard churches grew.[1] I began attending the church when it met in the Los Angeles suburb of Reseda, just a few miles from my childhood home in Woodland Hills. It was an exciting place to grow as a young Christian. I was mesmerized by Kenn's teaching and by the worship at church. Occasionally Keith Green, then an elder at the church, would minister in music, and his passion for the Lord was powerful and contagious.

The first time I attended this church, I was amazed by the passion of the people as they poured out their worship. They weren't just reciting words, they were experiencing God. It wasn't highly emotional, but

God was there and the church *knew it*. It was as if they could touch him and taste his presence. I realized this was for me.

A few years after attending the West Los Angeles Vineyard, I became an intern pastor for a year. During my internship, I did some counseling, teaching in small groups and lots of worship leading. It was during this time that I first came in contact with John Wimber. We visited Calvary Chapel of Yorba Linda, where John was the pastor. We attended a few Sunday night worship services in the gymnasium at Canyon High School and got a taste of God's powerful visitation in those worship and ministry times. John also came to the West Los Angeles area to conduct some healing meetings. Learning to minister in the gifts of the Holy Spirit was part of the package of what God was doing in our lives.

Like all other small-group worship leaders, I learned songs one at a time and figured out how to lead worship by a process of trial and error. For me, learning to lead worship was a natural byproduct of learning to worship. The most effective trait of a worship leader is a deep love for God and a willingness to express it. Having some musical ability is essential, but a multitude of musical errors are covered by a burning passion for God.

After a year or two of leading worship in small groups, I began leading worship with other musicians in larger gatherings. I had no training in leading a band; I just started doing it. At first the groups consisted of piano, bass and guitar. I had a minimal understanding of arranging music for a band. All we did was learn the words and chords and start playing! In those days, there was no such thing as a worship seminar. I slowly learned by watching people lead and listening to worship music—on vinyl and cassette.

In 1978 I was invited to lead worship on Sunday mornings at the West Los Angeles Vineyard. That was quite an experience—I was twenty years old and was leading worship in a large church. My team consisted of me on the guitar and two other singers. Worship bands hadn't yet become commonplace. We received lots of encouraging words from church members who felt that God was really blessing our worship leading.

But the joy ended several months later when we were informed that we didn't have the musical skill to be leading on Sunday mornings. A big factor in this decision was the influence of the professional musicians attending our church who wanted to see a higher level of expertise and a full band on Sundays. Though I had some natural talent, I was young and musically undeveloped. Sometimes our vocals were off-pitch. I didn't have the experience and equity with people to recruit a band to back me up. So the pastor decided to let the professionals have a go at it and develop a band.

This was the first of many disappointing experiences that helped develop godly character in me. Despite this setback, I stayed with the church and served in other capacities. If I had left the church in anger, I would have short-circuited an important lesson that God was teaching me—to humble myself even when I don't fully agree with or understand a pastoral decision.

Around 1980 I did my first musical recording, which included worship and message songs exhorting the church toward active participation in Christian mission. I wrote another song based on Psalm 67: "God be gracious unto us and bless us and cause his face to shine on us, that your way may be known on the earth, your salvation among all nations . . . let the peoples praise you, oh God, let all the people praise you."[2] The combination of worship and mission became a major theme in my life that has stuck with me through the years.

I really had no idea how to record an album, but I jumped into it with both feet. Thankfully, the studio engineer was very helpful and covered for much of my ignorance. When this project was over, I toured a bit, giving concerts in Southern California and up the West Coast into Oregon and Washington.

Hoping to get a big break as a young songwriter-performer, I sent my songs to Christian record companies. I did get a few nibbles, but nothing ever materialized. Before long I gave up the pursuit of a record deal and focused on local church ministry. I went through some periods of deep discouragement as I waited for some clear direction for my life. There was nothing I could do to create the right opportunities for a music ministry of wider scope and impact. But through the waiting, God was testing me and forming me.

After graduating from university, I worked as a teacher's aid in a few different elementary schools. Instead of forging my way into a career that promised good pay and a chance to climb the corporate ladder, I took the low road, working part-time jobs to survive while I trained in pastoral and worship ministry. Often I had barely enough money to keep the bills paid.

While working in these elementary schools, I would escape on my lunch breaks to a piano—sometimes in an auditorium, sometimes in a secluded storage room—where I would worship. These brief interludes of worship were an oasis to me. God soothed the pain of being in a very humble situation. In my brokenness and desperation for God, I found him through worship.

In the midst of this period of waiting for a door of opportunity to open, God gave me one of the few open-eyed visions I've ever had. Sitting on my bed during a time of prayer, I saw on the wall a simple but clear vision of Jesus on the cross in a hazy white hue. For several minutes I looked at Jesus, and I knew God was telling me that he saw my pain and he was with me. He knew I was bearing a cross, and I was following his example by sharing in the fellowship of his sufferings. I was surrendering myself.

I wrote a song, "I Am His," that expressed my surrender to God:

I am my beloved's own, I am his, I am his
I am my beloved's own, I am his, I am his
I am his, I am not my own
I've been bought with a price,
His precious blood
I will glorify the Lord in my body for I am his.
My beloved is my own, he is mine, he is mine.[3]

Santa Barbara
In 1983, while driving down the freeway toward the desert, God spoke to me about moving to Santa Barbara to help with a young Vineyard

church, even though I had never met Jack Little, the pastor of that church. After meeting him, Linda and I decided to join him. We moved to Santa Barbara after almost eight years in two Vineyards in the Los Angeles area. We were excited to be moving out of the big city and into a new adventure in church growth.

I wasn't crazy about the way the Sunday morning worship leaders at the Santa Barbara Vineyard led worship. Some of the songs seemed shallow to me. I had been leading worship for about seven years, and I felt I knew what worship was all about. At the ripe old age of twenty-five, I was angrily stomping around the back of the church as they led worship. I thought I knew how worship should be led, so I was critical of anybody who did differently.

When we first moved to Santa Barbara, the pastor invited me to lead worship in a weekly evening service. But for some reason, I felt I should get preferential treatment. I wanted to run the show. Looking back, I guess I thought I had it all together. I didn't understand Jack's respect for the leaders who had served for years before me. He wisely didn't want to bring about too much change too quickly. So it was my turn to wait and serve in other capacities. This was one of my many opportunities to get rid of some selfish pride.

However, functioning as an intern pastor, I received valuable ministry experience in the next year. But would it lead to a career in ministry? I didn't know. Though I was willing to do anything God wanted, no doors of opportunity were opening up for me.

Feeling anxious about my future, I felt it was time for a decision. Though I had applied to a graduate school program and was accepted, I *knew* it wasn't the right thing to do, so I passed it by. I was capable of pursuing lots of different paths in life, but I wanted to choose the best path. In academics I was a high achiever, but learning in the school of the Spirit involves working hard and also waiting. God's primary assignment for me in that season of my life was to simply trust him and patiently serve where he had placed me.

Many times I felt like taking matters into my own hands. I had worked hard for my college degree. I was tired of doing menial jobs while training for a ministry that I might never have! It was humbling for me to bide my time as an intern pastor while Linda brought home the bacon through her job as a registered nurse. Meanwhile God continued to purge me of impure motives for ministry. I watched as other pastors-in-training were given salaried positions. Rejoicing in the success of others isn't easy when you feel like you're at the bottom of the heap—a lesson that God taught me over and over again.

Once I was invited to lead worship at a conference in Sweden. While we were waiting at the airport for our baggage to arrive, I struck up a conversation with a young couple. The girl told me she would be leading the worship that week. I thought, *What? You've got to be kidding!* The pastor had asked *me* to lead the worship.

It so happened that just then I was listening to a worship song on a portable cassette player—the words were about humbling oneself before the Lord. As it turned out, we both led some worship that week— another opportunity to learn about being a servant, not the center of attention.

Being content while others receive more opportunities and favor from people and God has to be one of the top ten most important issues for a worship leader. Over and over again, I've had to repent of jealousy and criticism of other worship leaders and pastors.

Heading North

In 1984 Linda and I headed north on a concert tour. Before we left, God whispered to me that this tour would lead to something more than just a six-week trip. One of our concert engagements was in Canada, hosted by Gary Best. Half a year later, Gary spearheaded planting the first Canadian Vineyard church and invited us to join the team. Though Linda and I sensed God's stamp of approval on this opportunity, it was a big step of faith for us to head north to a foreign country.

When Linda and I left California, we were leaving behind all that was familiar—family, friends and country—to join a young church in a foreign country. It wasn't a *huge* leap since it was a First World country with a culture very similar to our own. But I can remember thinking as I drove up Interstate 5 in the rented moving van, *What in the world are we doing? We barely know these people. How do we know what will be happening a few months from now?* We *didn't* know. God was requiring us to trust him.

We didn't have any guarantee that the Langley Vineyard would really make it. We were part of a faith-risk adventure. I had lots of friends who had valiantly launched out to plant a church, only to see their church-planting teams fall to pieces. I didn't want to leave home and family to be a part of that kind of fiasco.

As it turned out, the Langley Vineyard grew quickly and became a flagship church in western Canada. The time of waiting for a ministry opportunity was over. As the church grew, we grew with it.

Starting a new job is difficult, and this was no exception. Training and pastoring small-group worship leaders and worship team members was a new challenge. Fitting into a new team of leaders was a challenge. Being a typical young male, who was eager to prove himself, I drove myself pretty hard. I was trying intensely to succeed in my new staff position. My body reacted to the high stress—I had bad headaches almost every day for two years. Spiritual warfare figured into this equation as well—God was blessing and Satan resisting this church that would plant many churches and become a hub for the Vineyard movement in Canada.

Beginning in 1985 I was invited to lead worship at some of John Wimber's equipping conferences in the United States, Canada and other countries. All of a sudden I was launched into a much greater level of visibility, which carried with it a spiritual test. John Wimber used to say that tough times are not the greatest test for a leader—the times of exaltation and success are. The big question is, "What are you going to do when everything is going right?" One of my favorite proverbs says, "The crucible for silver and the furnace for gold, but man is tested by the praise he receives" (Prov 27:21).

After doing several worship recordings in the years following, I received many invitations to lead worship conferences in the United States and other countries. While it's flattering to be invited to minister, it's also a test of character. Flattery appeals to the ego, but in worship there is no place for ego. Leading worship can truly get us in touch with God, but being in front of crowds gives a rush of adrenaline that can be addictive. And so I must remember the prayer of the psalmist: "Not to us, O Lord, not to us but to your name be the glory, because of your love and faithfulness" (Ps 115:1).

The Alluring Power of Performance

I once dreamt I was walking down a path arm in arm with a woman—a would-be mistress. As I observed myself in the dream, I thought, *What, no restraint? You dummy, what are you doing? What about your wife?* I woke up and asked the Lord what the dream meant. He said the mistress represented the alluring power of musical performance—self-aggrandizing performance. I've never had a problem with running after other women, but I have found fame to be a tantalizing temptation.

When I started leading worship in large conferences and my songs were appreciated, I found myself tempted to use the leverage of my position to extend my influence. I saw that I had an appetite for success that constantly had to be tempered and purified. Being careful not to use too many of my own worship songs is one way I've reined in my human ambition.

When I lead a worship set, people will know if I am driven by a spirit of self-promoting performance. Worship leaders impart not only the *words* of a song, but the *spirit* behind the performance of a song. I want to impart a spirit of worship when I lead. I hate the thought of stealing glory from Jesus. Musicians *should* pursue excellence in their performance. But here's the trick—never let the musical presentation take precedence over the heart of worship. If I get too intent on being musically innovative, the essence of worship sometimes goes out the window. But if I jealously guard the jewel of worship, the music isn't a distraction.

Matt Redman is a well-known British worship leader whose songs are sung in churches all over the world. He has adopted John the Baptist's statement, "He must become greater; I must become less" (Jn

3:30), as a worship leader's motto. Matt encourages worship leaders to write key biblical phrases like this one in a place where you can see them often—in your diary or the book you use every time you prepare for worship leading.[4] Fixing your thoughts on this verse will keep you from developing an addiction to leading worship and being in front of people.

It's All About Jesus, Not Us

This is a difficult lesson to learn, especially for musicians. When we work hard at refining a skill, we want to be able to use it. Everybody likes to do what they can do well. Using my gifts brings great fulfillment since I really enjoy leading worship. But having a feel-good experience isn't the main goal. These days I have a more profound sense of privilege in leading worship. It's not a right; it's a privilege.

But it's still a challenge for me to always remember that worship leading is all about making *Jesus* look good. It's all about *his* reputation, *his* name. So when I'm planning a set, I consider how I can serve the people and which songs will create an opening for God to come near and for the people to reach up to him.

Serving others is at the heart of Jesus' teaching. He redefined the path to greatness by saying, "Whoever wants to become great among you must be your servant" (Mt 20:26). To worship is to serve. One of the most frequently used Greek words in the Bible is *latreuein*, meaning "to worship" or "to serve." Another Greek word, *douleuein*, which is often found in the New Testament, describes our bond-service to God. It conveys the notion of "total dependence and obedience without any right of personal choice."[5] When I catch myself feeling unfairly treated, I stop short and remember that I really don't *have* any rights. Servants exist for the benefit of others, not themselves.

Music Was an Afterthought

When Jesus captured my heart, music wasn't in the picture. Because I didn't have any ambition to become a successful singer-songwriter, it wasn't something I had to surrender at that time. I played guitar, but it was only a sidelight. I didn't spend my teenage years playing in bands, hoping to make it big. I was on a path to a much more typical middle-class American career.

But within months after meeting the Lord, new music began exploding out of me. I had never written music before. My first songs weren't so great, and my first attempts to share my music were shaky. But as I gained confidence and skill, it was clear that my music was blessing people. When it became clear that I might actually get somewhere with my music, I began a journey of allowing God's revealing light to illumine my motives for writing and singing.

A huge challenge for any musician is the constant tension of putting forth our best effort to write, play and lead worship while surrendering the results to God. Many musicians I know have become frustrated because they haven't reached their musical goals in the church. It's so easy to let personal goals become our all-consuming passion instead of serving others and trusting God for the results.

The Human Need to Feel Appreciated

I still have to resist a tendency to find my value as a person through my ministry. There are always people around me who are more gifted in certain spiritual gifts like teaching and pastoring. When I see people with prominent ministries, the enemy whispers a lie: "If you could do what *that* person does, you would really be loved and appreciated. You would really find fulfillment."

In his first letter to the Corinthians, Paul talks about having a sense of *belonging*. There were people who felt like they weren't a valuable part of the body because they were a "foot" and not a "hand" (1 Cor 12:15). Like the people in Corinth, many Christians today (myself included) feel insignificant in the body of Christ because we're not prominent.

We long for appreciation and recognition. All of us have an insatiable need to feel significant, and one way we try to get it is through using our spiritual and musical gifts. But the truth is, God values each of us regardless of our role in the church.

I also feel valued through my personal relationships in the church.

Some of my most satisfying times are spent with friends who know the real me and like me for who I am, not for what I do in the church. All of us long for this kind of intimate fellowship, and it's available for all of us, not just the extraordinarily gifted.

Like everyone else, I have a deep need for unconditional acceptance. But no amount of prominence in ministry can satisfy this need. I find that people-pleasing is like a fire-breathing dragon whose appetite is never satisfied. I can never get enough strokes from people to make me feel secure and satisfied. So I look to God and find fellowship with friends.

When we accept ourselves for who we are, we decrease our hunger for power or the acceptance of others because our self-intimacy reinforces our inner sense of security. We are no longer preoccupied with being powerful or popular. We no longer fear criticism because we accept the reality of our human limitations. Once integrated, we are less often plagued with the desire to please others because simply being true to ourselves brings lasting peace. We are grateful for life, and we deeply appreciate and love ourselves.[6]

Obsession with Gifts and the Gifted

The church in Corinth made the mistake of exalting the gifts of the Holy Spirit and exalting gifted people. Those who spoke in tongues felt they were part of an elite group in the church. Factions were formed in the church around different gifted leaders. Prophets hogged the platform instead of deferring to one another. Paul sarcastically confronts their attitude with the cutting question, "Did the word of God originate with you? Or are you the only people it has reached?" (1 Cor 14:36).

Although Paul affirms the Corinthians for not lacking any spiritual gift (1 Cor 1:7), he later delivers a stinging rebuke: "Your meetings do more harm than good" (1 Cor 11:17). This was largely because they were more focused on the gifts than on the people the gifts were intended to help. Instead of using the gifts as a way of loving and serving one another, they used them to gain spiritual status.

The Corinthian church had a false teaching that if people spoke in tongues, they were equal to the angels; hence the obsession with this gift. In a similar vein, worship leaders have to be careful to not fall into the trap of becoming obsessed with musical gifts.

The Ladder of Success

Contemporary worship music has skyrocketed in popularity in the last few decades. The church has been revived through thousands of songs birthed by different church denominations and movements. In Western commercial culture, especially in America, a wave of church renewal is followed by a wave of marketing.

One byproduct of this commercial system is the artist/worship leader. The songwriter/worship leader makes CDs that are distributed locally, regionally, nationally or internationally. Adulation of worship leaders is partly a byproduct of our media/marketing-driven society. If your name is on a song or a CD, people are more likely to look up to you. Since we live in a highly commercial culture, we experience the strange intersection of worship music and marketing; the intersection of sacred devotion and commercialism.

God uses gifted worship leaders, but there's an inherent challenge in the system. To remain rooted in biblical values, we have to fight hard against the feeling that success is determined by having a good reputation among a wide audience.

The Worship Leader as an Icon

Sadly, there is a tendency in human nature to idolize gifted leaders. We need worship leaders who are role models, but admiration can easily be distorted into hero worship. Then we find a whole crop of young worship leaders who think they've "made it" if they can emulate the sound of the worship leader who is the flavor of the year.

At least since the time of King Saul, people have wanted human heroes. I've found that the idolization of worship leaders happens on both the small and large scale—in local churches, and in big conferences and conventions. Some people who see a gifted singer leading the church in worship get a distorted picture about the spirituality and stature of that person. I have to stifle a laugh at conferences when people treat me like I'm one of the holiest people they've ever met.

When I was in my twenties I thought I knew a lot and was pretty mature in my faith. Now that I'm in my forties, I'm much less impressed with myself. It's impossible to take myself too seriously because I know what I'm made of. I have weaknesses in my character just like everyone else. So when someone venerates me, I shrug it off because I know the *real me* that's not visible to most people.

Paul, the most prominent apostle of all, saw himself as the worst of all sinners, saved by grace (1 Tim 1:15). John Wimber often described himself as "a fat man trying to get to heaven." We ought to have this attitude of continual amazement that God would have mercy on us. This will fuel our gratitude for God's unmerited favor and save us from an over-inflated perception of ourselves.

Most worship leaders will never write a song that is sung outside their own local church. Is that cause for dismay? Is that an earmark of failure? According to worldly values, yes. According to Jesus' definition of success, absolutely not.

Here are some better measurements of success: believing God loves you unconditionally, being thankful for Jesus' sacrifice, being kind to your coworkers in the church, loving your children and giving to the poor.

My friend Graham Ord is a gifted worship leader and songwriter. He told me a touching story of God speaking to him through his children. After a long day's work he came home, walked in the front door and was tackled by his three young children who were excited that he was home. Amidst the love and kisses they poured on him, the Lord spoke to Graham, "This is as famous as you'll ever need to be."

God's Friend

Several years ago, while living in Anaheim, California, I was smitten by the words of the song "Draw Me Close."[7] As I was repairing my kitchen floor, I heard the song drifting in from the stereo in the living room. My heart was pierced when I heard the words, "I lay it all down again, to hear you say that I'm your friend." What a line, especially for worship leaders and other visible leaders who are always reaching for the next plateau in ministry. How easy it is to be distracted from my pure, simple devotion to Jesus.

Sometimes my work can be so consuming that I forget about being God's friend. Whose ministry is it anyway? Once, a pastor asked John Wimber how he could grow *his* ministry. John's answer was something like this: "It's not *your* ministry, it's Jesus' ministry." We don't build a monument to our own name through ministry; we simply participate in the ongoing ministry of Jesus, both behind the scenes and in full view. Time and time again I've caught myself lusting after a bigger ministry and envying those who have a wider impact in ministry.

The words of David are helpful for the worship leader with big aspirations:

> My heart is not proud, O Lord,
>   my eyes are not haughty;
> I do not concern myself with great matters
>   or things too wonderful for me.
> But I have stilled and quieted my soul;
>   like a weaned child with its mother,
>   like a weaned child is my soul within me. (Ps 131:1-2)

I've watched my babies be satisfied and quieted at their mother's breast. What a wonderful picture of security, trust and rest. Sometimes the babies seem drunk with delight after a good meal; there is no striving, just contentment. May this picture be an inspiration to us to draw close to our Father (and indeed the tender "mother" side of) God.

2

THE DOOR
TO INTIMACY

Repentance

IN 1986 VANCOUVER HOSTED "Expo '86." People from all over the world came to see impressive displays of art, culture and technology. The expo site has now been transformed into a complex of luxury apartments and commercial developments. But at the entrance to the grounds stands a large geodesic dome that was built for the exposition. An imposing silver structure, it towers above Main Street. Hundreds of triangular facets cover the surface of the dome. Some facets shine brilliantly in the sun, and some remain temporarily darkened.

To me this is a picture of the many-faceted nature of God. As with the geodesic dome, you can't see all the facets at once. There is too much of God to take in all at once. As the sun moves through the sky, different facets of the dome are highlighted. Similarly, as we worship, the Spirit of God enlightens us about different aspects of God's nature.

At times, he illumines my understanding about God's unconditional love. I catch a glimpse of the Father's heart of tender mercy. Over and over again I am amazed that his love is not like human love—it is never conditional on our performance. At other times I am awestruck by his holiness, his majesty and his transcendent power.

Occasionally God gives me a bigger-than-average glimpse of his holiness. In April 2000 I attended an evening of worship in Surrey, British Columbia. The worship was being recorded, and the room was electric with anticipation. People from all over the lower mainland gathered with great expectations for the evening. It was like a mini-reunion as I visited with friends from the greater Vancouver area, many of whom I hadn't seen in years.

During the very first song, I was overwhelmed by God's greatness and majesty. I felt like a tiny speck of dust, standing before the immeasurable greatness of the Almighty One. In that moment I felt the power of God towering above me. My *immediate* reaction was repentance. I was cut to the heart for my pettiness and selfishness. My response was not measured or calculated; it was *involuntary*.

God came near, and I was engulfed in him. Real worship reveals God's holiness, and in the presence of this holiness we bow down. This action expresses the essence of the word *proskynein,* the Greek word most commonly translated as "to worship" in the New Testament. This word expresses the Asian custom of "casting oneself on the ground, as a total bodily gesture of respect before a great one, kissing his feet, the hem of his garment, or the ground."[1]

When we humble ourselves before the *living God*, his word cuts sharper than the sharpest knife, revealing our innermost thoughts and desires. His word "exposes us for what we really are" (Heb 4:12 NLT), and we know we can't hide from him.

I love the prayer in the Episcopal liturgy that so beautifully acknowledges our nakedness before God: "Almighty God, unto whom all hearts are open, all desires known, and from whom no secrets are hid: Cleanse the thoughts of our hearts by the inspiration of thy Holy Spirit, that we may perfectly love thee, and worthily magnify thy holy

Name; through Christ our Lord. Amen."[2]

Worship isn't a place to hide from God; it's a place to be found by God. It's not a place to numb us to reality; it's a place to look honestly at ourselves in the light of God. In drawing near to God, we have nothing to be afraid of except our own denial and resistance to his holy love.

Gary Best, the national director for the Association of Vineyard Churches in Canada, inverts a popular colloquialism by saying that in worship we "put our *worst* foot forward." When we approach God, we let him see the ugliest side of us, and we *still* find acceptance. God's grace doesn't make sense—it's way too gracious. It's insanely generous, and it opens the door to an intimate relationship with Jesus.

We see a picture of this radically unfair love in the life and parables of Jesus. We see him forgiving a thief on the cross next to him. Was it fair for him to forgive this man just because of his last minute confession? Is it fair for a father to come running toward his wayward child when he has returned from wasting his inheritance on wine and women? Is it fair for a vineyard owner to pay the latecomers the same wage as the ones who worked all day? Apparently God's definition of "fair" is different from ours. When we catch a glimpse of this, we won't cower before him, afraid of being punished.

A classic picture of worship and repentance is found in Isaiah 6. Isaiah sees the Lord, sitting on a lofty throne, shrouded in glory. Angelic worship fills the room as the mighty seraphim sing, "Holy, holy, holy." The foundation stones of the temple shake, and the entire sanctuary fills with smoke (Is 6:4).

Isaiah's response is utter disgust at his own sinfulness. The searing brightness of God's holiness cuts into his heart, and he cries out, "I am a man of unclean lips, and I live among a people of unclean lips" (Is 6:5). Then Isaiah confesses his sin, and God sends a seraphim with a purifying coal from God's altar. The coal touches his lips and God forgives him.

Here is an amazing combination of God's attributes—his majesty and his mercy; his perfect holiness and tender compassion. He never ceases to be all of these things, and this paradox brings us to our knees.

The repentant words from Isaiah's mouth are paraphrased in the song "Change My Heart, O God."[3] It's the cry of every devoted Christian who wants to be more like Jesus. It's the cry of my heart as I struggle with temptations and indifference to the things of God. I need the ongoing transforming work of God in my life. Although I have been a worshiper for twenty-six years, it's still a *fight* of faith for me. The fight is won with a soft, contrite heart.

In October 2000 I attended a retreat for Vineyard worship leaders from Canada. In the opening worship session, God melted me with his loving presence. Once again God visited me in a powerful but tender way, assuring me of his presence and fatherly care. The worship set began with the song "Hungry"—"I'm falling on my knees, offering all of me."[4] The words of the song were alive with power. I deeply knew the truth of what I was saying to God—he is my all in all, and I belong to him. Again I intuitively reacted to God's felt presence by humbling myself before him.

A. W. Tozer says that worship involves "a humbling but delightful sense of admiring awe and astonished wonder. It is delightful to worship God, but it is also a humbling thing; and the man who has not been humbled in the presence of God will never be a worshiper of God at all. He may be a church member who keeps the rules and obeys the discipline, and who tithes and goes to conference, but he'll never be a worshiper unless he is deeply humbled."[5]

Worship is always intertwined with humility. If we are impressed with ourselves and our good works, we have little room for worship—a principle that is beautifully illustrated in the parable of the Pharisee and the tax collector (Lk 18:10-14).

In the story, the Pharisee approached God, confident that he had earned God's favor through his strict observance of Jewish laws. He was faithful to tithe and fast, and he looked down on others who were less religious. In contrast, the tax collector approached God hesitantly, with a contrite heart. He simply said, "God, have mercy on me, a sinner" (Lk 18:13). This man, not the Pharisee, "went home justified before God" (Lk 18:14).

Jesus turned upside down the popular views of what made a person acceptable before God. In Jesus' day, the Pharisee was considered the model religious person, while the tax collector was seen as the scum of the earth. The tax collector wasn't even allowed to bring a sacrifice to the temple because of his low place in society.

But Jesus' point is this: "All who exalt themselves will be humbled, but all who humble themselves will be exalted" (Lk 18:14 NRSV). When we're not impressed with ourselves and our own righteousness, it's much easier to be impressed with God. Being in awe of God goes hand in hand with being realistic about our shortcomings.

Repentance—the Normal Christian Life

In worship, the first and often-repeated step is repentance. As John Wimber said, "repentance is the way *in* and the way *on*." Walking with God is like a marriage—the goal is intimacy and fidelity, and the way to that goal is regular renewal of the marriage vows. Intimate relationships require ongoing maintenance. When I mess up, I sometimes need to apologize to Linda. I hate that wall of separation between us when we've had angry words. I like to deal with it quickly. Similarly, I like to get rid of my sin before God as quickly as I can.

The analogy of love between bride and groom is used often in Scripture to express Christ's relationship with his church. The imagery of physical and emotional love is powerful, but it's only a shadow of the intimacy that we have with God *in the Spirit*. Paul says, "He who unites himself with the Lord is one with him in spirit" (1 Cor 6:17).

Intimacy with God is about being faithful—having no other gods. Without obedience, we won't experience true intimacy—"They who have my commandments and keep them are those who love me; and those who love me will be loved by my Father, and I will love them and reveal myself to them" (Jn 14:21 NRSV).

The imagery of intimacy is one way of describing a deep, interactive life with God. A benefit of intimacy with God is being filled with the tangible knowledge of his love. It's having a hope of heaven that energizes us to keep pressing on. It's also letting God into the deepest part of who we are and turning from those things that hinder our relationship with him.

You can't become intimate with someone if you refuse to be honest and open. I fell in love with Linda by sharing my deepest hopes, fears and dreams with her. If she hadn't responded with the same openness, our relationship would have ended. During our courtship, she chose to listen to me and accept me in my moments of deepest vulnerability. When I was struggling to find the right career path, she stayed with me. When I wrestled with insecurities and doubts about my calling to the ministry, she accepted me. She loved me in spite of my fears of failure. She proved that I could trust her, and the foundation was set for a lifelong relationship.

Early in my journey of knowing God, I powerfully experienced God's love and acceptance. Like David I can say, "I have seen you in the sanctuary and beheld your power and glory. Because your love is better than life, my lips will glorify you" (Ps 63:2-3).

Despite the many ways God has shown his love to me, I still need regular doses of his tangible love to keep me healthy. I'm like a computer that needs to be regularly reprogrammed to see God as the one who *is* love. He lovingly coaxes me into the truth again and again—he loves me as I am, not as I should be.

Daring to Draw Near

Jesus made himself vulnerable for our sake. He laid aside the privileges of divinity to die for us. He subjected himself to terrible agony that we might know the love of God. By unselfishly giving his life for us, he has proven that I can trust him. I can openly respond to him, unafraid of his reaction to my sin. I can approach him boldly and with confidence. "What a merciful, merciful, merciful God."[6]

Without vulnerability and humility, we can't worship. When David was caught in adultery and murder, he came to God with a broken and contrite heart and was restored to fellowship with God. When Jesus told the Samaritan woman about her sordid past, she didn't deny her sin—she acknowledged him as the Savior of the world. When Paul, a fierce persecutor of Christians, experienced Jesus' mercy, he entered a deep knowledge of God's love that far surpassed any other treasure or delight. But without honest vulnerability before God, we can't pass through the door of knowing him.

Sometimes God catches us off balance when he comes near. In the early 1980s there was a young woman in a Vineyard church in Southern California who was furious with me because I did so many slow, intimate worship songs. She preferred the upbeat, joyful songs.

I don't think she understood why the songs of self-examination made her feel uncomfortable. I could sense that she felt threatened by the nearness of God's Spirit that is often felt during songs of repentance and consecration. She had a troubled life and marriage. God was inviting her to a place of repentance and healing, but she felt afraid and threatened. If we're not ready to humble ourselves, repent and be healed, the illumination of the Holy Spirit can feel like an intrusion, not a welcome revelation.

What was happening to her? The kingdom of God was drawing near to her. When we submit ourselves to God through worship, we place ourselves within the range of his grace. When the words of a song invite God to *change us,* he shines his searchlight on us to expose the shame and brokenness. That is our invitation to renewed intimacy with him. Confession, repentance and forgiveness.

I don't have tons of close friends. I don't let a lot of people know the deepest things I struggle with. Something that sets apart my casual relationships from the deeper ones is the level of mutual self-disclosure. If I confess my struggle with anger or lust to a brother, and he does the same with me, we're going to be true comrades. When I'm honest about my deepest disappointments, our friendship deepens.

In a much bigger way, God is a friend who responds to honesty. Without transparency before God, worship is a farce; it's only a ritual. Isaiah describes a people who come near to God with words but with hearts far from him (Is 29:13). God isn't interested in shallow "lip service" worship. In fact he hates it. He is looking for people who will be brutally honest with him and not hide anything. That's the pathway to intimacy with God.

Convicted by our own words. At the end of Moses' ministry, God gave the Israelites a song that would convict them of their sin when they forgot to honor God in the Promised Land.

> Now write down for yourselves this song and teach it to the Israelites and *have them sing it, so that it may be a witness for me against them.* When I have brought them into the land flowing with milk and honey, the land I promised on oath to their forefathers, and when they eat their fill and thrive, they will turn to other gods and worship them, rejecting me and breaking my covenant. (Deut 31:19-20, emphasis added)

We may come to God and sing, "You're all I want, you're all I've ever needed,"[7] and realize he's *not* all we want. There are other things competing with our love for him. We want the words of the song to be an accurate description of our hearts, but sometimes they show us where we're missing the mark. That's part of God's intention for worship songs. They lead us back to the Father over and over again. We turn from our wayward thoughts and desires, and change our direction. Worship points us back to the priorities of God's kingdom. "I am reaching for the highest goal, that I might receive the prize/Pressing onward, pushing every hindrance aside, out of my way, 'cause I want to know you more."[8]

Words of devotion in song are a powerful weapon in the fight of faith. They show us when our compass is off, and they point us back to true north.

A turning point. "Work out your salvation with fear and trembling" (Phil 2:12). Walking with God means getting rid of any competing loves that become idols. Consecration to God means that everything belongs to him. Whether it is fame, pride, chemical addictions or sensual temptation, there are always lions crouching at our door. Repentance and consecration lead the way back to Jesus.

For any Christian and for every worship leader, money will always be a lever of power. Whether we are scraping by with barely enough money to eat and pay the rent or whether we are living in a luxurious home, our faith must find expression through our spending, giving and restraint.

For North American worship leaders, the power of this materialism looms especially large. We have so much *stuff* in the United States and Canada! Our standard of material living is way above most countries I've visited. We're surrounded by comforts—homes, cars, air-conditioning, TVs and all kinds of entertainment. None of these things are inherently bad. In fact they're all a blessing. But they can make us so satisfied with our earthly life that we lose perspective on eternity.

Jesus' words, as revealed to John the revelator, are so appropriate for our culture: "You say, 'I am rich. I have everything I want. I don't need a thing!'" (Rev 3:17 NLT); "Be diligent and turn from your indifference" (Rev 3:19 NLT). It is only by continually exposing myself to biblical truth and vital Christian fellowship that I can keep on course. The world, the flesh and the devil are always prowling around, ready to devour.

Every time I visit a less privileged country, reality comes crashing in on me—I am rich in the things of this world! I am amazed that there are so many poor people in the world, yet their lives are marked by joy and gratitude. They must be *real* Christians! When I see such thankfulness in people who have a fraction of the wealth that I have, I wonder who the privileged ones really are.

North Americans think that freedom is found in riches, independence and power. The reality is, possessions can be like a chain around the neck. Like the man in the gospels whose wealth increased, we spend all our time building bigger barns in order to store our stuff. The maintenance required on a house and two cars (the middle-class American standard) can be demanding, let alone all the other toys we may amass.

The illusion of the American dream is to find happiness through wealth, but the Bible paints a different picture: material wealth cannot satisfy the needs of the human heart—it can be a huge stumbling block to finding God and persevering in the faith.

His grace and my flaws—fuel for worship. After being a Christian for twenty-seven years, I'm still amazed at how petty and selfish I can be. But even if I'm shocked at my repeated failures, God is not shocked. When he saved me, he knew exactly what he was getting—not a brand new, high-performance saint, but a flawed and fickle sinner. Yet the very recognition of my flaws provides fuel for worship. Every time I think of what Jesus has done for me, I'm thankful.

This contrast of human darkness and divine light is what produces worship in Paul: "How thankful I am to Christ Jesus our Lord for considering me trustworthy and appointing me to serve him, even though I used to scoff at the name of Christ. I hunted down his people, harming them in every way I could. . . . Oh, how kind and gracious the Lord was! He filled me completely with faith and the love of Christ Jesus!" (1 Tim 1:12-14 NLT).

I don't think God is looking for superstar Christians to be worship leaders. If that were the requirement, I wouldn't qualify. He's looking for people who will work out their salvation with fear and trembling all the way to the end of their lives. He's looking for people who will walk humbly and, like the tax collector, will look up to God and say, "God, have mercy on me, a sinner" (Lk 18:13).

To the indifferent Laodiceans, Jesus calls, "Look! Here I stand at the door and knock. If you hear me calling and open the door, I will come in, and we will share a meal as friends" (Rev 3:20 NLT).

What a beautiful picture of reconciliation with Jesus. The way of repentance is described as an intimate meal with a close friend! Eating with someone you love is one of the most intimate pictures of fellowship in the ancient Near East. We sit with Jesus in the living room, enjoying conversation and being warmed by the fire. I can say anything that comes to my mind because I know he knows my thoughts and motives and yet he fully accepts me. I feel free to confess my sin because I know he'll forgive me. I don't have to run and hide from him. I don't have to shove my secrets into the closet, afraid that he will reject me.

The Father is not waiting for chance to hammer us. He is the Father of the prodigal, running toward us with open arms, ready to throw a party in celebration of our return to him.

3

THE FRUIT
OF INTIMACY

The Father's Love

> *For a disciple of Jesus the process of spiritual growth is*
> *a gradual repudiation of the unreal image of God, and*
> *an increasing openness to the true and living God.*
> BRENNAN MANNING

P AUL PRAYS FOR HIS CHURCH in Ephesus that they would experience God's love: "And may you have the power to understand, as all God's people should, how wide, how long, how high, and how deep his love really is. May you experience the love of Christ, though it is so great you will never fully understand it. Then you will be filled with the fullness of life and power that comes from God" (Eph 3:18-19 NLT).

Is this passage written by a man who *experienced* God? Obviously. Remember, he is writing to the church—not to unbelievers but to regenerated, Spirit-filled believers. Then why does he ask that they "experience the love of Christ"? Because we all need to experience God's love over and over again. For Paul, tangibly encountering God's love is the normal Christian life. Certainly in God's "glorious riches" (Eph 3:16) he can strengthen us again and again as we draw near to him in worship.

Over the last several years, I have helped lead many worship seminars and conferences. Although I've consistently seen God bring great blessing to the conference attendees, sometimes the travel can be wearying. A few years ago I was leading worship and teaching at a worship seminar in Washington State. Since I didn't have any responsibilities in the first session, I sat in the front row, waiting for the worship to begin. I thought, *Is it really necessary to keep coming to these events? Is it really worth the effort?*

In that moment of reevaluation, the worship music began, and God overwhelmed me with his love and words of affirmation. Waves of divine love washed over me as he filled my mind with his love for me and good plans for me. There it was again—the "spirit of wisdom and revelation" that Paul had asked God to lavish on the church. God knew that I needed to be strengthened with power through his Spirit in my inner being (Eph 3:16). We need to be continually directed into God's love (2 Thess 3:5).

Constructing Distorted Pictures of God

Having a wrong understanding of God's personality is a huge barrier to the freedom and delight of worship. A. W. Tozer describes the importance of this: "The essence of idolatry is the entertainment of thoughts about God that are unworthy of Him. To think rightly about God is in an important sense, to have everything right. To think wrongly about God is in an important sense to have everything wrong."[1]

How do we form our view of God and the way he feels about us? One of the big factors in forming a picture of God is our relationship with earthly authority figures. It works both ways—if we have loving parents who affirm us, it's much easier to experience God's love. I thank God for giving me parents with strong character and morals—they put me way ahead in the game of life because they loved me and pointed me in the right direction. Their love enabled me to easily believe that my heavenly Father loved me.

But we also transfer painful experiences with parents, teachers and bosses onto God. Somewhere in the deep recesses of our soul, we remember being punished for our disobedience, and we can still feel the anger and manipulation. Even loving parents and good bosses make mistakes that leave us scarred.

When I was in my early twenties, I had a boss who was dishonest and unfair. In addition, he treated his employees, especially the women, with little patience and respect. He advertised a job opening at a particular salary rate and then reduced the amount when I came for the interview. From the very start it was hard for me to trust this man. Do you think I felt like throwing my arms open to him when I saw him coming down the hall? No, I felt hiding or running the other way.

Time after time, we see people in power who abuse their privileges and abuse the people below them. So we harden our hearts to authority and refuse to be vulnerable to people. Somehow this can be transferred to our relationship with God.

We have another strike against us if we have received bad teaching about who God is. If we've been taught that God is an angry tyrant, how can we bear to be in the same room with him? Sadly, some church traditions present God as a dour headmaster who loves to find faults in his students. Do you see him as a "mathematical God who weighs our good and bad deeds on a set of scales and always finds us lacking"?[2] How can we possibly *trust* a god like this? How can we make ourselves vulnerable to a god like this? We can't. Unless we're convinced of God's love, it's too scary to get near him.

Before he understood God's grace, Martin Luther walked a torturous path of feeling condemned by God. He describes his anguish in his journal:

> Although I lived a blameless life as a monk, I felt that I was a sinner with an uneasy conscience before God. I also could not believe that I had pleased him with my works. Far from loving that righteous God who punished sinners, I actually loathed him. I was a good monk, and kept my order so strictly that if ever a monk could get to heaven by monastic discipline, I was that monk. All my companions in the monastery

would confirm this. . . . And yet my conscience would not give me certainty, but I always doubted and said, "You didn't do that right. You
weren't contrite enough. You left that out of your confession."[3]

The sense of unworthiness that Luther felt is common to many Christians. If we are trying to earn God's approval by our good works, we
can never quite tip the scales far enough to feel that our good works
outweigh our faults.

David Seamands, a well-known Christian counselor, describes the
centrality of knowing God's grace: "Many years ago I was driven to the
conclusion that the two major causes of most emotional problems
among evangelical Christians are these: the failure to understand, receive, and live out God's unconditional grace and forgiveness; and the
failure to give out that unconditional love, forgiveness and grace to
other people. . . . We read, we hear, we believe a good theology of
grace. But that's not the way we live. The good news of the Gospel of
grace has not penetrated the level of our emotions."[4]

Dismantling Distorted Pictures of God

But God is in the business of healing our image of himself so we can
confidently look him in the eye. God is in the business of giving us the
power to understand the real depth of his love (Eph 3:18). It's one
thing to agree with the biblical definition of God's character, it's quite
another to *know God experientially* in this way. God isn't satisfied with
letting us have a cognitive understanding of his love—he wants to cut
down into the deepest part of our souls to uncover our fears, our
shame and our pain. He wants to heal us.

I brought a strong work ethic into my relationship with God. I grew
up in the system that is common to us all: the only way you make
progress in life—at work, academics, sports or church—is through
hard work. You get what you earn. The only way you climb the ladder
of success is by the sweat of your brow. If we make a mistake, we get
our hands slapped. Our world is very competitive, and if we don't
outdo one another, we don't come out on top.

It took me a long time to grasp God's grace. In my first ten years of following the Lord, I received much teaching about his unconditional love. Through wonderful encounters with God in worship and prayer, I experienced his grace. I came to the realization that I had done nothing to earn the gift of God's love and revelation. God sought me out, not the other way around. I was no different than anyone I judged as being less spiritual—we're all in need of God's mercy.

But I had much more to learn. In 1985 I began working as a worship pastor at the Langley Vineyard in British Columbia. Because of my type-A hard-driving nature, I put a lot of pressure on myself to perform as a spiritual leader. I was being crushed under the weight of my own desire to succeed in the ministry. One Saturday night in 1985, as I was preparing for a worship service, the Lord's love broke through to me in a new song about his grace:

Precious Child
Show me, dear Lord, how you see me through your eyes
So that I can realize your great love for me
Teach me, oh Lord, that I am precious in your sight
That as a father loves his child, so you love me.

I am yours because you have chosen me
I'm your child because you've called my name
And your steadfast love will never change
And I will always be your precious child.

Show me, dear Lord, that I can never earn your love
That a gift cannot be earned, only given
Teach me, oh Lord, that your love will never fade
That I can never drive away your great mercy.[5]

As I sang that song, the revelation of God's unconditional love flooded my heart. It was a moment when God's grace became real and tangible to me and when God redefined my view of him. He wanted me to see and *know* him as the loving God he really is, instead of worshiping a God of my own imagination. To know and worship anything else would be idolatry. He was dismantling my distorted view of him.

Seeing God As He Really Is

It can be frightening for people to sense God's presence in the midst of worship because, at the deepest level, they really don't know if God accepts them. The manifest presence of God isn't something we imagine, it's a real thing that has power. Jesus said the Holy Spirit would convict people of sin, righteousness and judgment. When the Holy Spirit falls on his people, we can sense what's wrong inside of us. One of the things we have to get right is our understanding of who God is, how he sees us.

Once, as an exercise, I imagined my fiftieth wedding anniversary party.[6] I imagined who would be present and what I would want them to say about me. I wondered what qualities of my character would stand out to them and what they would remember about my life and work. I immediately thought of my own children—I wanted them to *like me*. I wanted them to be not just my children but my friends. I wanted them to see integrity in my life—to see me practicing the things I write and sing about. I wanted them to know that I love them unconditionally.

I specifically thought of David, my second son. He is his own man. He's talented, creative, funny, enthusiastic and kind of zany. He cracks us up with his jokes and wonderful weirdness. When he gets an inspiration (to build a go-kart or a skateboard ramp), he gives himself to it passionately until the next inspiration (like snowboarding) comes along.

As I reflected on David's sensitivity, I wanted him to know that it didn't matter what career he chose or how his path in life compared to that of the other children. His personality is very different from Zachary, my first son. Zac is the typical first-born—responsible, organized and hard-working. Zac is successful at lots of things—school, music and sports.

In his pre-teen years, I was concerned about David feeling like an underachiever in his older brother's shadow. I wanted David to know I love him just as he is. It didn't matter what he would become as an adult—I would love him no matter what.

A song for David was born out of this time of imagining what long-term impact my life would have. I wanted David to know that if his achievements weren't as impressive as some of the other kids, it wouldn't matter. I wanted him to be confident that no matter how he performed in life, I would still love him. So I wrote this song for him and sang it to him in the presence of the whole family:

> My son David, I love you; my son David
> There are so many things that I like about you;
> You have a sensitive heart and a bright mind and a keen imagination;
> You make me laugh with the things that you say and do.
>
> My son David, I love you; my son David,
> There are so many things that I like about you;
> But no matter what you become in this life,
> No matter what you do, there's one thing that will always be true;
> I will always, always, always love you.

When David was about six years old, I sang this song to him in the gathered circle of our whole family. As I looked into his eyes and sang these words, I could see his eyes fill with tears. It was a powerful affirmation of my love for him in front of his siblings.

This picture reminds me of looking into the eyes of Father God and hearing his song of love over me. In worship, this is a place we can go.

This is what can happen in worship when we're looking into the Father's face. All of a sudden, he lets us *see him*. It's the presence of the Father in the room with us that makes the difference. It's not just a one-way recitation of song lyrics. It's a dialogue with the most loving Person in the universe. In worship we can experience God's delight in us and have the false images of God erased from our hearts.

Why are we reluctant to approach God and to ask his forgiveness? Part of our problem is that we attribute human imperfections to our holy, loving God. Since our closest friends and family have a hard time forgiving us if we hurt them repeatedly, we assume God must be the same way. Because our failures outweigh our goodness, we think he is reluctant to bless us.

How could anyone possibly forgive us again and again and again? It makes no sense in human terms. But we're not dealing with a human God. If we're not convinced that he is always ready to forgive us, we push him away, thereby cutting ourselves off from his love.

We are made in God's image, yet God is so unlike us. We have a hard time forgiving someone three times, but God's forgiveness is without limit. We love people only when they are kind to us, only when we benefit from them somehow. God loved the thief on the cross next to Jesus as much as he loved Peter, James and John. It takes a gift of God's revelation for us to truly know him this way.

But here is the key: "The love of God embodied in Jesus is radically different from our natural human way of loving. . . . When I love as a man I am drawn by the good perceived in the other. I love someone for what I find in him or her . . . unlike ourselves, the Father of Jesus loves men and women, not for what He finds in them, but for what lies within Himself. . . . The Father is a source. He acts; he does not react. He initiates love. He is love without motive."[7]

Brennan Manning, a Christian author and former Catholic priest whose books are loved by thousands, has a wonderful grasp on the lavish grace of God:

> God loves me in a creative, intimate, unique, reliable and *tender* way. Creative: out of His love I came forth; through His love I am who I am. Intimate: His love reaches out to the deepest in me. Unique: His love embraces me as I am, not as I am considered to be by other people or supposed to be in my own self-image. Reliable: His love will never let me down. Tenderness is what happens to you when you know you are deeply and sincerely *liked* by someone. . . . Your acceptance of me banishes my fears. My defense mechanisms—sarcasm, aloofness, self-righteousness, giving the appearance of having it all together—start to fall. . . . You instill self-confidence in me and allow me to smile at my weaknesses and absurdities. . . . I become more open, sincere, vulnerable and affectionate. I too grow tender.[8]

Manning continues: "If you could honestly say that God *likes you*, not only loves you, if you could say "The Father is very fond of me," there would come a relaxedness, a serenity, and a compassionate attitude toward yourself that is a reflection of God's own tenderness."[9]

There is no greater motivation to pursue righteousness than knowing I'm loved by God. Experiencing God's love makes me zealous to please him and free to worship him in front of others.

Climbing into the Father's Lap

As we come to the Father again and again, he reminds us who he really is. He gently washes away our fears and reminds us how amazingly gracious he is.

A collection of hymns called the *Odes of Solomon,* written in the second century after Christ, express many of the themes contained in modern worship songs. The worshiper who penned the *Odes of Solomon* describes well the Father's tender love:

> For there is a Helper for me, the Lord
> He has generously shown Himself to me in His simplicity
> Because His kindness has diminished His dreadfulness
> He became like me, that I might receive Him
> In form he was considered like me, that I might put him on
> And I trembled not when I saw Him,
> Because He was gracious to me. (Ode 7)[10]

One person at the Anaheim Vineyard described their experience of worship: "It's a very private time between God and me, a place where no one, or anything else, can interrupt the healing, assurance, approval, strength or whatever God is doing at the time. It's a place where I can look into the Father's eyes and see His soul."[11]

Our first and foremost role in life is not as a *worship leader,* but as a *child of God.* God is first of all interested in loving us. If we receive his love, we have something to give away.

To be really free in worship leading, I have to know that God is fond of me. Without confidence before God, I can't function in any capacity—as a child of God, a husband, father or worship leader. How can I confidently worship and lead others if I'm not sure how he feels about me? Unless I know I'm right with God, I can't have peace. All the tricks of the trade in worship leading won't help me if I'm not sure that God loves and accepts me.

4

THE LIFESTYLE PRODUCES THE LANGUAGE

Concentrate on doing your best for God,
work you won't be ashamed of,
laying out the truth plain and simple.
Stay clear of pious talk that is only talk. Words are not
mere words, you know.
It they're not backed by a godly life, they accumulate as
poison in the soul.

2 TIMOTHY 2:15-16 (THE MESSAGE)

Music is your own experience, your thoughts,
your wisdom. If you don't live it,
it won't come out of your horn.

CHARLIE PARKER

WHAT WE SEE MODELED in the biblical leaders' lives is crucial in gaining an accurate picture of genuine worship. These men and women encountered God, and their lives were changed forever. God's revelation of himself left an indelible impression on their hearts. Their identity, direction and purpose for living radically changed. The lives of the great Christian leaders of church history echo these biblical themes.

Their total commitment to God's purposes led them into taking great risks to extend his kingdom. In situations of despair and life-threatening danger, they called out to God for help. When we have left all to follow Christ, we are hungry for him, dependent on him and willing to make sacrifices to obey him.

Changed Forever

This immersion into Christ is the fountainhead of our songs of worship. To stay on course as worship leaders, we must revisit the reasons we sing. If our song leading is really motivated and marked by our pursuit of Jesus and his purposes, we'll be singing with a right heart. In this chapter, I highlight the importance of integrity between the lyrics of our songs and our lives.

Born again. Conversion is the first experience that causes worship to spring up from the Christian's soul. Paul is the best example of radical conversion resulting in radical praise. Because of his pre-Christian pride and persecution of the church, he calls himself the "worst of sinners." He writes this to Timothy: "Here is a trustworthy saying that deserves full acceptance: Christ Jesus came into the world to save sinners—of whom I am the *very worst*. But for that very reason I was shown mercy that in me, the worst of sinners, Christ Jesus might display his unlimited patience as an example for those who believe on him and receive eternal life" (1 Tim 1:15-16, emphasis added).

Meditating on God's mercy made Paul overflow with thanks: "Now to the King eternal, immortal, invisible, the only God, be honor and glory forever and ever. Amen" (1 Tim 1: 17).

True worship comes from the heart that recognizes its desperate need for God's mercy. But if we see that he is the source of every blessing—whether physical, spiritual, relational or otherwise, we won't be able to keep ourselves from worshiping him. Before Paul met Christ, he was proud of his own accomplishments as a "Hebrew of Hebrews." If we are impressed with the good works we have done instead of the salvation he has wrought on our behalf, we won't be able to worship God appropriately.

Paul is flabbergasted by the boundless mercy of God. In the midst of writing about God's mercy on Jews and Gentiles alike (Rom 11:28-32), he explodes with worship.

"Oh, the depth of the riches of the
    wisdom and knowledge of God!
  How unsearchable his judgments,
  and his paths beyond tracing out!
"Who has known the mind of the Lord?
  Or who has been his counselor?"
"Who has ever given to God,
  that God should repay him?"
For from him and through him and to him are all things.
  To him be the glory forever! Amen. (Rom 11:33-36)

The heart overwhelmed with God's mercy is a worshiping heart. Songs about the mercy of God and the cross and blood of Jesus should top our priority list. The song "This Is Love" is a great example:

Nail pierced hands
A wounded side
This is love, this is love.

The holy heart
Was sacrificed
This is love, this is love.

I bow down to the holy One
I bow down to the Lamb
I bow down to the worthy One.
I bow down to the Lamb.

The Son of God
Died for us
This is love, this is love.
He walked the hill
He bore the cross
This is love, this is love.[1]

His mercy, our humility. I've already highlighted the importance of humility in a previous chapter. The mightiest leaders in the Bible are examples of this kind of humility. Moses was called the humblest man on earth (Num 12:3). One expression of humility is obedience to God despite the way we feel. Moses was not interested in confronting Pharaoh and leading the Hebrews out of Egypt. Yet we see Moses humbly obeying God's command to lead a stubborn people through the wilderness. I have to believe that Moses' humility was the primary reason that "the Lord would speak to Moses face to face, as a man speaks with his friend" (Ex 33:11). God resists the proud but gives grace to the humble (1 Pet 5:5).

David, another Old Testament leader, served his earthly father and faithfully served Saul in every way he was asked to. Yet he considered himself unworthy to take the king's daughter as his wife (1 Sam 18:18). Though he made some serious mistakes, he repented thoroughly (Ps 51). David's humble prayer after committing adultery and murder has become a standard for the Christian church throughout the ages:

> Have mercy on me, O God,
>   according to your unfailing love;
> according to your great compassion
>   blot out my transgressions. . . .
> Create in me a pure heart, O God,
>   and renew a steadfast spirit within me. (Ps 51:1, 10)

Songs of surrender must be sung over and over again. A few examples are "Refiner's Fire," the hymn "I Surrender All" and "Change My Heart O God":

> Change my heart O God, make it ever true
> Change my heart O God, may I be like you
> You are the potter, I am the clay
> Mold me and make me, this is what I pray.[2]

The prayer of repentance for small and great sins alike is pleasing worship to the Father. When I react to my children in anger, I often confess my sin directly to my kids as well as to the Lord, and I ask their forgiveness. In the struggle to stay pure in our Godward and human relationships, the language of confession is essential. The attitudes of our hearts reveal themselves in the words of our lips.

Worship—Giving What Is Most Precious to Us

There is nothing more precious to a mother than her child. Hannah made the ultimate sacrifice that a mother could make. After waiting several years to conceive and bear a child, she presented her son, Samuel, to serve the Lord in the temple. After that time, she visited Samuel only once each year.

In giving her son to the Lord, she demonstrated her trust in God. She showed that she valued his lordship more than her right to control what was most important to her. She rejoiced in the Lord's gift of a child, knowing that only the Lord could open her womb. She named her son Samuel, acknowledging that he was born "because I asked the Lord for him" (1 Sam 1:20).

Trusting in God's sovereignty in all circumstances is another topic that should be on our play list. Every Christian is challenged with trusting God for things we can't control. A great song on this theme is "Faithful One."

> Faithful One, so unchanging
> Ageless One
> You're my Rock of Peace
> Lord of all I depend on you.
>
> I call out to you again and again;
> I call out to you again and again.
>
> You are my rock in times of trouble
> You lift me up when I fall down
> All through the storm
> Your love is the anchor
> My hope is in you alone.[3]

Gratitude for God's Favor

The story of God's visitation to the Virgin Mary is one of the most moving Bible stories of all. The angel appears to Mary, saying, "Greetings, you who are highly favored! The Lord is with you. . . . Do not be afraid, Mary, you have found favor with God" (Lk 1:28-30). Mary is overwhelmed and honored all at once. She pours out her gratitude in a song: "My soul glorifies the Lord and my spirit rejoices in God my Savior, for he has been mindful of the humble state of his servant. From now on all generations will call me blessed, for the Mighty One has done great things for me—holy is his name" (Lk 1:46-49).

Mary the mother of Jesus received a divine visitation and was impregnated by the Spirit of God. This picture aptly describes the ministry of the Holy Spirit in the lives of those he calls and empowers to minister. He plants a seed of his own desire in our spirits, and we carry the vision with us until it is time for the "baby" to be born.

The baby might be a new song, a new home group, a new worship team or a new church. To know that "the Mighty One has done great things for me" (Lk 1:49) makes me want to explode with worship to him. Once again we see an encounter with the holy God producing a song of worship in the one whom he visits.

Did you ever stop to think that Mary had a choice in the matter of bearing the Messiah? She could have said no. Her response to the angel's prophecy about her indicates her willingness to venture into the unknown: "I am the Lord's servant. . . . May it be to me as you have said" (Lk 1:38).

This type of willingness to take great risks in obedience to God was characteristic of Moses, David, Paul and many others in the Bible. Moses risked his life by coming before Pharaoh to make an unthinkable request—to let the Hebrew people go free. David repeatedly risked his life by going into battle to defend the people of Israel and to extend the reign of God in the Mediterranean basin. Paul was beaten, shipwrecked and imprisoned while on his missionary journeys to the Gentiles. When the living God encounters us, he conscripts us into his army. With kindness, gentleness and perseverance as our weapons, we can be vessels of the compassion he has shown us.

Humble King

Oh kneel me down again, here at your feet
Show me how much you love humility
Oh Spirit be the star that leads me to
The humble heart of love I see in you.

You are the God of the broken
The friend of the weak
You wash the feet of the weary
Embrace the ones in need
I want to be like You Jesus
To have this heart in me
You are the God of the humble
You are the humble King.[4]

Cry for Help

Real conversion leads to service; service leads to prayers, petition and intercession for God's help. When God makes the way clear to us, we give thanks. In his ordeal with King Saul, David cried out for help. "In my distress I called to the LORD; I cried to my God for help. From his temple he heard my voice; my cry came before him, into his ears (Ps 18:6). Then he praises God for the victory: "The LORD lives! Praise be to my Rock! Exalted be God my Savior! He is the God who avenges me, who subdues nations under me, who saves me from my enemies"(Ps 18:46-48). If David didn't dare to fight the fight, he would never have had a victory song to sing.

More than any other biblical character, David shows us the language of worship flowing out of the trials of life. Psalm 63 is one of my favorite Davidic psalms. The part I like best is about seeing God's power. But the context of this is so easily overlooked: "My soul clings to you; your right hand upholds me. Those who seek my life will be destroyed; they will go down to the depths of the earth" (Ps 63:8-9). David was in trouble in the desert. His life was threatened because he was on a mission from God. This propelled him to seek God's face. The language of worship was born in his lifestyle.

If we never step out in obedience to God's words to us, we'll never know what it means to trust him. If we only attempt to accomplish things within the limits of our own strength, we'll never experience God's empowering to do something far beyond our own capability. We'll never have a personal victory song of praise to sing.

Hungry

When people diligently pursue God's will in everyday life, worshiping in church takes on a whole new dimension. When a farmer works hard in the field, he comes home hungry for dinner. For the Christian worker, plowing the field, planting the seed and taking in the harvest develops an appetite for God that is satisfied in worship.

Proverbs 27:7 says, "He who is full loathes honey, but to the hungry even what is bitter tastes sweet." When I've ministered in Hong Kong to former drug addicts and the workers who minister with them, I see people hungry for God, and the intensity of their worship astounds me. I am reduced to tears by the deep cry for God gushing out of them. Sitting there during their worship, I think, *Why did they ask me to teach them about worship?* "God blesses those who realize their need for him, for the Kingdom of Heaven is given to them" (Matt 5:3 NLT).

We have lots of songs in which we cry out for more of God—more intimate knowledge of him, more revelation, more of his love. Great songs for this heart cry include "There's No One Like You," "Nothing Is As Wonderful" and "Hungry":

Hungry I come to you
For I know you satisfy
I am empty, but I know
Your love does not run dry

And so I wait for you
So I wait for you
I'm falling on my knees
Offering all of me
Jesus you're all I'm living for.

Broken I run to you
For your arms are open wide
I am weary, but I know
Your touch restores my life
And so I wait for you
So I wait for you.[5]

Guidance

Making Jesus the Lord of our lives means we look to him for marching orders. David, Paul and Jesus are good examples of this. David inquired of the Lord as to whether he should go into battle (1 Sam 23:4; 30:8) and where he should live (2 Sam 2:1). Jesus was always doing what he saw his Father doing (Jn 5:19). Paul was always looking for the Holy Spirit's leading in his travels (Acts 16:6-10).

If we are running our own lives, we have little need to inquire of the Lord. This is especially true in the modern-day Western world. We have unbelievable creature comforts and entertainment to keep us distracted from pursuing God's call on our lives. But if we are on a mission from God, we are totally dependent on him to accomplish our task—we *must* call out to him. The prayer of petition is readily found on the lips of the soldier in battle.

I find that the Lord is always putting me in new situations that require me to trust him in new ways. Whenever I travel to minister in a new location, I have to keep my ears open to the Lord's voice. Being a disciple means we are learning from him and dependent on him. Being a student in the school of the Spirit requires humility and forces us to depend on God instead of ourselves.

Prayers for guidance are found in the songs "Be the Centre," "Still Small Voice" and "Jesus Lead On":

This is my cry
This is my song
You are my guiding light
When the way is unknown
And when these sunny skies
Turn shades of gray

I'll stay close by your side
As you lead the way.

Jesus lead on, I will follow
Jesus lead on
Let your love light the way
Jesus lead on I will follow
Jesus lead on.[6]

Going to the Well

So many of our worship songs—songs like "One Thing I Ask" and "Only You"—are cries for intimate union with the Lord.

One Thing I Ask

One thing I ask, one thing I seek—
That I may dwell in your house, O Lord.
All of my days, all of my life,
That I may see you, Lord.[7]

Only You

No one but you, Lord, can satisfy the longing in my heart
Nothing I do, Lord, can take the place of drawing near to you.

Only you can fill my deepest longing
Only you can breathe in me new life
Only you can fill my heart with laughter
Only you can answer my heart's cry.[8]

It seems like I spend a lot my life "coming back to the heart of worship," as Matt Redman puts it. I need to recenter my life on Jesus everyday. I'm just like everyone else—I feel pulled away from the pursuit of God by the counterfeit gods of this world. So I go directly to God's word to find what is real, what is lasting. There I find my Father and his instructions for living my life.

There's nothing like being with God, meditating on his marvelous attributes and thanking him for all he has done for me. I find great refreshment in singing simple songs of love and devotion—just God, me and the guitar or piano. The simple joy of melody lifts my soul and enlightens my mind to the presence of Jesus. I see that Jesus is alive.

It would be folly to sing "I want to know you, I want to hear your voice, I want to know you more. I want to touch you, I want to see your face"[9] unless we actually spend time listening, waiting and seeking. I relearn the lesson again and again that I can't let my industrious, busy life squeeze out time with God.

I like to work. I like to be productive—to plan and complete projects of all kinds, whether for ministry or my family. But that is both a strength and a weakness. If I'm not careful, I never stop long enough to drink in the love and truth of God. Ultimately I find fulfillment not in *doing* but in *being*—being God's son, his beloved, his servant. In slowing down long enough to absorb God again, I find food for my soul and nourishment for the journey.

Can We Get By Without It?

Is it possible to have the language of worship without the lifestyle to go with it? Yes, of course it is! We can be model church-attenders who know all the right lingo, but without righteous living, the words don't mean a thing.

The prophets show us God's disdain for worship that is only dead, dry ritual. The prophet Amos reprimands God's people: "I hate, I despise your religious feasts; I cannot stand your assemblies. . . . Away with the noise of your songs! I will not listen to the music of your harps. But let justice roll like a river, righteousness like a never-failing stream!" (Amos 5:21, 23-24).

As worship leaders we should regularly ask ourselves whether we are leading worship through our lives or just through our music. What are we doing to bring justice to the world in a practical way? Have we helped anybody recently in a tangible way—have we shared a meal or provided a room for someone for a night?

I'm aware of the danger of having a ministry that is confined only to the "platform." We who are accustomed to church services can slip into thinking that having good meetings is the sole goal of our ministries. If we think we've arrived as Christians simply by having a good meeting, we're fooling ourselves. If the working out of our faith is confined to believers' meetings, then we numb ourselves to the needs of the lost and the poor. Apparently this overemphasis on religious meetings was big in the time of Isaiah and Amos. God wasn't impressed, because there was no justice.

Matt Redman shared one of his models for worship with me: revelation, response, reunion and revolution. The revolution part describes what we're going to *do* about the songs we've sung now that God has changed our hearts. Matt describes the fruit of a changed heart: "When you get some of the Father's heart for you, you're going to get some of his heart for the lost as well. When you see something of God's glory, you're going to care that he's not glorified in the whole world. In worship, God captures your heart; when he's got it, then the real work can begin."[10]

Our worship songs must remind us of our responsibility to share what God has given us. We're reminded of our call to give it away in "Spirit of the Sovereign Lord" and "Let Your Glory Fall":

Father of creation
Unfold your sovereign plan
Raise up a chosen generation
That will march through the land
All of creation is longing
For your unveiling of power
Would you release your anointing?
O God, let this be the hour
Let your glory fall in the room
Let it go forth from here to the nations
Let your fragrance rest in this place
As we gather to seek your face.

Ruler of the nations
The world has yet to see
The full release of your promise
The church in victory
Turn to us Lord and touch us

Make us strong in your might
Overcome our weakness
That we could stand up and fight
Let your kingdom come
Let your will be done
Let us see on earth
The glory of your Son.[11]

We see a thorough integration of worship-words with lifestyle in the life of Paul. Paul saw his work of evangelizing the Gentiles as *worship*, as a "priestly duty" (Rom 15:16). The lifestyle *is* worship. "And whatever you do, whether in word or deed, do it all in the name of the Lord Jesus, giving thanks to God the Father through him" (Col 3:17). For the Christian who can say with Paul, "To live is Christ and to die is gain" (Phil 1:21), the language of worship is a natural byproduct of life.

The song "Take My Life" aptly paraphrases one of Paul's defining Scriptures on the all-encompassing reach of worship (Rom 12:1-2).

Holiness, Holiness is what I long for
Holiness is what I need
Holiness, Holiness is what you want from me

Take my heart and form it
Take my mind, transform it
Take my will, conform it
To yours, to yours, O Lord

Faithfulness is what I long for . . .
Righteousness is what I long for . . .[12]

Day by Day

My wife and I are devoted to our children; they are our pride and joy. Raising our kids is probably the most important part of our "ministry." When I take Linda on a date, we talk a lot about how the kids are doing—their progress, their struggles, the funny things they say. Because of her devotion to them, she is effusive about them in conversation. The Bible says, "For out of the overflow of his heart his mouth speaks" (Lk 6:45). You can tell what people love by what they talk about. So it is with words of praise. If we frequently mention the name of Jesus in our conversations, it's a good sign that we're crazy about him.

I trust that God will continue to lead me into maturity as a Christian. I hope to see more of the fruit of the Spirit in my life as I pastor and disciple younger believers and as I continue the pilgrimage of being a father and a husband. I look forward to seeing many people come to the Lord and many impoverished people having their needs met.

I'll have to cry for help, wisdom and endurance when I feel weak. I'll have to pour out my frustration when nothing seems to be going right. I'll sing praises to God in hard times and good times. I'll bow in worship when he reveals himself to me afresh. If I walk the walk of devotion to God and his purposes, I'll be able to talk the talk of worship.

If we follow the examples of the godly leaders through the history of the church, our lives will produce the fruit of righteousness, and our lips will produce the fruit of praise that pleases God.

5

THE MINISTRIES
OF PRIEST,
PROPHECY & HEALING

It was he who gave some to be apostles,
some to be prophets, some to be evangelists,
and some to be pastors and teachers,
to prepare God's people for works of service,
so that the body of Christ may be built up
until we all reach unity in the faith and in the
knowledge of the Son of God
and become mature, attaining to the whole measure
of the fullness of Christ.
EPHESIANS 4:11-13

WHERE IN THE NEW TESTAMENT do you see the terms "worship leader," "song leader" or "psalmist"? Nowhere. Moreover there is scarcely any mention of musical worship forms in the New Testament. There are several passages that appear to be quotations of hymns that were sung in the early church (Phil 2; 1 Tim 3:16). We also have a few brief exhortations to sing psalms, hymns and spiritual songs as a way of thanking God and encouraging one another.

Nowhere in the New Testament is the emphasis on any particular person filling the role of worship leader. If anything, worship leading was done by anyone who came to a meeting with something to share—a song, a word or a prayer. There are no methods, formats or orders of service to be found. A study of early church history shows the gradual development of tradition. But in the fledgling church of the first century, there was little formalization of any kind of tradition—in worship and even in such matters as how a church was to be governed.

What we *do* have is instruction on the essence of worship, the heart of worship, instead of the how-tos. Romans 12, for example, distills the heart of worship as a lifestyle. The examples of many dedicated servants of God point the way for us, such as brief prayers of worship by Paul and other apostles. Out of this, all kinds of praise, thanks, repentance and celebration will flow. And of course, the Old Testament Psalms are a treasury to draw from.

In every nation and generation down through the ages, worship styles change based on many factors—church culture, national and local culture, and the ebb and flow of renewal and revival. Christian worship is a living thing; its form can never be packaged and finalized. If we had a prescribed order of service or format to follow, we would worship *it* instead of God. Our worship would become stale—a rote religious exercise.

The how-tos change. But the basic theology and emphasis of biblical worship should stay the same.

What Am I Going to Be When I Grow Up?

All of us want to know who we are and what we're here *for*. When I was a little kid, I was often asked what I wanted to be when I grew up. I really wanted to know that too. Our primary identity is, of course, found in being children of God. But we get a lot of our sense of purpose in life from what we *do*, so this is a big issue.

I have functioned in many of the leadership roles and spiritual gifts listed in the New Testament—pastoring, teaching and prophesying. But most of all, I've specialized in worship ministry. The Epistles legitimize the roles of teachers, pastors and evangelists, but where do the worship leaders fit in?

When it became clear to me that worship music was my natural niche, I wanted to know how this role fit into the New Testament pattern of biblical ministry. How does contemporary song leading fit into biblical ministry? What are we really accomplishing when we lead people in singing? Is it a worthy pursuit of one's time, gifts and talents?

If I was going to devote much of my life's work to writing songs, leading worship and training worship leaders, I had to find out whether this worship style was just a trend of the late twentieth century or if there were biblical roots to what I was doing. How does our style of worship compare to highlights of worship music throughout church history?

To answer these questions, I began by looking at various roles and gifts of spiritual leadership, mostly from the New Testament. I think it's easy to see many of the equipping gifts—teaching, prophecy, evangelism and pastoring—flowing through worship leaders. Another big one is the gift of healing through worship. I see today's worship leaders intertwining the power of music with these core spiritual gifts for equipping and strengthening the church. Also, worship leaders function as part of the New Testament priesthood, with a few strong parallels to the Old Testament priest. All these gifts function within the framework of the active rule and reign of God's kingdom.

Worship Invites God's Kingdom to Come

"The kingdom is near you" was the heartbeat of Jesus' message as he walked the hills of Galilee and Judea. Numerous people were healed of all kinds of physical ailments; souls were set free of spiritual blindness. Demonic oppression was broken as Jesus spoke powerful *words* of truth, followed by the *works* of the kingdom.

When John the Baptist sent a message to Jesus, asking, "Are you the one who was to come?" (Mt 11:3), Jesus simply answered, "The blind receive sight, the lame walk . . . and the good news is preached to the poor" (Mt 11:5). It was more than words—the kingdom was also manifest in God's compassionate touch.

The way into the kingdom is repentance. John the Baptist said, "Repent, for the kingdom of heaven is near" (Mt 3:2). The presence of the kingdom *in us* and *near us* is a framework for all we do. We respond moment by moment to God's activity in our lives.

Worship has everything to do with the kingdom of God. Because the kingdom of God is an overarching theme for any kind of ministry, it is a key framework for the worship leader. We are subjects of the King, submitted to his rule. Every spiritual gift we employ in worship leading is a product of God's kingdom near us and in us. The worship leader invites God's kingdom to come and invites people to submit to God's benevolent reign.

If we're *under* God's authority, we can be *vessels* or *ambassadors* of his authority. As we minister under his kingship, all kinds of things happen. His glory appears to people; hearts are pierced with a tangible sense of the Father's love; unbelievers sense the divine presence, they realize that this is *real,* and they want to be a part of it. *All of these things happen by the eruption of God's kingdom during worship*—I've seen it happen over and over again.

Here is an extraordinary story of God's power working through the great old hymn "All Hail the Power of Jesus' Name." The Reverend E. P. Scott, a missionary in India, saw a strange-looking man on the street. He found out that the man belonged to a mountain tribe that had never heard about Jesus. Reverend Scott prayed about it and decided to visit that tribe. As soon as he reached their mountain home, he met a band of warriors who were on a war expedition. They seized him and pointed their spears at his heart.

Immediately the missionary drew out the violin that he always carried with him, and began to play and sing "All Hail the Power of Jesus' Name" in the native language. He closed his eyes, expecting death at any minute. When he reached the third stanza of the hymn, nothing had happened yet. He opened his eyes and was amazed to see that the spears had fallen from the hands of the warriors and their eyes were filled with tears. "They invited Reverend Scott to their homes and he spent two and a half years among them, winning many of them to Christ."[1] The Holy Spirit melted the hearts of the attackers and caused them to weep as they heard the worship music.

The Priestly Worship Leader—Inviting People to Come to the Unshakable Kingdom

In the book of Revelation, John tells us that Jesus has made us his kingdom and his priests who serve before God his Father (Rev 5:10). Unlike the Old Testament priesthood, the Christian priesthood is not reserved for a few special people, but is for all believers. As we walk under God's authority, we all have the privilege of ministering in his name. Because Jesus has opened the way to the Father for all of us, worship leaders don't function as mediators between people and God. But through the gift of music, we invite the church to confidently and humbly approach him. We make it easier for people to approach God through our music, lyrics and prayers.

In the time of Joshua, the priests had the crucial task of carrying the ark of the Lord, which was a symbol of God's presence, favor and power. As the priests carried the Ark of the Covenant into the Jordan River, God stopped the flow of water, creating an open path for people to cross to the other side. This is an apt picture of the modern worship leader as priest. We clear a path for people through the art of song; we lead as servant-priests, holding up the "ark" while people move forward in their journey of following God.

What a privilege it is to invoke the presence of God on behalf of the people. It's a miracle every time God touches his people in worship. The priestly function of invoking God's presence through worship goes back to the time of Moses. God gave Moses instructions for offering sacrifices twice every day and promised that he would respond to Moses' worship by revealing himself. In the day of Moses, this was how God's kingdom came to his people: "This burnt offering is to be made regularly at the entrance to the Tent of Meeting before the LORD. There I will *meet you* and *speak to you; there also will I meet with the Israelites*, and the *place will be consecrated by my glory.* . . . *Then I will dwell among the Israelites* and be their God. *They will know that I am the LORD their God,* who brought them out of Egypt so that I might dwell among them. I am the LORD their God" (Ex 29:42-43, 45-46, emphasis added).

Every day, twice a day, God responded actively to the worship of Moses and the Israelites. It wasn't to be an occasional appearance of God, but a regular one. We see this theme echoed throughout biblical history as God speaks to his worshipers. In the Prophets, the Psalms and into the New Testament, God visits those who bow to him. The priests are catalysts in these holy moments of fellowship with God. Worship leaders today have the privilege of being instrumental in creating a place of communion between God and the church—everyday and every week.

In the early 1990s some doctoral students from the University of Southern California, who were studying why people were drawn to megachurches, conducted a survey at the Anaheim Vineyard. A high percentage of people indicated that they were drawn to the Vineyard because they experienced the presence of God during the musical worship times. In the questionnaire, people were asked to describe their feelings during Vineyard worship. One person responded, "I know that I am touching heaven and that heaven is there with us. God reaches in and touches my heart. He frees me and releases me from anxiety, fear and stress. I get to express my deep love and gratitude to God and His Son, Jesus . . . God is so good . . . I love him so much!!"[2]

Worship—Center Stage in a Spiritual Power Struggle

We're in a war, whether we like it or not. Paul describes the war we wage: "Fight the good fight of the faith" (1 Tim 6:12); "The weapons of our warfare are . . . mighty in God for pulling down strongholds" (2 Cor 10:4 NKJV); and "Endure hardship with us like a good soldier of Christ Jesus. No one serving as a soldier gets involved in civilian affairs—he wants to please his commanding officer" (2 Tim 2:3-4).

For worship leaders, this means two things. We must be dedicated soldiers, and we must rally the troops to be loyal to our commander-in-chief. To do this, we continually consecrate ourselves to his service. We can't lead people there unless we go there ourselves.

"God, put a hook in their jaws!" is a prayer I heard John Wimber pray many times during prayer-ministry times. This was John's way of asking God to write his Word on our hearts, to make us his devoted servants wholly dedicated to his purposes. When the Holy Spirit visits a meeting, he calls people to radical commitment.[3] As set-apart worship leaders, we sound the clarion call to consecration. We call people to wholehearted submission to Jesus. You can't enjoy the benefits of the kingdom without becoming a loyal subject of the King. Therefore songs of consecration and devotion are a crucial part of our arsenal for fighting this spiritual war.

As servants of the King, we relinquish our control and let him have the power. Corporate worship is a lever of God's kingdom power. The crucial role of this lever can be illustrated negatively by examining Satan's resistance to the worship of Yahweh. If worship is real, people who pledge their life to God are removed from Satan's grasp. If Satan loses the battle over worship, he has lost his grip on the believer—whether it's a new convert or a mature Christian. No wonder the enemy so vehemently opposes worship. The power struggle over worship is a recurring biblical theme and it is through this paradigm that we must view our own worship.

Lucifer was a chief angel who was surrounded by God's power. His purity was perverted by his own ambition. He couldn't handle being that close to God's glory. He tried to grasp it for himself—to be the object of praise rather than a giver of praise. So God rejected him.

We see Pharaoh resisting Moses' wish to take the Hebrews to the desert to worship. The Egyptian monarch didn't want to lose his work force, but in the end he couldn't resist God's delivering power. God was calling his people to worship him, to follow him. In weakness and halting obedience, Moses led his people into freedom and worship, out of the grip of the enemy and onto a journey of faith.

Nebuchadnezzar was enraged when Shadrach, Meshach and Abednego refused to worship the golden statue made in his likeness. The three Hebrew men resisted the temptation to bow down to an earthly idol and were thrown into the fire because of it. God delivered them from the fiery furnace. They were making a statement—they belonged to God and would be true to him and would submit to no other power regardless of what happened to them. Their worship was expressed through making a choice for God—this should be the essence of our worship today.

When Christ was born, Herod was deeply disturbed when he found out that the Magi were making a pilgrimage to worship the newborn king. So he made a decree that all boys under the age of two be killed. He took no chances, but did everything in his power to eliminate a competing king who would call worshipers to himself (Mt 2:1-17). Though Herod was an earthly king, leading an earthly kingdom, there was evil power behind him. Through him, Satan was opposing the unveiling of the Messiah, the object of our worship.

Why am I rambling on with these biblical illustrations? Because worship leaders in our day and age are in the center of the same power clash we see in the Bible. When we worship, *we are not just singing songs!* Look behind the physical exterior to the underlying spiritual reality. Like warriors on a battlefield, we are raising a standard of holiness. When we sing to Jesus "I am yours," we are calling people away from the counterfeit realities of this world. We call them to stand under the banner of Jesus. We call them to find their life by losing it in Jesus instead of numbing themselves with a dozen different addictions.

There Is Warfare in Worship

Kingdom revelation floods our minds as the sword of the Spirit, the living Word, pierces our hearts. When we sing lyrics like "Jesus is Lord and I will follow him," we "demolish arguments and every pretension that sets itself up against the knowledge of God" (2 Cor 10:5). Worship is a hammer that chips away at our hardness of heart. The only way to stay free from an "unbelieving heart that turns away from the living God" (Heb 3:12) is to daily encourage one another. Songs of worship are powerful in placing the truth before our eyes daily. The worship leader is indeed a spiritual warrior.

The flip side of the worship leader as warrior is staying free from the lust for power. This is one of the major themes of my life: not clinging to my rights but choosing the humble road. Not pulling out a list of credentials as my right to a high position but serving like everyone else in the local church. Serving my wife, my kids and my friends. Never feeling that I'm above doing the menial tasks of setting up a PA system or cleaning up after a meeting. Not looking down on those who are in lower positions, but treating them with honor.

I've been around a lot of power. I've had the privilege of holding important positions in worship leading. I've been around lots of significant leaders; I've been around the world lots of times, leading worship in large conferences. People know my name everywhere because of my songs.

But God is not impressed with earthly reputation. Having my name on songs and CDs doesn't give me a higher spiritual status than a counselor, a truck driver or a housewife. I have to walk in humility like everyone else, honoring and preferring others above myself and laying down the power.

Old Testament priests were called to purity. They were set apart for their God. Moses' brother and right hand man, Aaron, was such a priest—"Set [Aaron and his sons] apart as holy so they can serve as my priests" (Ex 28:41). The New Testament reflects this theme: "But you are a chosen people, a royal priesthood, a holy nation, *a people belonging to God*" (1 Pet 2:9, emphasis added). We are not our own; we're bought with a price.

As Priests, We Personally Go to Meet with the Lord

In the Old Testament priesthood, only the high priest could enter the holy of holies to meet with God face to face. But we have the privilege of going "into the presence of God, with true hearts fully trusting him" (Heb 10:22 NLT). But do we only do this in the midst of the congregation?

Despite the wonderful times I have had privately worshiping God over the past twenty-seven years, I have to relearn this lesson repeatedly—I need time alone with God. Without praying and reading the

Bible and other inspiring Christian books, I dry up. Since there are so many distractions that clamor for my attention, I need to push them aside and get alone with God.

I need to be formed by the word of God—both the written Word and God's personal word spoken to my heart. Otherwise I forget who I am and what my life is about. I end up going through the motions in ministry. I can still lead worship, but it is less genuine, less real.

Reconnecting with God through prayer, musical worship and reading gives me fuel to keep going and keep giving. When I sing a song in private and it comes alive, that song has much more meaning than when I do it in church. I sing with more passion and conviction when I have adopted the song into my personal worship vocabulary.

I love to work, and I get a lot of fulfillment from what I do. I have a lot of freedom in choosing how to invest my time. But it's easy for me to lose sight of the essential fact that I am first a worshiper and secondly a worship leader. So I take the time to meet with God in a variety of ways—I worship with guitar and piano early in the mornings, I go for prayer walks, and I read.

Recently I sat down to worship the Lord privately in song. My heart's cry was to come back again to simple and pure devotion to Jesus, to devote myself again to spending my life on him and his kingdom. What began as a personal song-prayer evolved into a congregational worship song called "Keep Me":

> Father, I can remember when
> I made a lifelong promise
> To follow you all the way
> But I hear so many other voices
> There are so many choices
> Pulling my heart away
> I am tempted by
> The worldly ways around me
> By philosophies and powers
> That surround me
> I need you to lead me.

Keep me in the narrow way
Keep me in the Jesus way
I need your help today
Keep me in the narrow way
Keep me in the Jesus way
I need your help today.

I hear wisdom is calling me
Leading me on the highway
Of righteousness and peace
I feel the battle is raging on
I'm asking you to be
The captain of my will
For I'm tempted by
The worldly ways around me
By philosophies and powers
That surround me
I need you to lead me.[4]

Physical Healing

In bowing to Jesus' authority in worship, we become eligible for all the blessings of his kingdom. We come within the range of his grace. When we invite God to rule over us, God's kingdom comes near us, sometimes touching our physical bodies.

Nancy Burns was one of the singers on my worship team at the Anaheim Vineyard. She had a condition called *ulcerative proctitis,* a long-standing ailment that caused her lots of pain, bleeding and inconvenience. The doctors told her, "You'll have it your whole life; there's nothing we can really do for you except give you drugs to control it." For an entire year, she couldn't work. She saw lots of doctors and nutritionists, and went on special diets, but everything she ate aggravated her condition.

One Saturday night she had a dream of the glory of the Lord visiting us during a worship time. The very next evening, while singing with our team in church, God healed her. On the morning prior to the worship time, she bled quite heavily, but during that worship time,

God touched her. Says Nancy, "The days of extended bleeding and pain have been completely gone since that night." Except for some bleeding during her pregnancies and the occasional short flare up, she has been free from the condition for several years.

Brenda Wesley, a friend from church, had stomach problems for years. She had experienced lots of pain, seen lots of doctors, adopted a special diet and taken medication. Many years ago she freely expressed worship for the first time and wonderfully experienced God's presence. As she was singing the words "His name is as ointment poured forth," God showed her a picture of the finger of Jesus applying ointment to the rough, red, sore lining of her stomach. After the meeting she wondered if she should dare eat a regular lunch or play it safe, take her medication and stay on her restricted diet. She decided to eat a normal lunch. She was healed and never had another problem!

When you hear stories like this, do you doubt their veracity? Do you think it's just coincidence or psychosomatic healing? For those who are skeptical of healing stories, here is a little scientific evidence of the power of music even apart from the power of the Holy Spirit:

> Marianne Strebely, severely injured in an auto accident, lay in the operating room of St. Luke's Hospital, awaiting anesthesia. She was hooked up to a computer that monitored her heart rate and brain waves. She was also hooked up, by earphones, to a tape recorder playing Vivaldi's *The Four Seasons*. "The music was better than the medication," Strebely claims, comparing this surgery with the previous one. "I remained calm before the operation and didn't need as much sedation." At home, convalescing to music, Strebely was even able to forgo her prescribed painkillers.
>
> Clinical researchers at the UCLA School of Nursing and at Georgia Baptist Medical Center in Atlanta found that premature babies gained weight faster and were able to use oxygen more efficiently when they listened to soothing music mixed with voices or womb sounds.
>
> At Baltimore's St. Agnes Hospital, classical music was provided in the critical care units. "Half an hour of music produced the same effect as ten milligrams of Valium," says Dr. Raymond Bahr, head of the coro-

nary-care unit. "Some patients who had been awake for three of four straight days were able to go into a deep sleep."[5]

God created music. This powerful art form is used for many different purposes—good and bad. But one of God's purposes was to use it as an agent of healing. Worship leaders play the role of the ancient bard—singing songs that contain the healing breath of God. If people are restored to wholeness more quickly through *secular* music, certainly God can use worship music to facilitate healing.

One person at the Anaheim Vineyard said, "[Worship is] a time of *relief*, as the music and words become a prayer from me to the Lord. Sometimes it becomes a very personal one-on-one experience where I feel the Lord holding and loving me."[6]

Healing for the Soul

A woman in our church recently received healing during the closing worship time of a Sunday service. As people were praying for her, the words of the songs were like arrows of love that penetrated into her heart. "It was extremely profound . . . it was like God speaking directly to me . . . to the deepest part where I didn't trust. I've been crying out for God to restore the things that have been stolen from me—rejection I experienced during my childhood. . . . God was telling me the things my father never said to me."

A day or two later, she asked me to send her a copy of the words of the songs I had been singing during her experience with the Holy Spirit. "Oceans of fear cannot conceal your love for me . . . many sorrows cannot quench your love . . . I will not fear, your love is here to comfort me" and "I am yours because you have chosen me, I'm your child because you've called my name . . . I will always be your precious child."[7] In her moment of healing, these words carried much more than information—they were empowered as tools of healing for the soul.

This is an example of seeing what God can do during a prayer ministry time and choosing songs that speak the Father's words of life and healing. We can provide a pathway for people to know the "Father of compassion" and the "God of all comfort" (2 Cor 1:3) as a real living person, not a distant theological truth. As members of the priesthood of believers, it is our privilege to declare his praises (1 Pet 2:9) through our music.

Here is one more story of a major turning point in the life of one of our church members at North Langley Vineyard. Again worship was the catalyst in this healing. In the autumn of 2000, Katherine went to a women's conference in Winnipeg, Canada. She had just been through a difficult time and was questioning her direction and purpose in life. She was so distraught that she didn't really feel like attending the conference. Nevertheless, she went.

Rita Springer, one of the worship leaders at the event, played a song called "Talitha Koum." This song, taken from the fifth chapter of Mark, narrates the story of Jesus raising a twelve-year-old girl from the dead. As Rita played the song, God came to Katherine. "My whole world stood still," she remembers.

Many memories from my childhood were flashing before my eyes. As the story of the resurrection of Talitha came alive, I realized I was like the little girl. I had the choice to stay dead or to reach up and receive the life that God had for me.

When I said to the Lord, "Yes, I want what you have for me," I burst into tears. While Rita sang, Cindy Rethmeier prayed for me. She didn't know what I was going through, but she prayed *exactly* what was needed.

While the Spirit of God filled me with his hope and life, all of my self-effort and despair were draining out of me. I felt that I had nothing left except what God was putting into me. I was falling to pieces emotionally, but my body was being strengthened by God's Spirit. It was for me the healing of my soul. I can always go back and revisit it. It was almost like an adult reconversion.

What I didn't know is that when I was about nine years old, as my parents prayed for me over my bed, God gave them this same Scripture, "Talitha Koum." They felt that later in life, when God gave me that Scripture, it would mark my crossing the threshold from childhood to adulthood. At that time, I would move on from the ways of the past, and come to life as an adult. They were right—this was the end of one season of my life and the beginning of a new season.[8]

An Anaheim church member interviewed in the USC survey shared this about healing in worship: "Almost all of the healing that has come to me has come through the Vineyard. Mostly during worship at kinship [a home group meeting] and in the services. . . . I know God is here, and I still want so much more of Him. I believe that here is where I become whole and also more holy."[9]

When the kingdom of God comes to the church, healing sometimes happens. Through our music, we invite God's rule and reign to break into our human sphere—physically, spiritually and emotionally. Worship leaders have the privilege of being a fulcrum on which the door to the kingdom of God can open.

The Mysterious Power of Music

"Music is a strange thing. I would almost say it is a miracle. For it stands halfway between thought and phenomenon, between spirit and matter," said Heinrich Heine.[10]

From as early as the time of King David, we see music employed as a healing balm for the human soul. As David played his harp, evil spirits were driven away from Saul. This wasn't music alone—it was the anointing of the Holy Spirit.

Music has the effect of bypassing our human defense mechanisms. Our hardened hearts soften up as we let melodies and harmonies wash over us. Music disarms us and taps into the sensitivities of our soul.

Martin Luther is full of praise for the gift of music. He speaks of the "winsome art of music—one of the fairest and most glorious gifts of God, to which Satan is hostile, since it drives away temptation and evil thoughts. . . . Music is one of the finest of the arts; the notes enliven the text, and it drives away the spirit of sadness, as you may behold with King Saul."[11] In 1521, when the imperial ban was placed on Luther, he took great comfort in playing his favorite instrument, the lute.

In 1530 Luther was excluded from participation in the Augsburg Diet, an important summit among leading theologians. Sequestered away at the Saxon border-fortress, he suffered spiritual doubts, insomnia and physical ills of all kinds. He was at the point of despair, even wishing to die. He wrote a letter to Ludwig Senfl, a respected church music composer, asking for a copy of a hymn called "I Will Both Lay Me Down in Peace and Sleep." He wrote to Senfl, "I hope that my end is near. The world has no use for me and despises me, and I am weary of the world and despise it; therefore let the Good Shepherd take my soul."[12]

Senfl sent a copy of the music, but he also sent a song based on Psalm 118:7: "I will not die, but live and will proclaim what God has done." The huge impact of this song on Luther was seen on the wall of his study in Coburg. On his wall, Luther wrote in large letters: *Non moriar sed vivum*—I will live and not die. "Luther, having freed himself of his afflictions and doubts, again became the man and the fighter. Music was the panacea that led him back to life and victory, and mankind to truth."[13]

Art impacts the emotions and feeds the spirit. Under the influence of songs of praise, our anxiety lifts, our mood changes and we get in touch with our inner person and feelings.

Ellie moved to Langley, British Columbia, from her native country of Taiwan. She lives with her young daughter while her husband spends most of his time working in Taiwan. She began to learn English only after relocating to Canada. She was very frustrated by not being able to communicate or understand what people were saying.

Yet when she came to our church and heard the worship music, she was deeply moved and began to cry. This was a new experience for her since she came from a very traditional church in Taiwan where no emotion was expressed. She couldn't understand the words of the songs, yet the Holy Spirit was showing her that God understood her loneliness and frustration. She felt connected to God and knew God was healing her deep hurts. Often the Holy Spirit touches her when she puts on a worship CD at home, bringing comfort in times of struggle.

Philip Yancey in his book *What's So Amazing About Grace?* describes his encounter with God's grace through music:

> I first experienced grace through music. At the Bible college I was at-
> tending, I was viewed as a deviant. People would publicly pray for me
> and ask me if I needed exorcism. I felt harassed, disordered, confused.
> Doors to the dormitory were locked at night, but fortunately I lived on
> the first floor. I would climb out the window of my room and sneak into
> the chapel, which contained a nine-foot Steinway grand piano. In a
> chapel dark but for a small light by which to read music, I would sit for
> an hour or so each night and play Beethoven's sonatas, Chopin's pre-
> ludes, and Schubert's impromptus. My own fingers pressed a kind of tac-
> tile order onto the world. My mind was confused, my body was
> confused, the world was confused—but here I sensed a hidden world of
> beauty, grace and wonder light as a cloud and startling as a butterfly
> wing.[14]

In his book *From Orphans to Heirs,* Mark Stibbe, an Anglican vicar
from England, tells the story of being engulfed by the Father's love
through a worship song. His big breakthrough came in 1987 when he
took his youth group to a rally.

The first song of the worship time, written by Ishmael, a well-
known children's worship leader from England, was about being
adopted into the family of God and placed in the loving care of the Father. Stibbe describes that life-changing moment:

> There was something not only in the melody but also in the words that
> moved me at first. Having been abandoned as a baby at birth, I have al-
> ways been particularly sensitive about being alone.
>
> The thought of the Father being always with us was hugely encourag-
> ing and heartwarming. But what struck me most was the statement
> about being "adopted" in God's family. I had never before sung a hymn
> or a song in which that word had appeared. As I sang out my praises to
> the Father for adopting me and making me his son, something was re-
> leased inside me. I felt my knees turning to jelly and I sank to the
> ground in front of my rebellious youth group. I was in floods of tears
> and I couldn't do anything about it. Nor did I want to do anything about
> it. I knew what was happening to me was the work of the Holy Spirit and
> that it was about the healing of lifelong wounds.[15]

Worship and the Prophetic

Who is there that, in logical words, can express the effect music has on us? A kind of inarticulate, unfathomable speech, which leads us to the edge of the Infinite and lets us for a moment gaze into that!
—THOMAS CARLYLE

In the ancient Near East, prophesying through music was common. Before Saul became king, he encountered a procession of prophets on the road who were playing lyres, tambourines, flutes and harps. The Spirit of the Lord came upon Saul powerfully and he prophesied with them (1 Sam 10:10).

David's chief musicians were "set apart . . . for the ministry of prophesying, accompanied by harps, lyres and cymbals" (1 Chron 25:1).

In the New Testament, prophecy is a gift that can be exercised by anyone and is for the purpose of "strengthening, encouragement and comfort" (1 Cor 14:3). God knows the needs of every person in a church gathering, and he often brings a specific message of prophetic encouragement through worship songs, prayers and Scripture readings.

On a Sunday morning not too long ago, some old friends who had moved to another city came to visit, looking for spiritual refreshing. As they came into the service, Ed said, "I am really thirsty for God." The words of the first song were "All who are thirsty, all who are weak, come to the fountain, dip your heart in the stream of life."[16]

This same couple had tragically lost a newborn grandchild two weeks prior to coming to visit us. The words of the final worship song brought them God's comfort: "I can't understand all that you allow, I just can't see the reason. But my life is in your hands; though I cannot see you, I choose to trust you. Even when my heart is torn, I will praise you, Lord."[17]

While we direct our songs vertically, singing to the Lord, there is a horizontal message that goes into the human heart. Sometimes these words are prophetic—they are anointed by the Holy Spirit to bring divine revelation. Jesus said, "The words I have spoken to you are *spirit and they are life*" (Jn 6:63, emphasis added). There is more than just a transfer of information as the prophetic word is spoken, prayed or sung—there is an impartation of God's living power that bursts into the human soul like a torpedo blasting into the hull of a ship.

The writer of Hebrews describes the Word of God as "full of living power. It is sharper than the sharpest knife, cutting deep into our innermost thoughts and desires. It exposes us for what we really are" (Heb 4:12 NLT). Many times I've been on the receiving end of this sword of God's Word. And many times I've seen this living power penetrate deep into the hearts of worshipers.

In the *Odes of Solomon,* a musician describes the prophetic wind of the Spirit speaking through his music:

> As the wind moves through the harp and the strings speak, so *the Spirit of the Lord speaks through my members*, and I speak through his love. (Ode 6, emphasis added)[18]

> I will open my mouth, and His Spirit will speak through me—the glory of the Lord and his beauty,
> The work of his hands, and the labor of his fingers,
> For the multitude of his mercies and the strength of his word. (Ode 15)[19]

Worship leaders use art to create an environment in which people can draw near to God. Good art pulls us into a higher level of perception. Art comes from the heart and goes into the heart. Music can make the imagination soar beyond the stars, taking us to other worlds.

Sting, the singer-songwriter, relates a childhood experience of music's power: "I remember sitting at my mother's feet as she played the piano, an upright with worn brass pedals. And when she played—always a tango—she seemed *transported to another world,* her feet rocking between loud and soft pedals. Her arms pumping to the odd rhythms, her eyes intent upon the sheet music . . . I knew some important ritual was being enacted."[20]

God can speak a specific word through many forms of music—congregational songs, solos and spontaneous music. The song "We Will Ride" came to me spontaneously when I was coleading worship at a conference in Germany in 1993. While another worship leader was singing, my heart started burning with a scene from the book of Revelation—it was Jesus, triumphantly riding on a white horse with fire in his eyes.

I was so gripped by this picture of the Lord that it was all I could do to wait until there was a pause in the worship to begin singing. As I sang one line at a time, I turned to the keyboardist and shouted out the chords I was about to play. I didn't know what I was going to sing until a few seconds before I sang each phrase. This is one of the few congregational songs I've written that began as a spontaneous song in a worship service. It was recorded live the first time I sang it and recorded again about a year later after some rewriting. This was an exceptional moment in my worship-leading journey. It was one of those serendipitous gifts from God that are unpredictable and impossible to reproduce. I wish this kind of thing happened to me more often!

Prophesying isn't meant for a few elite members of the church. Paul, in his letter to the Corinthians, said, "I wish you were *all* able to prophesy" (1 Cor 14:5 NLT, emphasis added). It takes courage to step out and share a thought that you think might be from God. But as you take the risk to bring words of encouragement, and you find that it was *exactly* what someone needed to hear, you are encouraged to keep taking risks.

6

THE MINISTRIES
OF TEACHING
& EVANGELISM

As the occupation of the ploughman is the ploughshare,
And the occupation of the helmsman is the steering of the ship,
So also my occupation is the psalm of the Lord by his hymns.
My art and service are in his hymns, because his love has
nourished my heart,
And his fruits he poured unto my lips.

THE ODES OF SOLOMON

ANOTHER HAT YOU WEAR in worship leading is that of the *teacher*. By singing songs filled with the Word of God, you have the privilege of holding the pen as God writes his word on the tablets of your church's heart. You equip the church by dispensing, proclaiming and preaching the word of God through music and other symbolic and artistic forms.

Paul emphasizes praying and singing with the mind *and* with the spirit (1 Cor 14:15). In worship, we gain understanding and give thanks by using our intellect. We speak *to one another* with psalms, hymns and spiritual songs. We pass on truth from one generation to the next through our songs (Ps 78:4-5).

As the church receives teaching through the songs it sings, the congregation's minds are being exercised along with their emotions. The way to our hearts is not just by a heightened experience of the Spirit connecting with our emotions. God reaches our hearts through our minds. "Let God transform you into a new person by *changing the way you think*. Then you will know what God wants you to do, and you will know how good and pleasing and perfect his will really is" (Rom 12:2 NLT, emphasis added).

The only way lasting change comes about is through changing people's minds. People make lifestyle choices based on careful consideration of the ideas presented to them. Together with the teachers and preachers, you function as one of the main outlets for God's truth in public meetings.

A survey taken in churches in the United States showed that people forget 80 percent of sermons they hear within three days after hearing them. Even the best of the sermon illustrations are usually forgotten. What do people remember? The songs! The words of songs stick in our heads because of the memorable melodies, rhymes and rhythms attached to them. Just as orthodox Jews bind phylacteries containing God's Word to their heads, the power of music binds the Word of God to our minds. So make sure you're giving them sound teaching in the songs you choose!

The New Testament hymns, which are woven into the fabric of the Gospels and Epistles and Revelation, teach many basic doctrines. Here are some highlights: the divinity and incarnation of Christ (Jn 1:1-18; Col 1:15-20; 1 Tim 3:16); Christ as the promised Messiah (Lk 1:68-79; 2:10-14); the sacrifice of Christ, which justifies us (1 Pet 2:22-25; 3:18-22; Heb 12:22-24); God's mercy (Lk 1:46-55, 68-69); the humility of Jesus (Phil 2:6-11); our call to humility (1 Pet 5:5-9; Jas 4:6-10); the nature of love (1 Cor 13:1-13); God's unshakable love for us (Rom 8:35-39); and God's faithfulness (Rom 16:25-27; 1 Pet 5:10-11). Some examples of New Testament hymns of praise can be found in Luke 19:38; Matthew 21:9; Mark 11:9-10; 1 Timothy 1:17; and Revelation 4:11; 5:12-13; 12:10-12; 15:3-4; and 19:1-9.

The song "Jude Doxology," which declares God's ability to keep us from stumbling, is taken from Jude 24 and 25:

And now all glory to him, who alone is God
Who saves us through his son, Jesus Christ our Lord
For he is able to keep us from falling away
He brings us into his presence with love and joy.

All power, authority, all splendor and majesty
Are his from the beginning and evermore, and evermore.[1]

The rich theological depth of these hymns sends us a clear message—teaching is an important part of singing hymns. In assembling song sets, we are proclaiming the truth about God's identity and our own identity as his heirs, servants and reconcilers of lost people.

In our culture, the value of the artistic is marginalized. Musicians aren't taken as seriously as teachers, doctors or professors. But the most predominant literary genres in the Bible are poetry, songs, stories and letters addressing specific situations in churches. There isn't a lot of didactic teaching in the Bible. In fact Jesus spoke in parables much of the time. This highlights the power of communicating through artistic literary forms.

In studying the great hymn writers of church history, from the early church, through the Reformation and in modern times, you find leading teachers and theologians using music as a teaching tool. Beginning with the early church fathers—Ignatius of Antioch, Saint Clement of Alexandria, Saint Gregory Nazianzus, Saint John Chrysostom, Saint Cyril of Alexandria, Saint Ambrose and Saint Gregory the Great—church leaders have penned songs of worship as a means of instructing their followers in basic Christian doctrine and devotion.

We Tell the Story of Jesus

Worship leading is a celebration of the birth, life, death and resurrection of Christ. Robert Webber describes the centrality of Christ in early church worship: "The Christ that was celebrated in worship was Christ the Creator, Christ the Incarnate one, Christ the inaugurator of the kingdom, Christ crucified, Christ risen, Christ ascended, Christ coming again to renew and restore the universe."[2]

The story of Jesus remains constant, and the message is timeless and relevant for all people of all cultures. But in postmodern society, the story is needed more than ever.

In current philosophical thought, the non-negotiables have become negotiable. There is no baseline Judeo-Christian understanding of a Creator God who calls people to morality. The rule of the day is to make your own rules. There is no fixed vision of eternity that creates a context for daily living.

Into the spirits of Christians and non-Christians challenged by changing values and beliefs, the worship leader injects the unchanging story of Jesus. "As far as the Christian is concerned, the story is wholly objective, not subjective to opinion, addition, or omission; it is constant. . . . The story of the gospel of Jesus Christ is the unchanging center of the life, work, and worship of the church. It is the thing that defines us, tests us, and judges us, as we seek to be faithful communicators of this gospel we serve."[3] Songs of worship are a primary means of telling the story of Jesus.

Through singing the story of Jesus—through rehearsing the acts of God in history—we give people a context for living. As we relive the coming of Christ into the world, our own lives make sense. In worship we see ourselves on the continuum of time—we live between the first and second comings of Christ.

The systematic telling of the Jesus story is one of the strengths of the liturgical church. The cross of Christ is at the center of the liturgy, and the Scripture readings gradually work through the Old and New Testaments year after year. Solid biblical teaching is built into the worship service.

This is more than an intellectual review of information. Within the worshiping community, we are formed by the incarnate Christ in our midst. In worship, we experience the essence of *family*. "This family is stamped by a character—the character of Christ delivered by the Spirit, especially in worship. From a human standpoint, this means that spiritual formation occurs not merely from being *at* worship, but allowing the vision rehearsed in worship—the vision that sweeps from creation to re-creation—to become the vision out of which and by which each worshiper lives."[4]

In worship we not only see who *God* is, we see who *we* are. As rays of revelation stream down from heaven, we say "Oh yeah! Jesus *is* alive! He is real, he is here, and he gives me purpose for living. I am not just a carpenter, a doctor, a truck driver, a mother of small children; I am an *eternal child of God.*"

As eternal citizens of heaven, everything we are springs out of everything God is. We are a "chosen race" because we are children of the Chosen One; we are a "royal priesthood" because we are followers of the great High Priest; we are a "holy nation" because we are subjects of the Holy One of Israel (1 Pet 2:9-10).

Peter goes on to say that we had *no identity* as a community of people until we were joined to the body of Christ: "Once you were not a people but now you are the people of God; once you had not received mercy, but now you have received mercy" (1 Pet 2:10).

"Worship is the *pathway* and the *atmosphere* for people—the saved and the unsaved alike—to discover their royal calling in Christ, their high destiny in life, their fullest personal worth and their deepest human fulfillment."[5] This is Jack Hayford's eloquent explanation of seeing our identity in Christ through worship.

Paradoxically worship is one of the most humbling, yet ennobling activities we can do. It's humbling because we bow before our Creator, and it is dignifying because in it we realize that we are heirs of the highest royalty.

> God wants the fullness of His power, the richness of his nature, the authority of his office and the wealth of His resources to ennoble our identity and determine our destiny! . . . Worshiping God brings the highest sense of dignity humanity can know, for the regal nature of His Majesty begins to flow downward and inward.[6]

In leading worship, we give people a window to heaven. Our songs are the vehicle of fixing our gaze on things above, not on things on the earth.

Fighting Doctrinal Battles Through Song

Most worship leaders wouldn't think of giving themselves the label theologian. Yet through our songs, we present the truth about who God is. We paint a picture of the personality of God and the way he relates to humanity. In an age where people get their information in quick, stimulating ways—through the Internet, TV and radio—worship songs are a hugely important source of theology.

To illustrate the theological power of songs, let's look at an example from church history. One of the most significant battles over doctrine in the early church was the Arian controversy in the fourth century A.D. The issue in question was the divinity of Jesus. Athanasius led the way in arguing that Jesus was "of one substance with the Father" (Nicene Creed)—that he was not created, but was eternal and infinite along with the Father and the Holy Spirit. His opponent, Arius, a presbyter in Alexandria, was viewed as an expert logician. He argued that the Son was created by the Father and was not equal to the Father.

This crucial doctrinal battle raged for many years. At times, popular opinion was on the side of Arius. His view held sway in the Eastern Orthodox churches. The Arian controversy was the main subject of debate at the council of Nicea in A.D. 325. This episode of church history is relevant to our discussion because the hymns written by Athansius and Arius were among their most powerful tools in fighting for their beliefs. Here are some excerpts from hymns by both of these theologian songwriters:

☐ From Athanasius:

The Father is made of none, neither created nor begotten.
The Son is of the Father alone, not made, nor created, but begotten.
The Holy Ghost is of the Father, and the Son:
Not made, nor created, nor begotten, but proceeding. . . .

We believe and confess that our Lord Jesus Christ, the Son of God, is
God and man. . .
Perfect God and perfect man: Of a reasonable soul and human flesh
subsisting:

Equal to his Father, as touching his Godhead:

Less than the Father, as touching his manhood

Who, although he be God and man, yet he is not two but one Christ.

☐ From Arius:

We praise him as without beginning because of him who has a beginning.

And adore him as everlasting, because of him who in time has come to be.

He that is without beginning made the Son *a beginning of things originated;*

And advanced him as the Son to himself by adoption.

He has nothing proper to God in proper subsistence.

For he is not equal, no, nor one is essence with him.

Wise is God, for he is the teacher of wisdom. [7]

Arius's hymn begins beautifully. But as the hymn unfolds, he strips Jesus of his divinity, thereby attacking the very foundation of Christianity. This song was sung by thousands of Christians in Arius's day. Let this be a lesson to us—if we are worship leaders, we *are* theologians, so we'd better be singing the real truth.

In the sixteenth-century Reformation, we see another example of the power of song. In a document by a Jesuit, we read, "Luther has murdered more souls with his songs than with his writings and sermons."[8] For an opponent of Reformation theology, the songs were the most devastating weapon, not Luther's sermons!

Through worship music, our souls are fed with a rich impartation of truth. The worship leaders' challenge is to serve good food to the church every week, giving them a nutritious diet of truth, encouragement and exhortation.

Every week, you *envision* people. You feed their minds. You tell them who God is, how God sees them and how God wants them to live. You challenge their minds; you confront them with truth. (Maybe that's one reason they often look pensive and thoughtful rather than always effusive and expressive). Remember, the worship you are hoping to foster goes far beyond the immediate reactions of people in a worship service. You are giving them food for thought, food for life.

Worship as Evangelism

"Ours is the culture of the artist, not the culture of the orator," said Eddie Gibbs, professor of church growth at Fuller Seminary, to a group of Vineyard songwriters in February 2001. He told us that our impact as worship leaders and songwriters is far greater than that of preachers or authors. He urged us to "respond to the challenge of biblical illiteracy," which is greatly on the increase today.

We face our own modern-day Arian controversy, since we live in a culture where the majority does not accept Jesus as God. Our job is not only to explain the nature of God to Christians but to present the gospel to the unconvinced.

Tony Campolo, who teaches at Eastern College in Pennsylvania, observes that in past years, the voluntary chapel services were largely neglected by the students. However, in recent years this has changed dramatically:

> Students are leading worship in forms that have come out of the charismatic movement. The worship time lasts for more than 30 minutes and it is drawing students together as never before. We had to move the chapel services out of the auditorium and into the gymnasium just to contain the student body. *Students are being converted by worship.* This is surprising to me because I always thought the sermons were the decisive factor in bringing people into a relationship with Christ. But, I am finding that worship can do that even more effectively and deeply. Young people are looking for a relationship with God more than a theology about God. Worship which is truly in the Spirit is giving that to them.[9]

Once again we see that worship touches the whole being—not just the mind, but the emotions and the spirit. The pathway to the mind is often through sensory, artistic experiences.

I have many friends who regularly lead worship music outside the four walls of the church. One friend in British Columbia leads worship every Friday night in the summertime after a church-sponsored barbeque for the needy in the town's central park. Other friends do worship songs at secular coffee houses (many of the songs don't emphasize the name of Jesus but are genuine songs about God). I've led worship on a beach boardwalk, in parks, in shopping centers and in apartment courtyards. Here is one story of the evangelistic power that works through worship in the marketplace.

In 1993 Gary Best took a ministry team to do some conferences and outreaches at a major European city that is known for its sordid red-light district. On the team were many teenagers and young adults. One day they did an evangelistic outreach in the town square. Some of the members of the team were doing free artwork—sketches of people's faces and other things—to offer to anyone passing by.

During these activities, the team members were meeting people. Gary met three young men from Morocco. Almost immediately the discussion turned toward a debate over the Bible versus the Koran. So Gary steered the conversation away from an antagonistic tone. "I'm not trying to coerce you into believing anything. But if you're around tonight, come and listen to the music. We have a pretty good band," he said.

That night, in the middle of the town square, the band started off with a couple of worship songs. Then Gary stepped up to the microphone and shared for about three minutes. More than two hundred people had gathered to hear the music. He knew that it would take much more than a nice musical presentation to draw anyone to Jesus.

"This is who we are—we're Christians. I know as soon as I say that, your first response is to tune us out. But we really believe what we're singing and we've experienced it. For us, this is genuine," he explained. Then Gary felt that God gave him an insight about the people in that city and their hunger for real love. "Listen to these songs. The love that you're searching for is what we're singing about."

After the band played about three more songs, Gary stepped up and gave some words of knowledge—insight from God intended specifically for a few people in the crowd. These words of knowledge were related to the lyrics of the songs. "There's a couple here—you were on your way to see a strip show. But you stopped to listen to the music, and the last song riveted you." Gary could sense people being gripped by these words. There was a ring of truth that people couldn't ignore.

"As the band continues to worship, some of us are going to be walking around; if you'd like to talk to us, we're here." The team members noticed lots of people in tears.

Gary walked up to a guy in his forties who had tears running down his cheeks. "Do you speak English?" Gary asked. The band had been singing the song "Father I Want You to Hold Me." The weeping man said, "I want to know the Father's love."

Joy, Gary's wife, had a long talk with the couple that had been on their way to the strip show. They didn't go to the show; instead, they talked about God and let Joy pray for them.

At the end of the last set of songs, Gary invited people to stay and talk. Lots of people wanted to stay and talk about what they had seen and felt. They hadn't been wowed by a concert; they had been struck by the spirit of worship. It wasn't a performance; it was a heart cry.

At the end of the worship, Gary found the three young Moroccan guys that he had met earlier in the day. He thanked them for coming and realized that they wanted to spend some time with the team. When Gary told them the team was leaving the next day, one of the men said, " I want to know Jesus. How can I know him?"

"You can know him right now," repled Gary. So three of the team members led them to the Lord.

About a year later, Gary found out that two of these men didn't even go back to Morocco. They joined a Discipleship Training School with Youth With A Mission. After taking the course, they went on an outreach trip with the school.

Christians and pre-Christian seekers are drawn to genuine worship. Today more than ever our cultural climate calls for genuine worship rather than glitzy shows or dry recitations of theological truth. People know the difference between a dead religion and a living relationship. So when they see people deeply engaged in worship, they take notice.

They see people expressing themselves as one group, yet individually. One is kneeling, one is sitting quietly, and others may be dancing. Someone is crying as a healing word comes to their heart. There is something tangible in the air, yet elusive. People aren't just singing to the ceiling; they are actually communing with God. When a pre-Christian who is hungry for God sees this happening, the light begins to dawn.

Jesus came to give light to every person (Jn 1:9). God gives everyone the capacity to know him from the heart. So when the Holy Spirit is mingling with worshipers' hearts, the seeker can sense something divine.

The Engel Scale, developed by James Engel, a noted social scientist, identifies the different degrees of a person's resistance to Christ or acceptance of him.[10] At the extreme negative end of the scale, a person is atheistic and strongly opposed to Christ. As he or she becomes open to Christian truth and entertains the idea that Jesus might be God, the person progresses toward conversion, or zero, on the scale. When the person makes a decision to receive and follow Christ, he or she moves into the positive side of the scale.

I see worship as a major factor in bringing people along this continuum from unbelief toward knowing God. With the added factors of hearing biblical truth and having friends who can personally interact with them, worship is a powerful tool for convincing and convicting people of God's existence and his love for them. Many people have told me that their crucial turning point of becoming Christians has been during worship times.

Walter Heidenreich, the leader of a Christian movement in Germany called FCJG *(Freie Christliche Jugendgemeinschaft)*, has visited Mongolia many times on missions trips. He tells the story of a Mongolian woman who heard a worship tape and unexplainably began to cry:

> In 1991 and 1992 I went to Anaheim, and John Wimber gave me quite a number of worship tapes. Some of these I took with me on my first journey to Mongolia. The story as I remember it was as following: The very, very, very primitively furnished hotel that we stayed at on that first journey to Mongolia also had a very, very, very primitive red-light bar in the basement. The lady working there was bored as she stood at the bar,

and we gave her your worship tape. Immediately she stopped the music and put in your tape. Never before had she heard of Jesus or Christianity at all, thus she didn't know that the tape contained Christian music. The atmosphere in the bar changed immediately when she played the worship music, and the lady started to cry. Our co-workers talked to her and after that prayed with her. I can't remember if that lady became a Christian, we haven't seen her ever since. However, what I can surely testify is that she experienced the love of God in such a strong way through your songs that she was deeply touched and moved.[11]

Here's another crosscultural example of evangelism through worship. I've had the privilege of going to the Vineyard church in Madras (Chennai), India. Every time I go, we conduct worship events in public venues and invite anyone who will come. Leaflets are passed out in the shopping centers, and posters are put up all over town. We've been to several cities—Bombay, Pune, Goa and Bangalore. Amazingly, non-Christians come by the droves to these events. In North America, it's like pulling teeth to get non-Christians to a Christian concert. If you have earned the trust of a pre-Christian person, they might consider coming to hear Christian music.

But in India it's not like that at all! They love to listen to *any kind* of music, especially if it's a band from North America. There is a cultural bridge that has been built through the secular media. The Indian people are enamored with Western rock music. So we use that bridge for evangelism.

Many people who first joined the Vineyard in Madras came because they had attended one of the many worship concerts. After an evening of worship, a Hindu remarked, "It seemed as if that guy [the worship leader] knew God personally." When we sing to God as a loving Father, it is a refreshing picture for the Hindu who has only known of a distant god who is appeased by impersonal rituals.

Pastor
King David was both a shepherd of Israel (see Ps 78:71) and "the man anointed by the God of Jacob, Israel's singer of songs" (see 2 Sam

23:1). This combination of gifts applies to us today.

Having a pastor's heart is essential for a worship leader. We care for the flock through our song service. We choose songs out of our desire to see people filled with God's love, walking under his protection and filled with his comfort.

When there is a tragedy in the church, we give people a musical language to express their grief. The lament is an important color in the spectrum of worship. We see many laments in the Psalms and many occasions for laments in the real life of our loved ones in the church. At any given point in time, a significant percentage of church members will be going through difficult times. Conversely when the church is celebrating a victory, we launch the congregation into joyfulness with jubilant songs.

The hands-on work of relating to people, counseling people and discipling people is a role that many worship leaders fill. Some worship leaders lean more toward a pure artist gift mix, while others are gifted pastors—they naturally gravitate toward spending lots of time encouraging and caring for others. Whether you are a people-person or a private person, you have to love people! Some of the caregiving issues for worship leader "pastors" are covered in other chapters of this book.

In summary, worship leaders have multiple functions—we invoke the presence of the Holy Spirit; we teach, prophesy and evangelize through the lyrics of our songs. Seeing worship leading through this multicolored lens heightens our awareness of the breadth and depth of our ministry through song. Through our music, the Holy Spirit writes on the hearts of men, women and children eternal truths of many colors and hues.

7

THE WORSHIP TEAM

Servants & Friends

Man strives for glory, honor, fame . . .
that all the world may know his name.
He amasses wealth by brain and hand
and becomes a power in the land.
But when he nears the end of life
and looks back over the years of strife,
he finds that happiness depends on none of these—
but love of friends.
AUTHOR UNKNOWN

WHAT IS A WORSHIP TEAM besides a musical group? Lots of things. It's a group of friends who mutually serve one another. It's a team of servants whose goal is to bless and encourage the entire church. It's a spiritual task force that has the job of bringing the people before their Father and Creator in worship. It all begins with inviting people to be part of a team.

Criteria for Choosing Worship Team Members

Musical skill. The level of skill required will depend on the number and expertise of all musicians in the church. At the very least, worship team members should be able to play from a chord chart, keep rhythm and stay on pitch.

Classical training versus playing by ear. There are two very different approaches to playing keyboards, woodwinds or strings—playing by ear and playing from a written score. While trained classical pianists may have great skillfulness in playing from a written score, playing on a worship team is an entirely different musical challenge. Some classically trained pianists (or violinists, flutists) can adapt to a contemporary worship-band setting. To do this, they must learn to follow the leader spontaneously—to skip around from verses to choruses to coda sections. The best solution is to learn to play by ear, not just from written scores. Another problem in being limited to playing written music is that often there are no written parts available for keyboards or symphonic instruments for contemporary songs.

Godly character in team members. Several traits come to mind: servant attitude and actions, freedom from selfish ambition, evidence of fruit of the spirit—love, joy, peace, patience, kindness, goodness, faithfulness, gentleness and self-control—and freedom from a need to find basic personal significance through playing music. Remember that nobody scores a perfect 10 in any of these areas, including the mature leader.

There are instances when you'll find a young Christian who is sincere and devoted to the Lord, but is still immature. I don't rule out the possibility of having young Christians on worship bands. As long as people are wholeheartedly pursuing God and are open to correction, I am open to including them on a worship team.

Godly parents and spouses. Do the parents on your team spend time with their kids? Are the husbands and wives serving each other? Are the husbands or wives plagued with jealousy over their partners hanging out with other people at worship practices and services?[1]

A heart that pursues God and a lifestyle that expresses the priority of that pursuit. How do people spend their time and money and energy? What are their goals in life? Do they do anything to reach out to the poor and needy? Do they spend more time in church or pursuing entertainment? For example, I know a couple whose path toward divorce was precipitated by spending time in line-dancing clubs.

Understanding of worship as a relational, interactive discourse with God.

Without experience in worshiping God this way, the approach to playing in a band can be far too performance oriented—playing primarily to entertain.

Church involvement—in a small group or another accountability group. Attendance at church is important even when musicians aren't in the band. Commitment to the overall vision and values of the local church is essential.

I usually require team members to have been actively involved in the local church for at least six months before becoming musically involved. If they are new to the church *and* if they have a good pastoral reference from another church, this requirement can be waived.

Personality compatibility with leader and team. In order to be comfortable leading a team, worship leaders need the freedom to choose people they can relate to easily. The worship team leaders' gut feelings about who they can work with are important. This doesn't mean the team members have to be best friends. Some churches have to pull together fifteen-year-olds and fifty-five-year-olds to form any kind of team. When the group is diverse in age and musical preferences, more love and deference is required to cover the lack of natural social and musical bonds. As always, a servant heart is the key issue.

A willingness to follow and serve under the leader's initiative. Few things are harder than trying to lead someone who doesn't want to follow you. Sometimes a worship leader will inherit a team and will find out the hard way that there is someone who is resisting his or her leadership every step of the way. I've been in the position of coming as the new leader among an already established team of musicians. I could feel the reluctance of the people to follow my leadership. Leading them sometimes felt like pulling a heavy weight up a hill.

Over time, team members need to accept a new leader, or else they can't stay on the team. The leader should be gracious and give the people room to accept the change in leadership. Hopefully they will gain an appreciation for the new leader. But if disunity starts to spread because of a resistant team member, the team really suffers.

A sense of leading from God in choosing team members. Sometimes I've had a distinct impression from God that I should include a certain person. Usually I make my decisions based on the naturally observable criteria that I've listed above. But once in a while God will plant faith in my heart for certain people and a strong feeling that they belong on the team.

Impartiality. Sometimes we can feel pressure to do a favor for someone who has connections in the church or is a long-standing faithful member, like a relative of the pastor. Those shouldn't be the reasons for putting someone on a worship team.

If you owe someone a favor, pay them back in another way. Remember, you have a responsibility to choose the instrumentalists and singers who will most effectively facilitate congregational worship. If you elevate to a worship team position a friend who doesn't have the required skill, you may eventually have to remove them. I do whatever I can to prevent those situations. It's much better to put people on teams for the right reasons. People should be on worship teams because they're musically gifted and they have a heart for worship.

The Audition Process

To join a performing group, musicians must compete for available openings. Before moving to the Anaheim Vineyard in 1992, I had never held a formal audition. The churches I had been in were always small enough to evaluate the ability of musicians in the context of informal tryouts. But I knew I would never find the musicians hiding in the woodwork at the Anaheim Vineyard unless I held a publicly announced audition.

Another reason to hold a public audition is that many singers and instrumentalists are too shy to come forward with their gifts. People are afraid of appearing competitive or self-promoting. Sometimes they underestimate their ability to be a contributing team member. The very same people who are shy about their gifts are sometimes the best choices for a worship team. Having an attitude of humility is a top priority.

At first I dreaded holding auditions because I knew I would have to tell some people that I didn't have a place for them on the worship team. But unless I held the audition, I would never have discovered the musicians hidden in the congregation or their musical skill levels.

I like to give people as much information as I can before an audition so they know what to expect. I hand out a few pages of written information about three weeks before the audition. Here's an example of the contents of that packet: "We're looking for electric guitar players and saxophonists who can play fills and solos, not the melody of the song." Then I explain that a fill is a short instrumental melodic line that complements the melody of the lyric. For classically trained musicians, this is sometimes new information. Playing from a written musical score is an entirely different thing than playing spontaneously by ear.

Musicians are usually pretty nervous when they're auditioning. To lower the intimidation factor, I have an entire band of candidates playing simultaneously so that the focus is never solely on one person. If there are only a few people auditioning, we bring regular band members in to play while the new people are trying out. I give them simple chord charts to songs that we do in church, and let them go at it.

To help minimize the disappointment for people who don't pass an audition, I clearly communicate beforehand that some people will not be chosen. Because of the size of our church and the number of musicians, I make it clear that we are primarily looking for people who have some previous band experience. Usually all of the Sunday worship leaders are present at an audition. After the audition we discuss the performance of the people. I usually respond to people after an audition by e-mail to let them know whether they have passed or not. I try to be specific in explaining what the different worship leaders perceived each person's musical strengths and weaknesses to be.

In church life, auditions are a tough issue because one of our general values is to include everyone. But if we are going to put our best foot forward in facilitating congregational worship, it follows that we should use our best musicians most of the time, while giving some opportunity for less experienced players and singers to develop.

A worship band is different from a church choir in this respect. In a choir there is room for as many people who can sing reasonably well. In a band there is only a handful of positions available. Raising up multiple bands includes more people, but there is still a basic skill requirement that must be met. The idea of competing for spots on a worship team may seem crass, but to me it's reality. Musical quality isn't everything in worship music, but it plays a big part. Christians come to worship, not just watch, we hope. They can't help but be influenced by the quality of the musical presentation—their spirits are inspired by God's Spirit *and* by what they hear.

How good does a singer or musician have to be to make the team? This standard is different depending on the size of the church and the caliber of the available musicians. In some larger churches, the caliber of musicians can be very high, therefore making it difficult for beginners to find a spot on a team. Conversely, in small churches there may be only a few musicians who attend the church. In that case, the skill level required is much lower.

At my church, there's a pretty high caliber of musicianship, so the bar is higher for new people coming in. Three out of our five Sunday worship leaders have sung on worship recordings that have been distributed internationally.

Where to draw the line isn't always easy. In assembling a team for a given Sunday, I sometimes try to mix in the less skilled players with the better ones. This way the overall strength of the team isn't compromised too much. If I have too many weak links at once, the music dips below a musical caliber that is needed to lead and stimulate the church to worship. The less skillful the players, the more stress I feel in leading the team. If a beginning electric guitarist gets a chance to play on the band and maybe play one short instrumental solo, they can learn a lot by hanging out with the rest of the band. They might not contribute a great deal to the overall sound, but they are adding something that's helpful in a few songs.

While I was at the Anaheim Vineyard, I experimented with having a trial period for new players. Sometimes my first step was to invite people to fill in for an absent band member. In a roundabout way, this is a type of audition. Even if I was pretty sure that someone was right for my team, I didn't promise them a permanent position. Instead I invited them to join us for a period of three to six months. I explained that either of us could opt out at the end of that time period. There are many potential reasons for discontinuing a person's involvement on a team:

- ☐ musical inability
- ☐ incompatibility between the leader and the team member
- ☐ lack of commitment to the team, like not coming to rehearsals
- ☐ attitude problems

Breaking the Bad News

In Paul's discourse on public worship in 1 Corinthians 11—14, he strategically places the famous "love chapter" right in the middle. Chapter 13 tells us exactly how to deal with the disappointments, jealousies and critical attitudes that rise up in us with regard to public worship. People were being hurt in the Corinthian church, and people get hurt today over the same issues.

How do you tell someone they don't sing well enough to participate on a worship team? You do it with gentleness, kindness and humility, with a good dose of sweat along the way. How do you resolve a personality clash between team members? You do it with great patience and perseverance. If the clash is never really resolved, you have to decide who goes and who stays on the team. At that point, it's time for all parties to "keep no record of wrongs" (1 Cor 13:5). I've personally experienced these types of conflicts, and it's really hard! I've stayed up nights worrying about some of those situations. Love and forgiveness have gotten me through. "Love always protects, always trusts, always hopes, always perseveres" (1 Cor 13:7).

There have been a few occasions when I've asked people not to continue in my worship team. One time the issue seemed to be a personality clash. Though I enjoyed the company of this friend outside the worship team, somehow there was tension when we rehearsed. Often I was rubbed wrong by the things this person said. I'm sure this was partly because I was a little on edge—I was anxious about doing well in my new position as a worship leader. At times I found it difficult to be at peace in rehearsals while working with this singer.

When I first asked her to sing on my team, she only had a few months experience of singing in a worship band. It was all a brand new experience for her—everything from using a microphone to singing harmony parts to worshiping spiritually with a team. Understandably, she felt tense. As a beginner working with a worship leader with high expectations for band members, she felt pressured.

So after several months of singing together, I had a personal meeting with this woman and her husband to let them know that it wasn't working for me. She had also been feeling the tension during our rehearsals and already had a sense that it wouldn't work out. She handled the situation with great maturity. She didn't stomp out of the church angrily blaming me for being a lousy worship pastor. It wasn't easy for her, but she made the right choice—she chose to believe the best about me. She didn't spread bad rumors about me. Whenever she felt a twinge of pain over the situation, she would ask God's blessing on me rather than being angry. She took it as an opportunity to grow in God—to become better, not bitter.

To break the news to her about discontinuing our working together, I had a face-to-face meeting with her and her husband, which was key to handling the situation. In conflict resolution, love and concern are best communicated in person, and this is so much better than writing a letter. Though face-to-face contact is the best, phone calls can also work well.

A few years later I invited her back to sing on the team, and it worked well. Both of us had matured enough so that the tension was gone. We continued singing together until my family moved away to another city.

Here's another conflict resolution situation. I had invited a singer to try out by singing with my team during a worship service. She had trouble staying on pitch, so I had to let her know that I wouldn't be inviting her to sing because of this. She took offense and felt hurt. Then she told her husband about our phone conversation. He was upset when he heard her version of what I had said, so I met with him in person. He was upset at the beginning of our meeting, but he softened when I gave him my version of my phone conversation with his wife. He could see that I really cared and that I had done my best to be kind and gentle with his wife.

There haven't been very many times when I've had to ask someone to leave a worship team, but there have been a few, and it's never easy. No matter how nicely you put it, you still have some bad news to break to people.

If I have to confront someone, I try to follow the biblical directive, "Clothe yourself with compassion, kindness, humility, gentleness and patience. Bear with each another and forgive whatever grievances you may have against one another" (Col 3:12-13). I don't like confrontation, but who does? Honesty is the best and only policy.

Different problems call for different kinds of intervention. If there are serious problems in the person's marriage or family, or problems with drugs or sexual immorality, I get the help of another pastor. When a really serious problem arises, sometimes the only choice is to discontinue the person's involvement immediately. But for less serious problems, I'd rather include the person on the team while we work through the issue.

Spiritual Warfare

Unless we address relational conflict on a worship team, sooner or later the Holy Spirit will be quenched in worship. If our relationships aren't pure, there is a foothold for the enemy. Most of the New Testament admonitions to resist the devil have to do with relational conflicts. Here are three primary examples of this:

☐ "In your anger, do not sin . . . and do not give the devil a foothold." (Eph 4:26-27)

☐ "What causes fights and quarrels among you? Don't they come from your desires that battle within you? . . . Submit yourselves, then, to God. Resist the devil, and he will flee from you." (Jas 4:17)

☐ "All of you, clothe yourselves with humility toward one another, because 'God opposes the proud but gives grace to the humble.' . . . Be self-controlled and alert. Your enemy the devil prowls around like a roaring lion looking for someone to devour." (1 Pet 5:5, 8)

The most grueling battles of spiritual warfare I've experienced have centered around strained relationships. Jealousy, competition and misunderstandings open the door to warfare. If we hold bitterness and anger toward one another, we are opening the door to our enemy, the roaring lion who wants to devour us and divide us.

I've heard some ugly stories about jealousy and competition on worship teams—people making threats because their territory on the worship team is being taken from their grasp. The worst story I've heard is of one sound man bringing a gun to a rehearsal and waving it around while sitting behind the sound board. This was his idea of a joke, his way of saying, "This is my turf and don't you dare mess with me." What's the message here? Surrender your rights.

There was another case involving a bass player/singer. When a new worship leader was appointed, he asked the person to play bass, but not to sing. The bass player raised a big stink, sending shock waves through the team. He was determined to hang on to his "right" to sing, not just to play bass. The unity of the team was destroyed through his angry self-centeredness.

To win this kind of war, the best defense is a good offense. "Do not be overcome by evil but overcome evil with good" (Rom 12:21). "Do nothing out of selfish ambition or vain conceit, but in humility consider others better than yourselves" (Phil 2:3). In the book of Philippians, Paul pleads with Euodia and Syntyche to "agree with each other in the Lord" (Phil 4:2). He saw that their disagreement was wreaking havoc in the church. Surrender your rights.

Imagine having to share your space—having to make decisions consultatively instead of all by yourself. Jesus walked in humility, following his Father's orders. Is the servant above the master? I don't think so. If two singers are struggling to hear themselves in the same monitor speaker, they need to communicate openly about it between themselves and the sound technician. Rather than accusing the other singer of trying to dominate, they need to talk it through in a non-threatening way. Small frustrations can turn into deep resentment if people fail to discuss issues like this.

What you need for right worship is humility. What you need for unity with your coworkers is humility. Humility and perseverance are the weapons that defeat pride and division. Paul wrote to Timothy, "I want men everywhere to lift up holy hands in prayer, without anger or disputing" (1 Tim 2:8). Disputes and prayer don't mix very well.

Maintaining Purity in Male-Female Relationships

God created us with sexual drive. Men are attracted to women and vice versa. In working together on a worship team, we have to face that reality. Men and women participate together in intense, passionate worship of God and may spend a lot of time together in rehearsal and ministry. I enjoy working with female musicians not only because of their musical ability, but because they are my friends. In rehearsal, worship and fellowship, we have a great time together as a team of friends. Close friendships can and should develop, but we have to safeguard against impurity.

Because of my role of working with men *and* women, I am forced to grapple with my own human frailties with regard to my sexuality. Maybe you saw the movie *Mr. Holland's Opus,* about a music teacher's struggle to be successful. But a subplot of the film is his attraction to a talented, attractive high school girl. Mr. Holland was drawn to her; he knew he had to act responsibly as a husband, father and teacher, yet he struggled with temptation.

Can you guess why this part of the story stood out to me? Because I am tempted in the same way he was. By the grace of God, I haven't dabbled in immoral relationships like this character did. But in twenty-seven years of worship leading, I've had to say no to sensual fantasies over and over again.

In this part of the chapter, I am speaking as a man and applying it primarily to men, with the hope that women can glean some wisdom and apply it to the female side of the equation. Here are some safeguards against impurity.

Don't spend too much time together. I wouldn't say that a man and woman should *never* be alone together for ministry purposes. If that were true, how could we work together? How could a man train a woman worship leader, or vice versa? You might say that same-sex relationships are the best for discipling. In regards to issues of general discipleship, I agree. But in a specialized ministry like worship, there will be times when there's not a man available in a local church to work with a male trainee, so the mentoring is done by a woman, or vice versa.

Most of the work I do with women is in the context of small group settings. But occasionally I have an appointment with a woman. We may go out for lunch or coffee. If I'm alone in an office, I use simple safeguards like leaving the door open. This is for the purpose of making the woman feel safe and avoiding the appearance of anything questionable.

Once I was on a trip to another city to do a worship seminar. There were two worship leaders for the weekend: a woman and me. We were given rooms in a hotel and a car to share to get to the meetings. The other team members were placed in homes, so we were the *only two* in the car and the *only two* in the hotel. When I figured out how this scenario was shaping up and how it might appear to others, I invited my bass player to share my hotel room with me. This removed the possibility of my being alone with the woman, and it provided accountability with another team member.

In the late 1980s I went on a ministry trip to a foreign country where English wasn't spoken. I worked with a young, attractive female interpreter when I was praying for people at the conference meetings. This woman also sang on the worship team. Though we were never alone together, I found that after a few days I had developed an emotional attachment to her that was impure. I should have confessed my struggles to one of the men on the team and asked him to pray for me right away; this would have broken the power of this temptation quickly. Instead I waited until I got home and then confessed my impure thoughts and feelings to my wife. God had been talking to her, letting her know that I was struggling with some kind of sensual temptation.

One of the lessons of this story is to avoid too close a working relationship with someone of the opposite sex. It is especially dangerous for people who do itinerant ministry. When we're on the road, the normal safety net of our family, friends and daily routine is gone, so we're far more vulnerable to temptation.

A second lesson is this: don't deceive yourself into thinking that just because you are never alone with a person, that you can't possibly be developing an unhealthy attachment. The seeds of lust and emotional bonding can be planted and fertilized even with no private contact between two people. Remember that Jesus said adultery is a sin of the heart, not just a physical act.

Signs that your friendship with a coworker is becoming too close:

☐ You find yourself always drawn to a person while in a group, and you *really enjoy* talking with them. There is electric excitement in talking to this person.

☐ You find yourself physically attracted to them, and you may struggle with lustful thoughts. It's not just an occasional glance, but a continued problem. There's a hook in you that keeps you coming back for more.

☐ You find yourself thinking about the person when you're apart. You picture yourself together with them, conversing and laughing together. You may even have dreams about the individual.

Getting your weakness and sin into the light:

☐ Confess your sin to God. He understands your humanity and is able to keep you from falling.

☐ Confess your struggles to a trusted friend of the same sex as yourself and request prayer. Make yourself accountable. It's a lot harder to lose yourself in sensual fantasy when you know that someone else knows about your problem.

☐ Avoid being alone at any time with any woman/man you are tempted to pursue.

☐ Don't be overly dependent on a person of the opposite sex as a ministry partner.

☐ Get your eyes off the person.

☐ Don't touch the person. Avoid a polite Christian hug if this stumbles you.

☐ Whenever a lustful thought comes up, do battle by praying for God's best for the person.

A Serving Arm of the Church

Playing on a worship team involves far more than a musical experience. It's a small network of relationships that's connected to the larger network of the church. We're all members of one another (see Rom 12:5), as Paul tells the Corinthians, and that means we have to be aware of how we fit in as individuals and as a worship team. There are some key things your team needs to understand about being part of your own worship team and the larger team of the church.

The worship team exists not unto itself but for the good of the whole church. What's the difference between a performing group and a worship group? First, pure performing groups exist for the purpose of putting on a good show. Performers want to look good. They're in it for what they can personally get out of it. Second, performers place a high value on having freedom to express their music however they feel inspired. They can play the songs of their own choice with all the intricacy and flash that they can muster.

Not so for the worship team. A key word for worship band members is restraint. Most of my instrumentalists and vocalists have *far more* ability than they show on any given Sunday. Because they understand the goal of our worship, they play to *support* the worship experience, not to *upstage* it. In moments of great exuberance and jubilation, more complex and aggressive playing and singing is appropriate. When the congregation is swept up into celebration, and *worship* is soaring, the instruments can also soar. This is why a sensitive heart is so essential for each musician. If the musicians are tuned in to the dialogue between God and his church, they will sense how to accent the worship time through musical embellishment.

The importance of teamwork. Each band member follows the cues of the leader to know when to crescendo and when to decrescendo. As the team communicates among itself through listening and simple glances and signals, members know whose turn it is to fill a hole with an instrumental interlude. This results from an attitude of servanthood and sensitivity.

Repeating old standard songs is one way of serving the church. It takes a lot of discipline for a worship team to play the same songs over and over again. The musician grows weary of a song much sooner than the average church member. I don't mean we should play a song to death, but in order to *facilitate worship*, the band must do the songs that are familiar, while gradually introducing new material. As a servant-team, we must swallow our artistic pride and repeat the songs that work for the church.

Respecting Your Church's Heritage

Every church makes a pilgrimage in its worship experience. Some major in traditional hymns; others sing exclusively contemporary music. Church traditions don't die easily. If you want to lead people in a form of worship that they can relate to and appreciate, you have to use the *language* they've come to love and appreciate. If you speak a different language (such as the wrong songs or too many new songs) people won't enter into worship very easily, and they may even get mad at you. Although *forms* of worship are really only *vessels* for sacred worship, people treat the forms as sacred in themselves. If you minimize their sacred experience, you'll get some serious resistance.

This should be an issue not of church politics but of getting the job of worship leading done. Decisions should be made by church leaders, not factions within the church. But the leadership should recognize the value of providing familiar forms of worship for their congregation. Familiarity is essential in congregational worship. Without it, people feel lost and unable to connect with God.

Being a Team Player

I've been in situations where the worship team struggled with an adversarial attitude toward the leadership of the church. If decisions that the worship team doesn't like are being made by the pastors, it's easy to take sides and become divisive. Church history shows us that divisions can happen over all kinds of issues. Sadly, history tells the story of people being murdered over the issue of how baptism should be done. In another case, one group didn't believe musical instruments should be used in church, so an axe was used to destroy some of the highest quality pipe organs of that day.

In hindsight it all seems so foolish. At the core of those arguments was an unwillingness to relinquish control of how worship was to be conducted. Insistence on personal opinions drove people to forsake love for one another. Brothers in Christ became enemies. The desire for power and control tainted the pursuit of godliness until hatred gave birth to murder. And it was all done in the name of sound doctrine.

It may seem crazy to draw parallels between contemporary church music issues and the tragic mistakes of church history. But the core issues are the same. An elitist mentality drove people to destructive behavior. The same can happen for us if we see ourselves as having all the answers for worship music. As a group of friends who perform together, it's possible to gain momentum as an exclusive group that is ruled by its own opinions and has its own agenda.

Matt Redman cautions worship leaders against falling into this pit: "It can be easy to get into an arrogance with all your muso mates; you all think you know the score on how the worship should be and what the church needs. . . . It can be so dangerous to get into that musical ghetto where it's the musos versus the pastors."[1]

What's the contentious issue in your church? More hymns or less hymns? More upbeat music or less? More intercession or less? More spontaneous prophetic worship or less? These issues are the source of many disagreements, sometimes leading to broken relationships. Rather than insisting on our own way, we ought to "submit to one another out of reverence for Christ" (Eph 5:21). There are lots of ways to worship God while remaining true to the biblical pattern. I think we're a lot more picky than God is about the *right* way to worship.

We'll always see things through colored lenses; we'll always have our own bias. So we need the input of nonmusicians to help us see the big picture accurately. The elders tend to be in tune with the needs of the church in regard to worship, partly because they're the ones that receive the complaints; so we should listen to them.

If critical opinions are shared among the band members about the elders' decisions, the Lord is grieved, and the unity of the church is disrupted. If that course is pursued, it will only be a matter of time before the anointing for worship dissipates. Nip these tendencies in the bud by refusing to speak against the leadership even if you disagree with some of the policies and decisions.

That's not always easy. But that's the way life is in the church. After all, the church is full of opinionated individuals. Maintaining the unity of the Spirit in the bond of peace takes *hard work and perseverance.* Paul knew how hard it was to get people to agree and cooperate. That's why he had to encourage his people with these words: "May the God who gives *endurance* and encouragement give you a spirit of unity among yourselves as you follow Christ Jesus, so that with one heart and mouth you may glorify the God and Father of our Lord Jesus Christ" (Rom 15:5-6, emphasis added). Without endurance and unity, we can't glorify him with "one heart and one mouth."

Sooner or later leaders will make decisions that you would have made differently had you been in their shoes. Having been a senior pastor for three years, I know a little bit about how hard it is to walk in those shoes! That experience has made me less critical of senior leadership. Worship team leaders have the power to influence band members toward pursuing peace and harmony with the leaders. If your friends entice you into making a critical comment, choose to bless and not curse. I've made the mistake of sharing opinions with team members that I should have kept to myself. Words are powerful. Used correctly, words are tools that can steer people toward an attitude of deference and humility, and build the unity of the church.

8

WORKING TOGETHER

Worship Leader & Pastor

> *Be completely humble and gentle; be patient,*
> *bearing with one another in love.*
> *Make every effort to keep the unity of the Spirit*
> *through the bond of peace.*
> EPHESIANS 4:2-3

I'VE BEEN IN SEVEN CHURCHES in the last twenty-seven years. I've worked under pastors of a wide variety of ages, personalities and leadership styles. In the late 1980s and early 1990s I worked with John Wimber during the last part of his life. John was a seasoned leader of a worldwide movement of churches. From 1983 to 1984 I worked with Jack Little when he was just turning thirty. Jack was the classic Southern California surfer-pastor. Jack had a winsome personality and was gifted at planting churches. I now work with Gary Best, who is the national director of the Vineyard churches in Canada and the pastor of the North Langley Vineyard.

I've had distant relationships with most of the pastors and closer friendships with only a few. What makes a coworking relationship a lasting and enjoyable experience?

Follow a Pastor You Respect and Trust

Why follow someone you don't trust and respect? I wouldn't go to a church, much less serve as a worship leader in a church, where I didn't trust the pastor. If I respect the character of a leader—the way he or she treats family, friends and the least visible person in the church—then I can consider following their leadership.

Moses appointed "wise and respected men" (Deut 1:15) to have authority to lead. Moses knew what kind of leader his people would trust and follow. The early church willingly brought their possessions to the elders to be distributed to the poor. They trusted their leaders to do the right thing with their gifts.

If I see my pastors serving wholeheartedly, then I can follow them and "hold them in the highest regard in love because of their work" (1 Thess 5:13). Some of the Christlike qualities I see in my pastor are generosity, freedom from selfish ambition, and a tremendous heart and lifestyle of serving God and the church and reaching the lost. Rather than a top-down leadership style, Gary emphasizes team leadership. When I see pastors exercising spiritual authority for the benefit of those they lead, instead of their own benefit, I can trust them. It's a privilege for me to serve with Gary and Joy because of their integrity.

Relationship

When you work together in the trenches of church life for several years, there's a depth of relationship that develops. In 1985, together with Gary and Joy Best, my wife and I experienced the rigors and joys of planting a church. Being comrades in planting a church draws you together. You make mistakes together and party together. You forgive one another and gain respect for one another.

So when I began to consider moving back to Canada, the established relationship with the Bests was a definite factor. Because of our history together, Gary isn't just an overseer and pastor; he's a friend. That's the best situation I know of for two coworkers.

When I asked Gary about the keys to nurturing worship leaders, he said, "Nothing fragments worship leaders like *using* them."[1] If a pastor has no relationship with the worship leader but uses his or her gifts as a means to create dynamic worship services, the leader can feel used. If the worship leader is wounded by the pastor, trust deteriorates. If the pastor simply gives orders and expects the musician to perform, to achieve a goal, the foundation for a lasting relationship isn't built.

But *friendship* isn't the first word I'd use to describe most of my relationships with pastors I've worked with—*coworker, leader, mentor, overseer* and *authority* would be more accurate. Sure, there has been an element of friendship with each pastor, but a deeper friendship only develops with a special set of circumstances—things like having time to play together, whether it be going out to dinner or playing golf.

Having a compatible personality allows the relationship go deeper. I don't think worship leaders are necessarily entitled to a deep friendship with the pastor. It's more possible in a smaller church where the leadership core is smaller. But what about larger churches? You may have very little contact with the senior pastor if you're on a large church staff.

When I moved to Anaheim in 1992, I had very little expectation of one-on-one time with John Wimber. He had not only a local church to lead but a national and international movement of churches to pastor. I wasn't disappointed that our private meetings were few and far between.

Even now a few months can pass between my meetings with Gary. Both of us have busy schedules, including frequent travel. But because of our history, friendship and mutual trust, our relationship isn't shaken by long periods of noncontact.

God's Leading

Another huge factor in finding the right pastor to work with is God's leading. If you know God has led you to join a fellowship, you can put your hand to the plow and not look back unless God redirects you. When things got tough for me at Surrey Vineyard in 1991, I was comforted by remembering the certainty of God's leading us to move there a few years earlier.

I tend toward a spirit of wanderlust. It's easy to think of reasons why it would be better to live somewhere else. All kinds of things make us look for the greener grass on the other side of the fence. Part of that is the discomfort of being a pilgrim on the earth. The only place that will *really* be home is heaven.

Faithfulness over the long haul isn't easy, no matter where you are. No church is perfect—every church is full of people, and people are imperfect. Even when you're surrounded by wonderful people, life is challenging. The Christian life is a marathon.

Values, Priorities and Practices in Worship

Here are a few more huge factors in a compatible pastor/worship leader pairing: Do you share the same theology of worship? Do you speak the same musical worship language?

The spectrum of styles is very broad from one denomination to another. More importantly, there's great variety *within* movements and denominations. Within the Vineyard movement, for example, there are many churches that have a traditional Vineyard approach to worship, emphasizing intimate songs of love, adoration and exaltation. But some Vineyard churches have a more seeker-sensitive service, which emphasizes upbeat music that is more message-oriented, giving the gospel to the unchurched rather than providing an opportunity for personal communion with God.

On the other end of the spectrum, some Vineyard churches have more of an "anything goes" model of worship, which is more emotional and may include all kinds of things like running around the church and making lots of loud noises. Loud noises are actually a very biblical form of worship (Ps 47:1, 5; 100:5)!

Regarding song selection, I use mostly modern worship songs and a few hymns. I mostly use an acoustic rock band, but sometimes I don't use bass and drums. I sing gentle songs and high energy songs. I sing songs that proclaim the attributes of God and his saving work on the cross, and also simple songs of love and devotion.

But everything I do is within a narrow range of instrumentation—

guitars, keyboards, drums and bass, with the occasional acoustic instrument, such as flute, penny whistle or saxophone. I don't use a
choir (though I did occasionally in Anaheim), and I don't use hymn-
books.

The specifics of instrumentation and song style aren't issues of
right or wrong; they're issues of fitting in with your local church. As
long as the pastor and worship leader are comfortable with a certain
selection of songs and instrumentation, the partnership will be har-
monious.

Are You on the Same Page?

To know if you belong somewhere, you need to know the overarching
guidelines that the pastor has established. In some cases this may not
be clearly defined because the pastor implicitly trusts the worship
leader. The pastor knows that the worship leader is aware of the historical precedent of worship in that church, and that they will lead in a
manner that fits the personality of that church. This was the situation
for me in Anaheim and now in North Langley. Because I have a
shared history and a good track record with the pastors of these
churches, there is a mutual understanding and agreement between us
about what is acceptable in terms of song selection, length of the set
and other variables.

But in many other cases, there needs to be ongoing clarification regarding the philosophy of worship and worship leading. Clear expression of expectations between the pastor and worship leader is essential for the team to be working in unity. In my first few years in
Anaheim, I had a few of these sessions with the pastor. At one point
they felt I was putting too much emphasis on intercessory songs, so I
toned down that theme. I thought these songs were very relevant to
the church at that time, but the pastor asked for less intercession, so I
cooperated.

Here's a true story of two friends of mine—a pastor and worship
leader—who came to an impasse in their working relationship. The
pastor—let's call him James—had taken over a small church and was

going through the typical turmoil of leading church members through a transition. Before James came to pastor, the church had been through a season of holding renewal meetings. The ethos of the church was marked by a thirst for personal renewal.

James wanted renewal, but had a much stronger bent toward evangelism. He was looking for a worship leader who had the same values. He found out that a gifted worship leader, Jerry, was possibly interested in relocating to a church where he could lead worship.

James respected Jerry's musical gifts. When they met briefly together, they seemed to be on the same track. So Jerry relocated from a different region of the country, and they began working together.

As the months went by, conflict arose over a few major issues. First of all, James was looking for a more aggressive style of worship leading in which the worship leader directly addresses the congregation, exhorting them to express worship with enthusiasm. This clashed with Jerry's style, which was to simply let the people worship as they were drawn in by the Holy Spirit. Jerry emphasized contemplative songs with a sprinkling of joyful celebration, while James wanted to major on songs that were more upbeat and rousing.

James's commitment to his philosophy of worship was especially strong because he himself was a good worship leader. In the first church he pastored, James began as the main worship leader. He had found a style that worked well. In their initial meetings, James probably didn't realize how different his style was from Jerry's.

Second, after about a year in James's church, Jerry and his wife were uncomfortable with James's style of leadership and the overall direction of the church. It was hard to keep leading worship when they weren't sure it was the kind of church they wanted to help build.

Third, there was a personality conflict. James had a high-energy, sanguine personality, while Jerry was more like me—mellow, pensive and sometimes melancholy.

It wasn't a good marriage. Unfortunately they didn't have much of a courtship. If their process of getting to know one another had been longer and more thorough, maybe they would have figured out that it wasn't a match. But it's hard to dig deeper in a relationship when you live a thousand miles apart. Even the luxury of more get-to-know-you meetings might not have painted a realistic picture of working together day by day.

After a few years of trying to make it work, Jerry and his wife moved on to another church. Both leadership couples learned a lot through the experience and found God's help in the midst of the struggle. But it was a hard situation to go through.

The moral of the story is, are you on the same page as the pastor? Do you share a common background in worship style? I can work easily with Gary because our idea of a good worship service is pretty much the same. I don't have to be careful about staying within his boundaries for worship music; he gives a lot of freedom to the worship leaders to plan and lead their own song sets.

If you have a different church background from your pastor, do you have enough in common to work together? If you don't, you may finish a worship time and feel it was great. Meanwhile the pastor thinks you were really off track. In the past I've sung songs that I thought were prophetic, and later the pastor let me know he thought I was really off the mark.

None of these differences of opinion between my pastors and me have been fundamental differences that would give me a reason to leave the church. But at the time, I was discouraged by the requests to shift my direction. At one point I was asked not to emphasize spontaneous songs because I was told it excluded the congregation from participating.

Even though the pastors sometimes didn't like spontaneous songs that I thought were prophetic, they *did* believe in prophecy. They *did* allow people to prophesy in other ways, both in larger services and home meetings. Here is an example of a negotiable difference. I felt constricted in my freedom to sing spontaneously, but my basic theological view was the same as that of the pastors. We all believed prophecy was good and should be practiced. So I limited my freedom in order to be a team player and maintain unity. I didn't agree with their point of view, but I cooperated.

Input from the Senior Pastor on Song Selection

Empowered leadership is a high value for me. I come from a move-ment of churches that strongly believes in delegating authority to peo-ple to lead and letting them lead, not as a puppet of the senior leader, but as responsible decision makers.

On the issue of delegating leadership authority to worship lead-ers, my pastor says, "Always give them a little more freedom than they want and not enough so they can hang themselves. . . . Give them a little more than you and they are comfortable with." Gary's goal is not just an inspiring worship service for this week; it's to train *strong, capable leaders* who can lead responsibly. Children can carry out orders, but they'll never mature in leadership if they can't help steer the ship. Your goal isn't just musical skill acquisition; it's matu-rity and growth.

A big part of learning to lead is making mistakes. Releasing leaders involves risk. Sometimes they'll make decisions you don't like. If they never have a chance to learn from their mistakes, they won't grow. Oc-casionally I feel embarrassed by the leaders I release. They say the wrong things, they offend people, they sing songs that aren't appropri-ate for the moment. That's all part of the game—we risk our own rep-utation when we put people on the platform. But how else do people learn to lead?

Matt Redman recalls the acceptance and encouragement he re-ceived in his formational years: "I was allowed to try new things. I didn't get slammed down when things went wrong. They [the pastors] said 'well done for trying' when things didn't go so well."[2] If we slap the hands of young leaders when they make a bad decision, how will they have courage to spread their wings and fly?

If you're a senior pastor and you want to raise up worship leaders, you need to let them *really lead*. Delegating authority to lead isn't about repression and control; it's about envisioning and empowering. Un-der God's authority, people are mobilized into service, not confined to a narrow space of carrying out orders from an overseer. When leaders operate in God's authority, they don't have to give orders. Most often

Gary makes suggestions; he doesn't give orders. He influences, but he doesn't control.

It's one thing to theoretically hold to the value of equipping the saints (Eph 4:11-13); it's another thing to actually *do it*. Allowing others to minister means letting go and letting things get messy sometimes. I'd rather have lots of workers on the field learning to use their gifts than a perfectly polished presentation.

A strong preference of postmodernists is collegiality in leadership. Top-down leadership is less accepted today than it was twenty years ago. This applies to the church as much as to the business world. Gifted leaders don't want to be told what to do; they want to be part of a team that works and consults together.

Gifted worship leaders intrinsically have the ability to choose good songs and assemble good sets of music. One of the goals in a leader's development should be a high level of autonomy in choosing songs. Early in a worship leader's development, the pastor may need to give lots of input—even looking at the Sunday song list on Friday to make sure it's OK. That's reasonable. If the young leader has thirty minutes on a Sunday morning, the senior leader has good reason to be concerned about what songs will be sung and what message will be given.

As worship leaders develop a good track record by consistently leading inspiring worship that engages the congregation, they prove their readiness to have significant decision-making power in planning worship.

When is it OK for a pastor to give specific input to a worship leader? It can be very helpful for the senior leader to occasionally suggest a certain song, mood or theme. The pastor and worship leader can join forces by weaving a common theme into the sermon *and* the songs. This one-two punch is a powerful communication tool. During a prayer-ministry time, the pastor may suggest a specific song or two that will set the stage for the church to respond to the sermon message. Having led many prayer ministry times myself, I know how helpful it is when a worship leader does a song that releases *my* faith and points the way for the prayer time.

The roles of pastor and worship leader in worship leading are shaped by their church culture and tradition. If the pastor traditionally has had lots of input into the songs and other elements of Sunday worship, such as dance, video or special numbers, then it would be natural for that to continue, though it may evolve over time. If the church traditionally plans worship through a committee, I wouldn't throw out that model either. Each church has to respect its traditions and make changes gradually, if and when the leaders decide the old model is no longer helpful.

The Committee Planning Model
Typically the Sunday worship leaders in my church have only minimal contact with the speaker in planning for a Sunday morning service. The pastors communicate to the worship leaders what is being covered in an upcoming sermon series. Occasionally a pastor will suggest a certain song, but the majority of the music planning is left in the hands of the worship leader, who has a high level of independence in planning the specifics of a worship set.

In contrast to this model, many churches have a committee approach to worship planning, which involves the worship leader, the pastor and a worship leadership team. One such church is the Christian Church of Clarendon Hills, Illinois. Robert Locklear, appointed last year as the music director, explained to me how they work together as a team.[3]

First, the church's overall mission and vision is clearly communicated to all the workers in the church. Though the church has been in existence for several decades, they currently describe themselves as a church with a church-planting mentality. They are in the process of transitioning from a traditional model to an intentionally evangelistic one. They have also made a recent transition from a model of two worship planners per week to a centralized committee model for planning worship. The church is growing, and they are planning for much more growth in the years to come.

The musical worship at Clarendon Hills is piano-driven, with a synthesizer and bass. Occasionally they have drums and an acoustic guitar, and they plan to add electric guitar in the near future. Their goal is to soon be regularly using a full band. For special numbers, they use backing tracks.

The pastor provides broad input to Robert, painting a big picture of sermon series and topics. He plans his sermons at least five weeks in advance so Robert has plenty of time to research song possibilities. After meeting with the pastor, Robert sends out an outline of the message topics to his worship planning committee, asking them to come up with ideas on how to support and develop the theme.

The planning committee is made up of ten to twelve people. Included in the team are (1) a point person for musical solos and dramas, (2) a point person for the decoration of the sanctuary and other artistic enhancements and (3) several musicians who are taking responsibility as coplanners—background vocalists, pianists and others. Some of them serve as "efficiency directors," filling the role of a stage manager to help each phase and transition of the service run smoothly. (They avoid the term "stage director" to avoid a show biz mentality.)

Once every month, the committee has a planning meeting. They discuss ways of developing the theme of the sermon series through music, drama and other artistic expressions. All committee members have the freedom to suggest their ideas, and everyone's opinion is valued. Having worked together for several months with this model, they are gaining an increasing sense of teamwork.

As with any group of artists, everyone doesn't always see eye to eye on how to develop a theme. People are sensitive, and artists are especially sensitive. So they are careful to show respect to one another and not say, "You're wrong." Though there are tensions, they are healthy, and the committee is working together as a team.

A week before each Sunday service, Robert hands out all the music to the vocalists and instrumentalists. Toward the end of the week, Robert and his pastor meet to fine tune the service. Robert will ask the pastor to interject words and prayers at certain points in the service.

When Is It OK to Agree to Disagree?

I know a worship leader who was leading worship in a large highly visible Vineyard church (I'll call him Bob). His worship leading was very well received for the first few years. Bob did a great job working with band members and other worship leaders, and the pastors greatly appreciated his worship leading and his work—together with his wife—with young married couples.

But then his path of growth diverged from a new emphasis in the church. Bob gained an increasing hunger for more intensity in worship, more insertion of spontaneous prophetic songs and more freedom to expand the borders of his leadership style. At the same time, the church tightened up its guidelines for Sunday worship leaders. They began shooting for a model that was more seeker sensitive— more upbeat music, mostly declarative songs as opposed to songs of intimate communion with God, and a shorter and shorter time for worship. The time for worship decreased from about thirty minutes to about twenty-one or twenty-two minutes. The pastors made increasing requests to stay closer to the mark in both duration and content of the worship service.

Conflict of opinion between Bob and the pastor increased. The sense of trust they had in one another eroded through a few misunderstandings. After a year or so of declining involvement, Bob moved on to another church. Through his last year in the church, I counseled Bob to not make any sudden moves, to make sure he didn't speak against the pastor and to act with integrity in every way. It was clear it wouldn't work in the long haul. So he proceeded cautiously, carefully watching his words, both to the pastor and to church members who asked questions about his departure.

Here is a classic example of nobody being wrong. It was a divergence of paths—two people with different visions and convictions for Sunday worship, two people who loved God and had different ways of doing church. Was it difficult for Bob to leave? Absolutely. After several years of making friends, discipling people and worshiping together, there were close bonds of relationship. It wasn't easy for Bob and his wife to walk away from those friends.

In many cases the bonds of friendship will sway the decision of worship leaders to stay in a church even if they prefer a different style of worship. After all, the music is only one aspect of overall church life. There are many other values and practices that make up the essence of any local church. If you have spent many years worshiping with one church family, make sure you've spent lots of time praying and receiving counsel before leaving your church. If you're married, make sure you talk through the issues thoroughly with your spouse.

I don't believe in church hopping. I believe in staying committed to a local church even through the hard times. But if young worship leaders aspire to devote a good part of their time and energy to worship ministry, they have to be in a place that will allow growth and development of their gifts (not on their own terms, of course). There is no single model of worship that will work for everybody. The body of Christ is too diverse. Denominations and movements all have their own slant, their own repertoire, their own way of vocalizing praise to God. They breed worship leaders who lead in distinct styles.

Communication

How do you maintain unity with a pastor and solve conflicts? Talk about the issues. Have the courage to initiate discussions about pastoral decisions you don't understand or don't like. Begin by asking questions, not confronting. Seek to understand the pastor's viewpoint before you give your opinion. I have to fight against my natural tendency to defend my viewpoint, my turf and myself. If I go into a meeting with all guns blazing, I'm not pursuing peace.

Find out the difference between negotiables and nonnegotiables. Where is the line a hazy one, and where is it solid black?

I've found it can be intimidating to talk through policy issues with people in authority. But most of that fear comes from within me—it's not because my pastors have been ogres. All of my pastors have been ready to listen to my ideas and answer my questions. The great majority of my discussions with pastors have been peaceful and encouraging.

Here are some simple examples of how a worship leader can get feedback from the pastor: "How do you feel it's going with the song selection for Sunday worship?" "I've been experimenting with a slightly different approach on these songs—do you think it has been well-received?" Questions like these simply open the door for the pastors to give their opinion without having to force it on you. If you know the pastor feels good about how it's going, you'll feel more relaxed and secure as you continue to lead.

Before recording the album *The River Is Here,* I was getting a recurring word from God, or at least I thought it was from God. I was seeing myself doing an entire worship album, not just half of the CD, as was the custom with the *Touching the Father's Heart* series. I felt it would be arrogant and self-promoting to suggest that I do an entire album. I knew that John Wimber wanted to protect worship leaders from becoming enamored with themselves, and one of his ways was to have at least two worship leaders per album.

I dismissed these impulses about doing an entire album because I knew it didn't fit into the established policy. But the thought persistently came back to me that I would do an entire worship album. It got to the point where I felt I would be disobedient to God if I didn't at least bring up the subject with John, who was the executive producer for the worship series. I mustered my courage to bring up the subject. I began with a disclaimer. It went something like this: "I keep hearing something that might be from God, but it doesn't seem to make a lot of sense. I'm bringing it up because I don't want to ignore something God might be saying. I'm ready to hear you say, 'No, that's not a good idea,' but I at least have to discharge this thing that's on my heart."

He did say no and reviewed with me the policy of including as many worship leaders as possible. He said encouragingly, "I wish we could hear *all* the songs you've been writing." But he stuck with his policy of having two worship leaders on the recording. I was satisfied. I had fulfilled my responsibility of discussing with the pastor a leading from God that wouldn't go away.

Within a year after that episode, I recorded an entire acoustic worship album called *Eternity*. It wasn't my idea to do that album—I was invited to do it by Chris Wimber. A few years later I recorded another entire worship CD called *Name Above All*. I had the right idea in doing some solo projects, but the timing wasn't right for *The River Is Here*.

This is an example of hearing something from God and not understanding the application of the word. Discussing the word with a pastor was part of the process of interpreting the word. I let it go and did nothing more to pursue it. Then it came back to me in a way I couldn't have predicted—it *was* a promise from God after all.

My willingness to follow John's leadership goes back to God's leading. As clear as I've ever known anything, I knew that I was supposed to go to Anaheim to serve in the Vineyard. This became clear to me through words, dreams and visions from God that I had received between 1989 and 1992.

It was a privilege to serve under John's leadership. He impacted the church worldwide, was tremendously gifted and was a great encouragement to me. But I didn't agree with everything he said or did. That didn't matter because I knew that God had called me to work with him for a season. Serving God is worked out by serving under the leaders he raises up. I trusted God to express his authority in my life through the leadership. That's the only way to go.

As Paul says to servants with earthly masters, "Whatever you do, work at it with all your heart, *as working for the Lord, not for men,* since you know that you will receive an inheritance from the Lord as a reward. It is the Lord Christ you are serving" (Col 3:23-24, emphasis added).

Expectations

In 1979, at the age of twenty-one, I had my first position as a Sunday worship leader. I was a primary worship leader and an intern pastor as well. But I had almost no contact with the senior pastor. I was hoping he would be a friend and mentor to me, but he had hundreds of other people to attend to and dozens of other leaders.

Since then I've learned not to have unrealistic expectations of the role that a pastor will play in my life. If you look up to a pastor and have an aching need to be guided and fathered, you may find yourself craving attention from him. That might set you up for a big disappointment. Jesus himself only had eleven people that formed his most intimate group of friends, and only three of those eleven were his closest companions.

Pastors are human. They have a limited capacity to care for people, just like everyone else. So I don't expect them to be superhuman. I don't expect them to be mistake-free either. So if I feel hurt by something a pastor says, I forgive.

In more than one of churches I've served in, I've seen other young leaders receive more favor and attention from the pastor. Whose fault is that? Nobody's. But it's so easy to blame a pastor because you feel left out. At times I've felt slighted and ignored. I've struggled with jealousy. But it was a sifting experience for me; it produced godliness in me. Who was I serving? What was my goal? To serve Christ or to curry favor from a pastor who would reward me with his friendship and maybe a staff position?

I don't expect pastors or leaders to initiate contact with me. If I want to talk to someone, I take the first step. I have a busy life with my work and family, and so does everyone else. It's my job as a member of the body of Christ to *pursue fellowship*. I know people who sit around and feel sorry for themselves because nobody calls them. That's the sin of self-pity, and the way out is repentance and taking initiative by being the first to call someone else.

The Danger of Withdrawal

There have been times when I've felt like withdrawing from relationships with authority figures. I can remember sulking and letting my grievances boil to the point of bitterness. On a few occasions in the late 1980s I went to Gary (we were then at the Langley Vineyard) to confess sins of competition and jealousy.

I couldn't live with myself until I was free from my impure ambitions to succeed. I wanted to excel as a pastor, and I saw that my gifts were limited. In my late twenties, I was still finding out who I was as a leader and what my role in the church would be. In this insecure phase of life I was frustrated with my own limitations. (Not that I'm done with being frustrated in my forties!) I expressed this insecurity through comparing myself with other leaders. If I could do what another leader could do, I would get more responsibility and status, or so I thought.

Having the guts to get these things out into the open was key to my survival as a worship pastor. Exposing hidden sins to God's light breaks their power over us. Gaining freedom from these insecurities wasn't an overnight transformation—it took a lot of perseverance and relentless repentance. But confessing my weaknesses to my friends and elders was crucial. I found that they accepted me despite my insecurities; they didn't expect me to be a superpastor. They were happy to let me do what I was gifted and able to do.

The Independent, Artistic Temperament

Sometimes the pastor and worship leader are on two completely different wavelengths, so they have to work hard at understanding each other. The wise pastor will learn about and make room for the quirks of the artistic personality. Some traits of the artist are personality related, and some are just plain *sin*. So wise worship leaders will not let personality traits *or* sin become an obstacle to their responsibilities as a servant leader.

The first issue that can drive a wedge between worship leader and pastor is the tendency of artists to be highly independent, which can lead to a rebellious spirit.

My generation is famous for its resistance to authority. The culture of drugs, sex and rock 'n' roll from the 1960s and 1970s was all about freedom from authority. Being able to make one's own way in life is respected by our culture. These influences pull me away from being committed to the church. When you add to all of that the nonconformist artistic mindset and the rebellion that is in the heart of every son and daughter of Adam, you have a potential problem!

Independence and self-determination are high values for the modernist and postmodernist. I want to make my own plans and control my own destiny. But since I'm just one member of an integrated community, and I'm responsible to the other members, I can't make all the rules and always get my own way. I enjoy lots of artistic freedom in leading people and leading worship, and my pastors are happy to give me lots of freedom. But it's all within the greater context of *serving* in the church. I'm part of a body of people. I'm *joined* to Christ and his body. Though my personality tendency is to be solitary and self-sufficient, I am constrained by my connection to the greater whole.

If we import into Christianity the value of self-determination from the modern age, it's like oil on water—it doesn't mix. In the spirit of an entrepreneur, I would use every opportunity to promote myself and my music. The goal would be to gain as big a share of the market as I could. But is that what worship is all about? Not according to the Bible. As far as I can see, worship is about surrender—giving yourself as a living sacrifice.

The strange and challenging thing about worship leading is that we are using a musical model from our culture, but we are turning it upside down. In any secular concert, the guitar-playing, band-leading vocalists are *the focal point*. It's all about the skill, cleverness and magnetism of the performers. The performers are there to further their reputation, to demonstrate their prowess and to impress people.

In worship leading, we might engage in a popular form of music, but we come for the purpose of furthering the reputation of Jesus. We come to show off *his* exploits, to reveal *his* personality and to make people fall in love with *him*.

In his book *Music, the Brain, and Ecstasy,* Robert Jourdain describes the personality profile of the great composers of history. "Studies of the great classical composers show the same kinds of personality profile [sic] as all kinds of creative people. They show strong independence in every respect, tending to be solitary and socially reserved, shunning group activities and establishing few close friendships."[4]

Shades of these artistic traits can be seen in Charles Wesley, the preacher and hymn writer. "What are we to make of his paradoxical nature—patient yet impulsive; retiring, yet resolute; frail, yet a fighter; controversial and hot-tempered, yet gentle and forbearing; other-worldly, yet intensely human; introspective, yet exhilarating; a rigid conformist, yet a bold pioneer . . ."[5] Isaac Watts, the outstanding hymn-writer, "was fond of studious retirement, and so devoted to his books, that in the early part of his career he seldom went out."[6]

My generation, the baby-boomers, have an inbred desire for self-determination. We don't like it when people tell us what to do. Many of my peers have no sense of community or social obligation—all they're committed to is themselves. In 1979 sociologist Robert Bellah surveyed a few hundred middle-class Americans: "Many had no sense of community or social obligation. They saw the world as a frag-mented place of choice and freedom that yielded little meaning or comfort. They even seemed to have lost the language to express any kind of commitment to anything—church, family or community—other than themselves."[7]

Partly as a reaction to the emptiness that results from living in isola-tion, today's young people recognize their need for community. Gen-eration X values genuine relationships. "Busters (adults 18 to 31 years old) are the generation most likely to be seeking out good friendships (41% of Busters compared to 30% of seniors, 25% of Boomers, and 23% of Builders [those in their 50s and 60s])."[8]

Nevertheless, nowadays it's very common to find people who love God but have no felt need for the church. This flies in the face of the New Testament definition of church. The New Testament is filled with references to the community of believers, such as the saints in Christ Jesus, the people of God and the family of God. The believers are al-ways together—eating together, worshiping together, sharing their possessions and encouraging one another. The early church father Cyprian (A.D. 250) stated, "You cannot have God for your Father if you have not the church for your mother!"[9]

I know several people who have stopped going to church because they've had disagreements and disappointments in church relationships. Ironically the process of working through those misunderstandings is the *only way* to maturity. It's impossible to mature in Christ apart from being joined to the church.

Author Rodney Clapp describes "freelance" Christianity as a dangerous rejection of the body in which Christ dwells. The view that church is optional "misconstrues human personhood as fundamentally atomistic (rather than social) and the church as a collection of individuals—rather than as a corporate body whose members have identity and purpose by being part of a church."[10]

Unless I'm working and serving in the church, I won't grow. The only way I can mature is to serve others. "As each part [of the body of Christ] does its own special work, it helps the other parts grow, so that the whole body is healthy and growing and full of love" (Eph 4:16 NLT). There's not much room for the isolated "I am an island" musician in the biblical model of a church.

Unless I'm worshiping God, hearing Bible teaching and praying with others, I stagnate in my faith. When I attend a prayer meeting, I'm impacted by the zeal of other Christians as they intercede for the lost and cry out for more of God. My indifference is confronted as I hear their passion for the Lord and his work. My enthusiasm is like water in a leaky bucket—unless I keep filling up the bucket with more water, it all drains out. I find that water is fellowship with other Christians. The way I gain compassion for the poor and the lost is by being with people who have that kind of heart.

Several years ago I led worship at a conference in eastern Canada. The pastor who was the main speaker told me how surprised he was to see me taking notes on his sermons. In his church, the worship leader didn't even listen to the sermons, much less take notes! If I'm going to have my head in the ball game, I have to be renewed and transformed by God's Word just like everybody else.

If I spend too much time away from the vitality of Jesus' body, I become narrow sighted and focused on my own problems. I lose vision for God's kingdom. I am tempted to blend in with my culture rather than be about my Father's business. I am tempted to rationalize my indifference and make compromises.

I relate to John Piper's statement, "I wake up carnal every morning. I have to get saved all over again every day."[11] How do I do that? I push myself into prayer, worship, service and fellowship with Christians. I don't do these things because I always feel like doing them. I do them because it's the only right choice. Sometimes I don't feel like going to leadership meetings, but I do it because it's the only way I can play my part on the team.

John Wimber made it clear that he was interested in developing pastors who could lead worship, not narrow-minded musicians who have no pastoral heart. To follow this directive, I have to join hands with the other pastors in order to cooperate with the direction of the church, be sensitive to people's needs and benefit from the counsel of other leaders.

9

THE UPS & DOWNS
OF WORSHIP LEADING

However much, Lord, I would feel you,
it is still not you yourself I touch,
For my mind can touch nothing of your hiddenness:
It is just a visible, illuminated image
That I see in the symbol of you: for all investigation
into your being is hidden.
In you, Lord, may my mouth bear the fruit of praise
that is acceptable to you.[1]

SAINT EPHREM OF EDESSA

AS I PREPARE A LIST OF SONGS, I'm trying to follow
God's leading, but I certainly can't hear anything from God right now.
*Which songs should I choose? How can I possibly know which ones are right
for this worship time?* As I look through the list, it seems that I've sung so
many of them hundreds of times. Is it possible to squeeze any life out
of these songs one more time?

As the set begins I notice that most of the people haven't arrived at
church yet. Many of those who are present seem to look at me with va-
cant stares during worship. This doesn't encourage me.

Despite these emotions, I make the choice to worship. Midway
through the first song, a high-pitched squeal blasts from the moni-
tors, which leaves my ears ringing. At least everybody is now awake. It

takes the sound technician a while to find where the feedback is coming from, so the special shrieking sound accompanies us for half a minute.

I have worked up a pretty good sweat by the end of the second song, and I'm singing with as much gusto and sincerity as I can muster. I try to think about God, but I have a hard time getting my mind off the drummer. He's making the song go faster than I want it to go. I turn around and mouth the words "slow down" with exaggerated enunciation. I try to smile while I say it. It helps a little; the runaway train slows down a bit. The next song speeds up as well, so I grin and bear it.

Despite listening to the CD during rehearsal and trying to emulate that arrangement, I notice that the band sounds, well, quite different. I did my best to explain the parts I was looking for, but something got lost in the communication. The guitar and keyboards don't have the right kind of patches and amplifiers to get the sound I'm looking for.

By the fifth song there is some kind of breakthrough, and I actually feel that God is among us. He's letting us see a glimpse of his glory! Amazing! Despite this refreshing breeze of the Spirit, the congregation looks nonplused and lethargic. If God's presence seems so real on the platform, why is there so little response among the people? Maybe it has something to do with the fact that half of them arrived during the fourth song of the worship time instead of at the beginning.

I've painted a pretty negative picture in the above scenario. But sometimes it really does *feel* that way for the worship leader. Worship leading can be an emotional roller coaster. It's like rowing upstream without a paddle. At times I am plagued by self-doubt—I feel like a hypocrite; I don't really *feel* any love for God right now even though my posture would suggest that I'm peering right into the most holy place. I begin to wonder, *Am I just fooling myself? Does my worship leading really have any value? Does it really help people? Are we just going through the motions, running the same play over and over again?*

The Many Voices That We Hear

In the struggle to lead worship, I find many voices speaking to me. Some of these inner voices stem from the melancholy artistic temperament—the Eeyore complex. Have you seen *Winnie the Pooh*? Eeyore is always depressed, always expecting the worst to happen. He keeps losing his tail, and he doesn't see a chance in the world to get it back. When caught in the spirit of Eeyore, the worship leader has a bleak perspective—"No matter what I do, the people won't worship. Why sing joyful songs when no one is joyful? Maybe it's time to retire from worship leading."

It's true that musicians and artists are, on the whole, more sensitive and emotional. But can we use that as an excuse to roll over and die when things aren't going our way? I don't think so. If the set isn't going my way, that's OK because worship leading isn't about getting my way. It isn't about how I feel. It's not even about whether I personally benefit from doing it. It's about *faith* and *service*.

Charles Wesley, one of the greatest hymn writers of all time, was susceptible to moodiness. Here is an excerpt from his journal that reveals his melancholy:

> Thursday, June 1st. I was troubled today that I could not pray, being utterly dead at the sacrament.
>
> Friday, June 2nd. I was still unable to pray; still dead in communicating; full of a cowardly desire of death.
>
> Saturday, June 3rd. My deadness continued, and the next day increased. I was exceeding heavy and averse to prayer; so that I almost resolved not to go to church. . . . When I did go the prayers and sacrament were exceeding grievous to me; and I could not help asking myself, "Where is the difference between what I am now, and what I was before believing."[2]

Though we may feel depleted, we can't excuse faithless actions under the guise of being sensitive musicians. Of course we're sensitive. That's one of the God-given traits of the worship leader. We have a

Spirit-illumined intuition about what's happening spiritually in a group of people. When the Holy Spirit seems to be a million miles away during worship, we feel it. When God is drenching the people with dew from heaven, we feel it.

Sensitivity can be a strength and a weakness. If we feel the wind blowing, we have ways of musically putting up the sails so the ship, God's bride, can cut through the water with freedom and power. But when the heavens seem to be brass, and the words of our songs aren't imbued with power and revelation, it's just hard work. If we let our sensitivity rule us in moments like these, we'll collapse in a downward spiral of hopelessness.

Will we feel challenged by the task of worship leading? Of course we will. But in our weakness, God will be our strength. As a good soldier of Jesus Christ, I try to keep marching even if there are arrows flying at me from every direction.

This brings us to another of the voices that can plague us as worship leaders—the voice of the enemy.

Worship and Spiritual Warfare

We worship *in* and *by* the Holy Spirit. Our worship takes us into the realm of the Spirit. In that realm there are "rulers," "authorities" and "powers of this dark world . . . and spiritual forces of evil" (Eph 6:12). As leaders, we lead the people toward victory over these powers. Through the words of our songs and prayers, we lead people to deliverance from bondage to sin, and freedom from the one who "blinds the minds" (see 2 Cor 4:4) of the ungodly. Week by week, we call people to consecrate and reconsecrate themselves to God. In so doing, we are fighting a spiritual battle. Paradoxically God calls sensitive artists to be spiritual warriors.

Charles Wesley relates his experience of preaching with extraordinary power on Jesus' healing of blind Bartimaeus. After a second day of powerful preaching, Wesley records, "A messenger of Satan came. He seldom fails me after success."[3]

If we are inviting people to make vows of devotion to God, the enemy has good reason to resist us. We are encroaching on his territory. So he tries to defeat us with words of discouragement, taunting, accusation and intimidation.

When the enemy sees his hold on people slipping away, he makes threats and accusations to throw us off track. One evil tactic he uses is *condemnation:* "Who do you think you are to be leading people in worship when you have sin in your life?" Guess what? All of us have sin in our lives. We'll never completely conquer sin until we're out of this body. It's not by our own righteousness that we are made worthy to worship God. Forgiveness and acceptance are God's free gifts to us. If we confess our sin, he is faithful to forgive (1 John 1:9). As a sincere follower of Christ, I still stumble into sin, but God is there to help me get back up and keep walking in righteousness.

Charles Wesley struggled with condemnation: "I live in a continual storm. My soul is always in my hand. The enemy thrusts sore at me, that I may fall; and a worse enemy than the devil is my own heart." On the day of one of his greatest triumphs, when many were converted and the crowd would hardly let him go, he wrote, "Before the day was past [I] felt my own sinfulness so great, that I wished I had never been born."[4]

Does your mind ever wander while you lead worship? Mine does. Do you ever think sinful thoughts? I do. There's a pretty simple solution: repent and get your mind back on God and the task at hand. He's not surprised by your sin, and he's very quick to forgive and forget.

Should you feel like a failure when you're unable to have a deep connection with God while leading worship? I take a practical approach. When I'm leading a band *and* leading a congregation, I have a lot to think about. I have to give cues to the band, concentrate on playing my instrument and keep tabs on what is happening in the congregation. I do all of this while trying to have a conversation with God.

Sometimes a worship set unfolds effortlessly. But typically there is push and pull, moments of being in the zone and moments of dead air. I don't feel condemned for leading a less-than-perfect worship set or for having emotional ups and downs. I'm there to serve the people, to open the worship-door for them. So if I don't personally have my imagination stirred by the beauty of God every time I worship, it's OK.

And then there's *accusation* for not doing enough good deeds—not being spiritual enough, not praying enough, not witnessing enough or not giving enough. The bar is just too high for us to clear. So we feel defeated and unqualified to minister as spiritual priests.

These arguments from the evil one are dispelled when we remind ourselves of the gift of righteousness that comes through Jesus' sacrifice on the cross. We're not made right by our own good works, but by the good work of one man, Jesus. It's impossible to add to the righteousness that Jesus has secured for us. "In addition to all this, take up the shield of faith, with which you can extinguish all the flaming arrows of the evil one. Take the helmet of salvation and the sword of the Spirit, which is the word of God" (Eph 6:16-17).

The cornerstone of our faith is Jesus' work on the cross. Of all God's acts in history, it's the number one event that gives us good cause to worship God. As a worship leader you have to have that one figured out. Be convinced of the efficacy of Jesus' blood in securing God's favor on your life. You've been chosen as a *friend of God*. You've been adopted as a beloved child of the Father. Happy is the one whose sin is forgiven!

As a worship leader you have the privilege of pointing people to the glorious work of Jesus on the cross. You are a defender of the faith against the lies of the evil one. In your songs you dispense the truth of God to reinforce the rock-solid assurance of God's unfailing love.

On Christ the Solid Rock
My hope is built on nothing less
Than Jesus' blood and righteousness
I dare not trust the sweetest frame,
but wholly lean on Jesus' name.

On Christ the solid rock I stand
All other ground is sinking sand
All other ground is sinking sand

His oath, his covenant, his blood
Support me in the 'whelming flood
When all around my soul gives way
He then is all my hope and stay

When he shall come with trumpet sound,
O may I then in him be found
Dressed in his righteousness alone
Faultless to stand before the throne.[5]

Lessons from the life of Moses. The devil isn't the only source of discouraging words. Unfortunately it sometimes feels like our Christian friends are our enemies. To survive and thrive in the long haul of worship ministry, we must never treat our brother or sister as our enemy. For some valuable lessons in leadership, let's take a look at the life of Moses.

The life of Moses can teach us a lot about dealing with complainers. First, Moses had to deal with a group of people called the "rabble." They were discontented complainers. They craved "the good things of Egypt" they had left behind (Num 11:4 NLT). They longed for "the good old days."

Many churches have a contingent that complains because "it's not like it used to be." They love the style of the previous worship leader, and they're not afraid to let you know it: "Why can't we do the old songs? I just can't get into God's presence with these new songs." They focus on what they don't have. They come to be served, not to serve.

How do I respond to these people? I smile and listen and nod as they share their feelings. But I usually don't do anything to accommodate them. Though the rabble usually comprises a small percentage of the whole church, it can feel like more. You can't keep everybody happy all of the time. So love and accept them, but don't cater to them.

Second, the Israelites were required to collect manna everyday in the wilderness. God supernaturally sent manna from heaven, but picking it up required unglamorous work. This is a picture of leading worship. Sometimes the work involved in leading worship feels unsupernatural—practicing, setting up the PA, organizing the team members and preparing a set list. Through worship we can touch the supernatural manna from heaven, but it can be work to gather in what God wants to give us.

The actual definition of the Hebrew word for *manna* is "what is it," because manna was unlike anything the Hebrews had ever eaten. Sometimes when I'm trying to find the right solution for a worship service, I keep asking, "What is it?" I know God wants to give his blessing, but I have a hard time grasping what he wants to do! Worship ministry is a combination of the natural and the supernatural; sometimes it just feels like hard work.

A few years ago I came to the end of the year and was asking God for direction and help. He gave me a picture in my mind's eye of a baseball pitcher who was tired. It was late in the game, and the pitcher didn't feel like he had the stuff to get the ball over the plate. This was exactly how I felt. I was tired, and sometimes it was all I could do to drag myself out of bed to go to church.

The Lord said, "Just show up. Come to the pitching mound, and I'll give you the stuff you need to get the job done." The biggest test in any kind of ministry is this: will we keep showing up for work? Will we persevere?

Life is a marathon, not a sprint. Many of us are called by God to persevere in worship ministry for three or four decades. There will be ups and downs through the years. God doesn't call us to be flamboyant, just faithful. God doesn't call us to hit home runs every time at bat, just to show up and do the best we can. He promises to do the rest.

10

ENCOURAGING
EXPRESSION
IN WORSHIP

Sing lustily, and with a good courage.
Beware of singing as if you were half dead, or
half asleep; but lift up your voice with strength.
Be no more afraid of your voice now,
nor more ashamed of its being heard, than when you
sung the songs of Satan. . . .
Above all, sing spiritually. Have an eye to God in every
word you sing. Aim at pleasing him
more than yourself, or any other creature.
JOHN WESLEY

FROM THE PLATFORM, I often look out during a worship time and wonder, *Is anything happening with these people?* In an ideal church, we would look out over the rows of worshipers and see the whole gamut of biblical expressions of bodily praise. We would see kneeling, bowing, dancing, lifting hands, shouting, speaking and singing. For a variety of reasons, we don't see all these things in most churches, because there aren't many ideal churches.

I personally desire to see an increase of physical and emotional expressiveness in worship in my own church. But how do we respond to a group of people who seem to act more like an audience than an army?

There are many factors that influence the worship-expressiveness of a given church. I see the corporate expression of worship as a fountain that springs up out of a pool of water. The health of the water in the pool determines how the fountain will look. The water is made up of many things:

1. The overall spiritual momentum in a church. Is the kingdom of God advancing in the lives of the converted and unconverted?
2. The kind of worship that the leadership teaches and models.
3. The worship heritage. What normative patterns of worship have been established over many years?
4. God's sovereign visitations—salvation and healing, discipleship, evangelism, compassion, ministry, hearing from God, unity of the body.

The Overall Spiritual Momentum in Your Church

Let's take a look at the first of these ingredients in the water. Look at the most outstanding examples of worship in the Bible. Question: When is worship explosive in the history of God's people? Answer: When God is moving powerfully and when his people ardently follow him.

Why did Moses, Miriam and the Israelites sing and dance for joy? Because the Lord delivered them through the Red Sea. I'd dance too if my would-be murderers were swallowed up in the sea. Why did David dance with all of his might, leading the whole house of Israel in celebration? Because God enabled him to defeat Israel's enemies and bring the Ark of the Covenant, the symbol of God's power and favor, back to its rightful place in Jerusalem. As King David danced and whirled his way down the street, hundreds of Israelites followed behind him in jubilation. No one was pressuring them to dance—they just jumped into the procession.

Years later David received instructions from God to build a temple of worship. By God's direction he passed the task down to his son Solomon. The completion of the temple was the consummation of many years of work. On the day of dedication, the glory of God was so strong in that place that the priests could not even perform their ritual duties.

In this God-ordained building project, he sent a mighty outpouring of his Spirit to confirm his blessing. As a sign of his favor he rearranged the priests' plans for a worship service. This was a pinnacle of worship in the history of Israel—the people gave of themselves wholeheartedly, and God responded with his glorious presence.

When Jesus walked the earth, the kingdom of God came through him mightily. By his touch, thousands were fed, the blind could see, the lame could walk and the dead rose to life. When he entered Jerusalem riding on a donkey, no one could restrain the crowds who threw blankets, coats and palm branches in his path. Nothing could stop the cries of "Hosanna in the highest, blessed is he who comes in the name of the Lord" (see Mt 21:9). No worship leader was needed here. Exuberant praise was the spontaneous cry of a people that had been touched by the finger of God.

The signs and wonders and salvation continued to flow in the early church. People worshiped everyday in their homes and in the temple. They ate meals together and shared their possessions with anyone in need. A sense of awe rested on this community of believers that had been gripped by God's marvelous love.

In these snapshots of biblical history, worship rises up like a mighty billowing cloud, a pleasing aroma to the Lord. While it's true that we can't reproduce the historical events surrounding these worship events, there are principles at work in these stories that apply to us.

The fountain of worship rises out of a pool of believers who are experiencing and responding to God. We are touched by his love, forgiveness and healing power. We become hungry for him; we're eager to know him more and zealous to serve him. This stirring of personal and corporate revival produces a beautiful crescendo of praise and worship. In times like these, worship leaders have an easier job. But are these times of God's dramatic intervention the norm for every day and age?

Seasons of Silence, Seasons of Renewal
Unfortunately we don't live in a constant state of revival. We continue to worship no matter what the spiritual climate is.

The New Testament paints a picture of God's power poured out on his people. Paul's teaching is filled with references to God's power and love filling the church. Paul himself describes his experience of going to the third heaven and being caught up into heaven (2 Cor 12:2). (One must remember, however, that the New Testament writers recorded the highlights—the best stories—of the early church. Whenever you pick the best stories that span several years and compress them into a short document, it gives the impression that church life was *always* dynamic and powerful.)

Sometimes we feel the power of God, but there are many times when all we can *feel* is our own humanity. Instead of seeing God's glory, we only see the people on the other side of the room. God's love and majesty are theological truths, but not a felt reality.

Since the early church, there have been seasons of silence and seasons of renewal. In the 1700s revival spread throughout England through the Wesley brothers and Whitefield. In the early 1900s there were revivals in Azusa Street, California, and in Wales—not to mention the revivals in the United States in the 1940s, the charismatic renewal of the 1960s, the Jesus people of the 1970s and the revivals during the 1990s. The spread of the Pentecostal church has been accompanied by revivals all over the world in the last several decades, notably in Korea, China and South America.

In 1740 revival was breaking out through the Wesley brothers. Joseph Williams, an observer of the revival meetings, described the fervent worship:

> Never did I hear such praying, or such singing, never did I see or hear such evident marks of fervency of spirit in the service of God, as in that Society. At the close of every single petition, a serious Amen, like a rushing sound of waters, ran through the whole society. . . . They seemed to sing with melody in their hearts. . . . Such evident marks of a lively, genuine devotion, in any part of religious worship, I never was witness to in any place, or on any occasion. . . . I do not remember in my heart to have been so elevated in prayer or praise, either in collegiate, parochial or private worship, as it was there and then.[1]

As a songwriter, I went through a period of prolific writing in the mid-1990s while our church in Anaheim was undergoing renewal. I didn't write more songs because I scheduled more time to write, but because God was visiting us. One byproduct of his visitation was the outpouring of words and melodies. We had many marvelous times of worship; God's presence was so thick that it made us swoon, laugh and dance, sometimes all in the same five minutes.

What do you do when a wonderful wave of the Holy Spirit subsides? You can't help but be disappointed. Everybody loves being touched by God. Everybody loves to *feel* his power and *see* his glory, and we love it in extraordinary amounts. I've had all kinds of supernatural experiences in worship. God has touched my body powerfully, given me startling revelations and sent his angels to minister to me. There's nothing like having supernatural experiences. It encourages my faith and causes me to seek the Lord with greater zeal and fervency. But sometimes there are long periods between my strong sensory experiences with God. So I walk by faith.

We occupy the battlefield until Jesus comes again. We fight the fight of faith, obeying the main and plain teachings of Scripture. We still see people saved, healed and delivered. Like farmers who plant seed every season, worship leaders sing their song in great years and in lean years.

There is a built-in frustration in being a worship leader and, indeed, in being a Christian. When we taste of the Holy Spirit, we wish we could have heaven now. When God lifts us out of our doldrums in a magnificent time of worship, our eyes are opened to new possibilities. Then we come crashing back down to earth when the next worship time is wooden and inane in comparison.

We Can't Manipulate God

Why does God let it happen this way? Why doesn't he allow Pentecost to happen during every gathering? For one thing, he wants us to know that *he* has the power and we don't. He's God and we're not. We can't manipulate him. Though he proves himself over and over again as the self-revealing God, he reserves the right to remain silent.

During Abram's long sojourn in Canaan, there were long periods of silence, and then God would dramatically break through. After one of God's appearances, Abram built an altar to commemorate the Lord's visit (Gen 12:7). Apparently God expected Abraham to remember the times of great revelation to help him persevere in the silent times. Think back on the extraordinary times of worship God has given you. Build an altar in your memory to remind you that God has powerfully demonstrated his love to you.

I can't manipulate the supernatural. I can't conjure up the presence of God. So my walk of faith continues when the tide of the Spirit ebbs low. Even in the absence of a *season* of renewal, God ministers powerfully to his people. But the highs aren't quite as high, the visitations of God aren't quite as frequent, and there are less phenomena of the Holy Spirit.

In a fast-moving world of high-powered communication, technology and entertainment, we're used to getting everything right now. It's easy to forget the place of waiting quietly on God. We can't "click on" God and make him open a window of heaven. He has a myriad of ways of communicating with us and it's not all with fireworks and fanfare.

If God withholds his power in worship, we ought to draw from the well of living water he has already poured into us. Though we may not always "experience the love of Christ" (Eph 3:19 NLT) powerfully, his Word is always living and active with the ability to cut deep into our innermost thoughts and desires (Heb 4:12). When I sing the words "Refiner's fire, my heart's one desire is to be holy,"[2] I don't need a special revelation. The words of the song should be enough to cause me to search my heart.

Though we can't produce revival by our own efforts, we can emulate the pursuit of God that we see in the early church. We can pray often, be filled with the Word of God, give to the poor and build strong relationships of accountability. While none of these practices will guarantee a mighty move of God in our midst, it will at least open the door to all that God wants to do. We can never make God our debtor by doing good works. He will never be obligated to show us signs and wonders. But if we live our worship daily, we can expect a beautiful fountain of praise to appear in our meetings.

Factors That Influence the Tone and Intensity of Meetings

Teaching, modeling, tradition and style of music. To a large degree, congregational worship reflects the teaching and example of the leadership. The style of worship in a local church is like a cultural custom that has been passed down through the generations. Whether it's a style of home decor or a dialect common to your town, cultural norms are practiced because they've always been done that way.

I've occasionally visited churches that are predominantly non-Caucasian in their membership. I've worshiped in African American churches, Hispanic churches, Filipino churches and in many Asian cultures. While it's wrong to make sweeping generalizations regarding ethnicity and worship style, there are some patterns that emerge. Many African American and Hispanic worship traditions are very expressive and full of emotion. I think I have a lot more ingrained stiffness because of my Anglo-Saxon heritage.

Every church has its established patterns of worship, which have sometimes been passed down for generations. When you are born into a tradition and you see the same model of worship every week, it becomes part of you.

Customs and worship styles are established through teaching and modeling. In classic Vineyard worship, the emphasis is on consecration, adoration and a tender yielding to God. God captured the hearts of thousands of young people in the 1980s through tender intimate worship. Now many of those young people are leaders in Vineyard churches all over the world. Having met God through a certain style of worship, we tend to stick with it.

In classic Pentecostal worship, the model is more jubilant and joyful. Joyfulness has been the cultural norm for generations. Not a bad custom considering it's straight out of the Bible. In the last ten years or so, Vineyard music has slowly evolved to include a wider variety of musical styles and to embrace a wider biblical expression—more joy and celebration and proclamation. In the last decade we have produced music with aggressive rhythms that stir the soul and body. But we still have a lot more to learn—from the Bible and from other denominations and movements.

Physical expression—one measure of maturity in worship. Though it is certainly not the only indicator of the vitality and genuineness of worship, physical expression is an important aspect of worship. The Bible teaches us to worship with our bodies. The Psalms are replete with examples of physical acts of worship. When I kneel or lift my hands or dance, worship takes on a deeper meaning for me. Because my spirit, mind and body are interconnected, I can't help but be inspired in my heart when I move my body in worship.

To be honest, I usually stay monotonously still while leading worship. Since I'm not a big mover and shaker, I can't expect the congregation to shake, rattle and roll. If your worship leaders and elders aren't physically active during worship, the congregation will follow suit—people do what their leaders do.

At my church we welcome dance as a valid and biblical form of art in worship. We have a dance team that is gradually developing a repertoire of dances. Some of their dances are mostly spontaneous, and some are choreographed. But dance isn't limited to the dance team members. At times a few dozen people get out of their seats, form "conga lines" and really go for it.

This kind of joyful expression is exactly what we see in the Psalms. It's easy to show from the Bible that dance is a God-ordained form of worship. Psalm 149 enjoins us to worship God with dance: "Let them praise his name with dancing and make music to him with tambourine and harp" (Ps 149:3).[3] Other notable examples of dance in the Old Testament are when Miriam, the sister of Moses and Aaron, led a dance after the Hebrews passed through the Red Sea (Ex 15:20), and when David danced "with all his might" in leading a celebratory procession "while he and the entire house of Israel brought up the ark of the LORD with shouts and the sound of trumpets" (2 Sam 6:14-15).

I think dance is a great blessing for those who do it and for those who watch it. For those of us who rarely dance in worship, it is a heart-stirring sight when others are leaping, spinning and bowing to Jesus. Engaging the whole body in worship is a prophetic picture of giving your whole heart to the Lord.

I find that I am more physically expressive in worship when I am around others who are. In December 2000 I visited the Philippines and helped lead a few worship conferences. The enthusiasm of the Filipinos in worship was amazing and contagious. Though I was in the position of leading, I was more of a follower as I was swept into the zeal and freedom of these delightful worshipers. In one set I was leading, I found myself unable to stop moving!

This example also illustrates the difference between *conference* worship and *Sunday morning* worship. At a conference people are spending their precious time, energy and money to attend an event that is over and above their weekly routine of worship. If there are special speakers or worship leaders coming from another city or country, the expectation and anticipation level is higher. When people are filled with unusual faith and expectancy, worship goes to greater heights.

Danceable music. If you come from a tradition of classical music in worship, you probably won't see a great outward display of emotion. If most of your music is soft and gentle, you won't see much exuberant dancing. If we want people to dance joyfully, we have to do joyful music.

When I'm at home, if I put on a CD with catchy music, I sometimes dance. When I listen to certain kinds of jazz, rock and black gospel, it's hard *not* to dance. So I'm always looking for songs to use in church that inspire celebration and dance. They have to be songs that fit within the limits of my musical ability and my band's expertise.

Having been in the Vineyard for twenty-six years, I've done a lot of mellow worship, and it has been the entry point for a deep relationship with God. We'll never abandon that kind of worship in the Vineyard. But mellow worship is one small slice of the whole pie of biblical worship. If all I do is mellow music, I get bored. One of the functions of music is to *stir us* into action.

When King David's band and choir of 288 were shouting to the Lord, beating the drums, crashing the cymbals and playing the pipes, it had to be pretty dramatic (1 Chron 25:6, 7). God created us not just with a mind and body, but with *emotions*. He gave our souls the capacity to be stirred by powerful music. I love to see everything from classical violins to techno-pop employed in worship. I personally love all of it.

Coming before God quietly and listening for his voice is paramount, but there is also a swath of biblical worship that is meant to be full of fun and hilarity. The Psalms have many different Hebrew words that are translated into the English words *praise* and *worship*. Some of those Hebrew words connote wildly exuberant praise. The word *halal* (translated as "praise" in 1 Chron 23:5) can also mean "to shine, boast; and thus to be clamorously foolish; to rave."[4]

The psalmists did something we don't do—shouting. The word *teruah* (Josh 6:5; Ezra 3:11; Ps 47:5) means "clamor, acclamation of joy, or battle-cry."[5] *Ruwa*, another word for shout, means "to split the ears with sound" (Ps 47:1).[6]

In Western culture, the cognitive is elevated and the emotional is downplayed. This can make us lopsided worshipers—we engage our minds but not our bodies and emotions. We are products of our culture—most of us like to be as cool as cucumbers. We like to hang loose and meditate on the words. Meditation is certainly valid and biblical. But if that's all we ever do, we miss out on the riches of expressive worship. It's hard to be immersed in a sea of worship if we don't get our feet wet.

Inviting people to go for it in worship. In an interview with *Worship Leader* magazine, Tony Campolo was asked if worship songs should necessarily teach us the doctrines of the faith. Here is his answer:

> I don't think that hymns have to be sermons set to music. It's about time that we recognized the legitimate role of emotion. Pouring out one's heart and soul with passionate intensity is what worship is about at its

best. When lovers finish talking to each other, I'm not convinced that they have communicated theologies or philosophies. I believe that they have exchanged the deepest feelings of their hearts and minds. So, I believe that worship is a time of loving Jesus, and in the words of the Apostle Paul, as recorded in Romans 8, the true worshiper has spiritual groanings that can not be put into words, and obviously that means they are beyond systematic theologies.[7]

So part of our job as worship leaders is to invite people to go for it. Not to coerce, but to invite. Not to manipulate people, but to stimulate them toward loving God. It's a biblical model.

The book of Psalms is one example of a literary style that was common in ancient Middle Eastern countries. Babylon, for instance, produced psalms to be used in religious rituals. One of the unique characteristics of biblical psalms is the *imperative*. In our Bible, it is common to see strong exhortations to praise such as "Come, let us sing for joy to the Lord"; "Come, let us bow down in worship" (Ps 95:1, 6); and "Sing to the Lord a new song, for he has done marvelous things"(Ps 98:1).

Following this biblical example, it is completely appropriate to encourage people to worship God. Historically, this hasn't been widely practiced in Vineyards, but some of our worship leaders do it. Reading a psalm or giving a short exhortation to people to draw near to God is a great idea. It isn't threatening, it's encouraging.

The longer I lead worship in middle-class North America, the more I want to find ways of jostling people out of spiritual sleepiness.

Speaking of being jostled during a worship time, several years ago I was in Hong Kong, leading worship at Hang Fook camp. This was the old location for St. Stephen's Ministries, led by Jackie Pullinger, an English woman who for over thirty years has been caring for drug addicts, prostitutes and street sleepers in Hong Kong.

As I led worship, I heard an extremely loud, shrill sound. At first I thought it was really bad feedback from the PA system. I looked around startled, wanting to cover my ears. Then I found the source of the piercing noise. It was Jackie, blowing a referee's whistle in the middle of a worship song! This was her way of exuberantly praising and interceding!

Maybe we need to be alarmed into deeper worship by people like Jackie. She is a prime example of a radical worshiper—as a teenager she left the safety and security of her homeland to give herself to missions work. She got on an ocean liner and asked God where to get off. When the ship approached Hong Kong, she knew she was in the right place. For more than thirty years, she has been evangelizing the poorest of the poor in Hong Kong. She and her team members have touched thousands of lives, helping many addicts get off drugs and bringing prostitutes off the street.

The Joy of the Lord, the Joy of Music and Endorphins

"Feeling the presence of the Lord," "being touched by God" and "being in the flow of God's anointing" are terms that are used a lot these days. You find them in all kinds of worship songs.

I think that a lot of what people call the "presence of the Lord" is actually adrenaline, endorphins and the joy of music. People are looking for a high and mistakenly measure the success of their worship time by how high they get. We all love to have euphoric feelings during worship. It has happened to me many times. What are the various sources of euphoria in a worship time? David Di Sabatino, managing editor of *Worship Leader* magazine, describes the human physiological response to music:

> When a person listens to music, the body releases special neurons—usually used to combat pain—called endorphins—into the brain's pathways that slow down activity. When endorphins are released in a response to music, a bodily euphoria ensues. In his book *Music, the Brain, and Ecstasy*, Robert Jourdain states that this euphoria is "like that produced by drugs like morphine. In fact, the opiates to which drug addicts are so devoted work their magic by approaching the same neurons influenced by the brain's own endorphins."

Di Sabatino goes on to say, "The pleasure garnered by a worshiper through the release of these endorphins constitutes part—at least, the physical element—of what is going on during a worship experience."

But how should these physiological realities influence what we do in worship? Should we be afraid that our music will release people's endorphins? No! God made our endorphins. He made our emotions, and he created us with adrenaline. He knew how our bodies would respond to music. God made music and he's smart enough to understand its power over us. Says Di Sabatino, "Those that clamor that music is 'manipulative' ignore both biblical and scientific reality. Music is simply a tool of influence."[8]

When the Israelites madly danced down the street, following king David, you can bet there were some endorphins being released and that people felt euphoric. When the psalmist says, "Make a joyful noise unto the Lord!" (Ps 100:1 KJV), he's not holding back his emotions.

But here is my main point: the God-given blessing of ecstatic feelings does not always accompany the worship experience, and when it does, it is not necessarily accompanied by the manifest presence of the Holy Spirit. So let's not falsely label our high emotions as a visitation of God's power. Emotion in worship is good, and the presence of God is good, but they are two different things that are not always experienced simultaneously.

To survive the long haul in worship ministry, we must have reasonable expectations. On one hand, we expect God to meet with and speak to us as he has done throughout history. On the other, we relinquish control of the *way* God chooses to minister to his church on a given day or in a given season. God the Holy Spirit is ultimately the worship leader because only he can soften hearts and ignite a flame of love for God.

The danger of focusing on the experience of worship rather than on God himself is not only a modern phenomenon. Jonathan Edwards, the preacher who led the Great Awakening in New England in the 1730s, warns against getting too caught up in our wonderful experiences instead of glorying in the person of Christ:

> The basis for the true delight that a real Christian has is in God and in
> His perfection. His delight is in Christ, and in His beauty. God appears

as He is in Himself, the chief among ten thousand and altogether lovely. . . . When false believers congratulate only themselves, they keep their eyes only upon themselves. Having received what they call spiritual discoveries or experiences, their minds are taken up with self and the admiration of their experiences. *What they are chiefly excited about is not the glory of God or the beauty of Christ but the thrill of their own experiences.* They keep thinking "what a wonderful experience this is! What a great discovery that is! What wonderful things I have encountered!" And so they put their experiences in the place of Christ and His beauty and all-sufficiency. Instead of rejoicing in Christ Jesus, they indulge in their own wonderful experiences. They are so caught up in their own imagination about these great and wonderful experiences that all their notion of God relates merely to them.[9]

These days, there are hundreds of songs with lyrics such as "I love your presence, I feel your presence, I long to be in your presence." Those are some of my favorite songs, but if we get too caught up in how much of God's presence we're feeling, we're missing the point of worship. Worship is first and foremost about giving glory to our matchless God and Savior, Jesus Christ.

11

PREPARING A WORSHIP SET

I poured out praise to the Lord,
Because I am his own.
And I will recite his holy ode,
Because my heart is with Him.
For His harp is in my hand,
And the odes of His rest shall not be silent.
I will call unto Him with all my heart,
I will praise and exalt Him with all my members.

THE ODES OF SOLOMON

WORSHIP LEADING IS a spiritual art. It has been said that the worship experience is more easily caught than taught. The same can be said of worship leading. Intuition, sensitivity and hearing the voice of the Spirit play a big part in knowing what to do and when to do it. We might say that some people have a gift of worship leading or an anointing to lead worship. This is certainly true.

But is worship leading purely a mystical art that is not definable in concrete terms? I don't think so. Worship leading does require spiritual sensitivity and God-given gifts, but it also requires practical skills that can be learned and developed through experience and instruction.

There are many rules of thumb that can be applied to the art of worship leading—there is some science mixed in with the art. Though it can't be reduced to a step-by-step process that guarantees success, there are many basic guidelines to follow and pitfalls to avoid.

My purpose in this chapter is to communicate the practical points that I've learned. Hopefully this will demystify the process and provide some handles on how to approach this musical/spiritual task.

Worship leading in many church traditions refers to the planning and leading of the entire worship service, including the sermon. In addressing the subject of worship leading, I'm not focusing on the teaching of Scripture or the celebration of the Lord's Supper. In my context it refers largely to the selection of songs for worship.

Song Selection

Because the role of a worship leader is to help a group of people approach God in worship, the particular characteristics of that group will determine a lot of the planning process. Knowing what songs the people know and love will strongly shape the selection of songs.

Repertoire is a big issue. One of my greatest challenges is to keep the right balance between old, familiar songs and newer songs that bring a fresh wind to the worship time. Matt Redman says, "Be aware of what's been done recently in your church: what's been overdone, what's been underdone, what's been done to death."[1]

If you entirely leave out the old classic worship songs, you're taking the risk of losing some or most of the people. Routine in worship is necessary for people to connect with God. They need to be able to sing songs that they've memorized, songs that are easy to sing. People love to pour out their hearts in worship without always having their eyes glued to the overhead screen. Because intimacy with God is such a big part of our worship experience, we have to let people use words that they've committed to memory. This is one reason that liturgical models of worship have endured throughout the centuries. The prayers I grew up with in the Episcopal church are powerful and full of biblical truth. The language of the prayer book became my own personal language of prayer. It still comes alive for me when I visit my parents' Episcopal church.

No Guarantees

Truthfully, no song is going to be absolutely "can't miss" every time you do it. The anointing of the Spirit and the response of the people is somewhat unpredictable, even with the familiar songs. Without the Holy Spirit's anointing and a ready response from the people, even great songs are not great at that moment. Therein lies the mystical nature of worship leading. One day we can sing the classic hymn "Great Is Thy Faithfulness" and all heaven seems to open up; the next day it can seem like just an average song. However, we would be foolish not to take note of the songs that have a great track record. If you find a great song, use it over and over again. If you want to reduce your chances of having your set flop, look for the "can't miss" songs.

What are the characteristics of great worship songs?

☐ People connect with God when they sing them. You can watch hands go up in the air, and you can hear the increased volume of their voices when you begin a song that is one of their favorites.

☐ You may notice an increase of the presence of God in the room. It's not just a matter of a catchy tune or a theologically sound lyric. What makes a good worship song is somewhat mysterious. In discussing songwriting for worship, Matt Redman says, "Sometimes you have all the right lyrics and it's clever musically but it doesn't have the spark."[2] Certain songs seem to *invoke the presence of God*. People love to meet with God!

☐ The melody and lyrics of the song are memorable and easily memorized. After several times of teaching the song, the people won't have to look at the printed words very much.

☐ Even after years of singing the song, it still has life and vitality. Use these kinds of songs if you want to be successful in worship leading!

It's important to note that no two people will have exactly the same list of songs. All of us have different taste in music, and we personally identify more strongly with some songs than with others. Some songs may be standard in one region or country, while in other parts they are relatively unknown. Part of the reason for this is the great number of worship songs that have been published by different denominations and music companies. Lots of factors shape our choice of songs, including ethnicity, church affiliation and age.

Worship leaders should choose songs that release faith *in their own heart* as they worship. You have to be able to find God through the song before you can use it as a tool for leading others. If you aren't encouraged, refreshed, renewed, touched or challenged by God in some way through a particular song, you probably shouldn't use it in your worship leading.

This brings up the issue of songs that work for *you* versus songs that work for your congregation or group. On one hand, you lead the people by personally entering into worship, so you have to choose songs that are meaningful to you. On the other hand, you have to choose songs that effectively *escort* people to the Lord. You might have five new songs that really excite you in your personal times of practicing and worshiping, but in order to *serve the people*, you have to give them a balanced diet of old standards with some newer material sprinkled in. You have to feed the sheep the type of food that they are willing to eat.

Preparing Your List

With all of the above in mind, I ask the Lord for guidance as I plan. Sometimes I feel that I get clear direction on a few songs that I'm supposed to do. Much of the time it doesn't seem that I'm getting any clear instruction from the Holy Spirit, so I make the best choices I can and proceed with faith that God is with me.

After years of leading worship, I have come to the conclusion that God enjoys my heartfelt offering of worship even when he doesn't tell me specifically what he wants me to do. On more than one occasion, when I've asked him what he wants me to do, it has seemed that he has countered with another question: "What do *you* want to do this Sunday?" We value hearing God's voice, but we also must realize that he has given us wisdom, sensitivity and the ability to *choose* to worship him. He gladly receives our sincere offerings of worship that are a choice of our own will.

Worship leading is like any other spiritual activity—you learn to do it through much experimentation. Over a period of years you gradually gain more confidence. You relax and believe that God wants to bless what you are doing. You see that God *really does* want to meet with his people as they worship, so you approach the planning process with more expectancy. On the days you don't *feel* inspired, you realize that God is nevertheless really with you.

I asked Matt Redman how he chooses songs for a worship set. Here are some of the key points of his response: "The main question I always ask is 'what can I do today that will be fresh?'"[3] Examples of that would be a new song, or an old song done in a new way, perhaps by moving a really big song down a few keys so it becomes tender. When you move a song down in pitch, the singers aren't able to sing as forcefully. Thus the song becomes more meditative.

Matt says that a key part of the worship leader's job is to try to "awaken something of the mystery of God in the worshipers. A lot of the other parts of worship fall into place when you tap into the mystery of God."[4] It's not enough to know Jesus as friend—we must also know the reverential fear of the Lord.

In regards to assembling a song list, Matt says, "I don't usually find that I get a list in which God has told me 'song 1, song 2 . . .' I usually get a sense to emphasize a certain theme. . . . The more you do it each week in your local church, it gets harder to know whether God has given you this list or if it's an idea that you came up with. And I don't think you have to make too much of a distinction between these two— God has given you wisdom and common sense."[5]

As a contemporary freestyle worship leader, I find it helpful to look at church history to see the wide variety of methods used in planning for worship. In surveying a variety of denominations, you see all kinds of philosophies of worship. Some churches plan their worship services a year in advance. Some use liturgies and guidelines for worship that have been used every year for generations. I believe there is wisdom in planning. There is nothing unspiritual about it: it's biblical, and we have a strong precedent from church history on planning for worship.

Building the Set

When possible I like to find out what the theme of the message is going to be. If I know what the sermon topic is, I will consider how to support the message through the choice of songs. Sometimes the speaker will request a song. This provides some definite guidelines which function as a starting place for planning the set. Doing a song that the speaker requests is a great way to be a team player with the pastor or speaker.

On special days and holidays like Thanksgiving, Christmas and Easter, it's obvious what we should emphasize. When we receive the Lord's Supper, we want to sing about the cross and blood of Christ. When we're doing worship during a prayer ministry time, we choose songs that set the stage for people to receive ministry.

What are some ways that God might try to get your attention as you plan for a set? He might put a theme strongly on your heart, like evangelism, holiness, repentance or the Father's love. He might say something very unreligious, like "Let's party." (I find that he speaks to me in terms that I can understand.) A song title might pop into your head. All of a sudden, "Holy and Anointed One" is clearly in your mind. It might be God speaking to you. You might envision a song working or get a strong feeling that something will work. Don't dismiss these kinds of impulses as merely your own ideas. Very often this is how God nudges us into doing the right thing.

As I wait on the Lord and play through options for songs, I see what grabs me. If it grabs me, it might be the Holy Spirit telling me to use the song, or it might just be a song that I really like! In either case I have reason to consider that song for the set. If I feel strongly about a few songs, I write them down and then search for songs that will be complementary to the first few.

The Curve of a Worship Set

What are the rules regarding the types of songs to use in the different phases of a set—beginning, middle and end? Should you *always* begin a set with up-tempo songs? Should you *always* progress from up-tempo songs to medium-tempo songs in the first half of the set?

In many respects, you can't have hard-and-fast rules in worship leading, and this is one of those areas. The biblical models for worship, and the experience I've had in worship leading, tell me that there's no *one* correct model for using slow songs in a certain place and fast songs in another place in the set.

Below I've listed several curves that a worship set can have. On the graphs, the vertical axis is the *energy* of the song—the product of beats per minute and the rhythmical feel of a song.

An example of a fast song would be "The River Is Here" at 115 beats per minute. A slow song would be "Refiner's Fire," at 72 beats per minute. (The number of beats per minute can be deceptive; the feel of a song like Brian Thiessen's "Name Above All" can be gentle even though it's over 100 bpm; a song like Darlene Zschech's "Shout to the Lord" is very powerful though it's only done at about 74 bpm.) The horizontal axis is the progression of the worship set from one song to another.

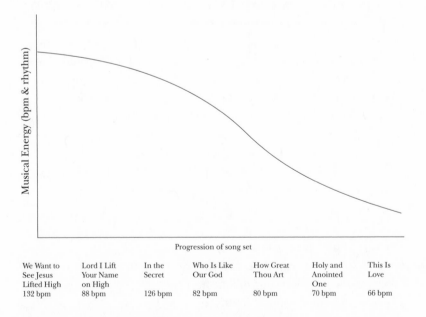

Figure 1. **The classic progression**

The classic progression (figure 1) is the most common curve of all. It is appropriate for Sunday mornings and other services when the people need their faith and their bodies to be stirred as they begin the worship time. Up-tempo songs which proclaim the works and attributes of God are good for this phase of worship.

The earthquake progression (figure 2) is the classic progression with an explosion at the end. After embracing God and being embraced by him for twenty to thirty minutes, a natural next step is to celebrate!

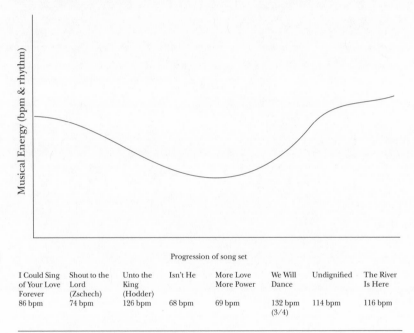

I Could Sing of Your Love Forever	Shout to the Lord (Zschech)	Unto the King (Hodder)	Isn't He	More Love More Power	We Will Dance	Undignified	The River Is Here
86 bpm	74 bpm	126 bpm	68 bpm	69 bpm	132 bpm (3/4)	114 bpm	116 bpm

Figure 2. The earthquake progression

The mild progression (figure 3) begins with medium-tempo songs and never moves to a fast tempo. Songs that proclaim the majesty and holiness of God in medium- to slow-tempo songs can be very powerful— for example, "Who Is Like Our God" and "Shout to the Lord." When we receive a revelation of God's holiness, we don't always need fast, loud music to bring us into worship. Sometimes it's appropriate to simply be in awe of God with reverence, bowing and kneeling.

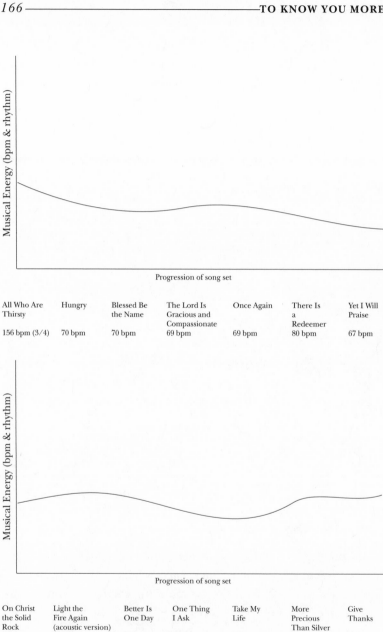

Figure 3. Two examples of the mild progression

Some people find it easier to engage with God through a slow- or medium-tempo song at the beginning of the set. People come to church in all sorts of mental, emotional and spiritual states. They may be depressed, angry, reluctant to worship or grieving over the loss of a loved one. For all these reasons, some people find it hard to begin worship with a bang. So a gentle, meditative song is one good way to begin a set.

This kind of set is begun with a medium-tempo song like "You Are Worthy of My Praise." In this song, people are gently led into making the decision to worship as they sing, "I *will* worship . . . I *will* praise you." During conferences, retreats or other worship gatherings that extend over more than one meeting, this kind of set can be very appropriate. People are very focused and ready to worship. When people are tuned into God, they don't necessarily need a high-energy song to kick start them into worship.

Elements That Provide Continuity

A worship set is like a conversation with God. Instead of abruptly jumping from one subject to another, there is a natural progression in the flow of thought and discussion. There are basic ways of building continuity into a worship set.

Before I jump into examples of elements of continuity, I must again emphasize that in the end, there are no rules. A skillful musician or band can play and sing musical interludes that will create continuity even if the methods below aren't used. Nevertheless, here are some helpful suggestions

Lyrical continuity. I often do two or more songs consecutively that have a similar theme. Here are some portions of worship sets that illustrate lyrical continuity. In the first set, the first two songs speak of the blood of Jesus. The third, fourth and fifth songs have the theme of consecrating one's life to God. In the second set, evangelism and faith-in-action are the themes of the first four songs. The third set has a theme of thanksgiving that runs throughout. The fourth set has a strong celebratory theme.

168 ————————————————————————————TO KNOW YOU MORE

Set #1
E "Once Again"
F "This Is Love"
C "Change My Heart O God"
E "Refiner's Fire"
E "When the Music Fades"

Set #2
G "Let Your Glory Fall"
D "I See the Lord"
E "Multiply Your Love"
Gm "Spirit of the Sovereign
   Lord"
G/A "Let It Rain"

Set #3
G "Give Thanks with a
   Grateful Heart"
A "Father of Lights"
A "All Creation"
E "Thank You Lord"
D "Amazing Love"

Set #4
F "The Happy Song"
G "Kingdom Celebration"
D "Undignified"
D "We Will Dance"
C/D "Did You Feel the
   Mountains Tremble?"

When we get to the end of a song about one of God's attributes, such as his *holiness*, we've only had a few minutes during that song to concentrate on that aspect of his nature. Just as we begin to catch a glimpse of God's self-revelation, the song ends—that's an opportune time to go into another song on the *same theme*. To switch to an unrelated topic would be to miss the opportunity to let God continue to reveal that aspect of his character to the church. The great hymn "Holy, Holy, Holy" and the song "Exalt the Lord" make a strong pair on the theme of holiness.

Key. In the following sets, notice the instances of doing songs in the same key consecutively:

Set #5
A "All Creation"
A "Holy Love "
A "You Are My King"
A "Eternity"

Set #6
G "There Is Joy in the Lord"
G "You Are Worthy of My Praise"
D "Humble King"
D "I Surrender All"

Set #7
E "I Could Sing of Your Love
    Forever"
E "Be the Centre"
E "Take My Life"
E "Better Is One Day"
E "Your Name Is Holy"

Set #8
G "Show Your Power"
G "I Give Thanks"
G "Give Thanks with a Grateful
    Heart"
A "Father of Lights"
A "All Creation"

Making a *segue*, or transition, between two songs is much easier when they are in the same key. When the music continues between songs or if there is a short gap between songs, the musical momentum is maintained.

Part of the power of stringing two songs together in the same key is the emotional and spiritual impact of the segue. Remember, our spirit, mind and emotions are integrated as one unified whole. We can't separate these components of our soul and psyche. When our emotions are impacted, our human spirit is automatically touched. Therefore we should build a worship set so as to tap into the sensitivities of the soul. Our goal is not to manipulate; it is to *call forth* worship from all that is within us.

As an example, in going from one celebrative song to another, like going from "All Your Promises" to "I Give Thanks," the momentum of the worship experience can go up a notch. Another example of this would be moving from the chorus of "We Exalt Your Name" to "Jude Doxology," which are both in the key of A (this transition is more difficult because one song is in 4/4 and the other is in 3/4.)

Using the *relative minor key* of the original major key is another good transitional tool. The relative minor key of any major key is the 6-minor of that key. For instance, Em is the relative minor of the key of G. Because of the musical compatibility of these two keys, a transition can be smoothly made between them. So I can move from the chorus of "Exalt the Lord," which is in G, to the verse of "Holy Is the Lord," which is in Em.

Tempo. If I am singing the chorus of "You Are Worthy of My Praise" (key of F or G) and I move to the chorus of "I Worship You," which can be done in the same key *and* is played at the same tempo *and* has the same lyrical theme, I am making a seamless transition that will enhance the beauty and power of the worship time.

Another example of this would be moving from the hymn "Great Is Thy Faithfulness" to the Vineyard song "Faithful One." These two songs can by played in the same key (D) at the same tempo, and they have the same theme of God's faithfulness. As a group of people are meditating on God's faithfulness while singing this old hymn, they can explode into another vein of worship when they move into the more contemporary expression of "Faithful One."

Style or rhythm. Two country-rock songs like "I Give Thanks" and "Amen Hallelujah" work well together not only because of the theme, key and tempo, but also because they are part of the same musical genre.

Whether or not to combine songs of different styles is partly a matter of personal taste. For some people it won't seem incongruous to link songs of diverse styles. I would personally lean away from changing too rapidly from one genre to another—for example, from country to light jazz to rock. I like each style, but if they are sandwiched in too tightly it can come across disjointed. For instance, I wouldn't move from a traditional hymn like "Holy, Holy, Holy" to a country song and then back to another hymn such as "All Hail the Power of Jesus' Name."

It is important to not overemphasize the value of a musical segue. Early in my worship leading experience, I mistakenly had the attitude that if I could assemble a set that was filled with smooth transitions, it was automatically going to be a good set. I found that as I finished a song that was strongly anointed and was eliciting a great response from the people, and I transitioned into the second song, the momentum of the worship took a severe nosedive.

This illustrates an essential point: don't do transitions just for the sake of having nice transitions. Every song we use has to *stand on it's own* as a strong worship song. To add a nice transition without having the right songs is to add trimming without having the meat.

12

DELIVERING A WORSHIP SET

As the wind moves through the harp
And the strings speak,
So the Spirit of the Lord speaks through my members,
And I speak through his love.
THE ODES OF SOLOMON

ALL WORSHIP LEADERS should feel a healthy dose of dependence on God as they begin a time of worship. Only God can make it happen in worship. He controls the release of the Holy Spirit, not us. Our job is to pray, prepare and trust him for the results. One week he may bring a glorious outpouring of his Spirit during worship; the next week it may be much less dynamic.

I believe that God purposely chooses to pour out his Spirit at one moment and to withhold it at other times to show that he cannot be controlled by us. This keeps us from worshiping the act of worship instead of worshiping God. Our job is to honor him, praise him and thank him. We should be grateful for whatever degree of self-revelation he bestows on us.

With this as a starting place, the worship leader can enter a place of rest during the worship time. Ultimately *God* is the worship leader. *He* stirs the hearts of people as he renews their minds and hearts. The job of the worship leader is to vigorously approach God in worship, thereby setting an example and clearing a path for the congregation to do the same.

Changing Your List

It's very common for me to make additions and deletions to my song list after the initial planning session. I will typically make changes the night before a Sunday morning set, one hour before the set (during rehearsal) and even five minutes before the set. This keeps my worship team on their toes! One reason for making last minute changes is that a song hasn't felt right in the rehearsal time. Sometimes a song feels flat—even though it seemed like a good idea to put it on the list, it doesn't have that special spark of life that makes me want to sing it. Another reason to cut a song is that the band can't successfully pull together the musical arrangement in the allotted time. Another reason is simply that some better song choices come to mind as the time for the set draws near. Finally, I may change my mind simply because I'm indecisive and unsure about what to do.

Even after tweaking the set list several times, I will often diverge from my plan once the set begins. I will make on-the-spot decisions to do things differently than I had planned. There are various reasons for changing your list. I've listed some of them below.

Momentum versus preparation. On one occasion when I led the song "Let It Rain" during a Sunday morning service, there was a strong spirit of intercession present as we sang. When we finished the song, it was obvious that we needed to continue on that theme; to go in a different direction would have been to stifle what God seemed to be doing in our midst. There was nothing on my list that provided the right vehicle for continued intercession, so I inserted another intercessory song called "Glorify."

This song had the right theme, and I knew that the band could play it even with no rehearsal. As we continued with "Glorify," the momentum in worship was still very high. It still would have been premature to bring the dynamics down to the gentle songs that I had planned for the end of the set, so I inserted another aggressive song that allowed the church to express the attitude and energy that had been unleashed in them.

How do you let the band know that you're changing the list? I have a very simple and direct approach. I turn around and tell them the title of the song we're going to do. Maybe it's not super smooth, but it works. If the song is in my master songbook, I tell them so. Then they scramble to find the right page. Usually it works fine for me to start the song alone on guitar. As the song builds, the other musicians join in. To help with spontaneous song choices, I've put together a songbook with words and chords for more than 180 songs. I bring about five copies of this book to every practice and worship time. I'm constantly updating the book as I add songs to my repertoire.

Another example of adding a song that fit the moment was a time when I was singing the song "Unending Love," a great song about God's unconditional love. The church seemed to be powerfully in touch with God's love as we sang. Despite my original plan, I then inserted the song "His Love" because it followed up so effectively on that theme.

These two examples are good illustrations of the spontaneous moving of the Holy Spirit. We never know when he's going to take a song that we've sung a hundred times and bring new life to it. In moments like these we should be ready to reset our sails to catch the wind of what the Lord is doing.

Responding to unresponsiveness. A common question I hear is, "Should the response of the people affect the way I lead?" If you sense that the people aren't really with you, what do you do? There are lots of factors that determine the right answer to this question.

First, what kind of tradition of worship does your group have? If your church is unfamiliar with a style of worship that emphasizes intimacy with God, it's going to take time for the people to catch it. For most uninitiated worshipers, the idea of communing with God through singing is new and strange. It will take time for them to enter in. They'll start by watching you and the people around them. If they are full of love for God and ready to take a risk, they'll go for it quickly.

But many people are much more cautious and will participate with reluctance for a while.

In any Sunday morning church service, some of the people will be in this category. Don't consider yourself a failure just because not everyone is waving their arms and jumping up and down. If you want to be encouraged during worship, look at the ones who *are* worshiping, not the ones who aren't. If you are in a new church plant where most of the people are just learning about worship, get ready to persevere as they figure out what they're supposed to be doing.

When the people *do* understand worship and they're *not* responding, what do we do? Sometimes the leader's lack of preparation and poor song selection is the reason the worship time is lagging. The solution to this problem is obvious—get prepared!

At other times the overall spiritual dynamics in the church hold sway over the liveliness of the worship time. The overall momentum and vitality in a church will be reflected in the corporate worship times. If a high percentage of church members are devoting their energies to seeking and serving God, they'll be ready to praise him when it's time to worship. If Jesus is the passion of their lives, it will be evident in corporate worship times.

Encountering nonworshipers challenges the worship leader to lead with a pastor's heart. We have to avoid the "us against them" mentality and realize that "they" *are* "us"! We're all on the same team. We are to "bear with the failings of the weak" (Rom 15:1) and be patient as the less mature take steps toward knowing God. There have been times when I've felt angry with people because they didn't seem to be worshiping. Over the years, however, I've come to have more of a pastor's heart. On any given Sunday, there are broken people who need a lot of mercy when they come to church. It's our job as worship leaders to get people in touch with the mercy of God. We can't do that very well if we're judging people because they don't seem to be engaged in worship.

This point brings up another important issue. How expressive does someone have to be in order to be genuinely worshiping? Where do we draw the line to determine whether someone's way of worshiping is valid? Do we require them to raise their hands at least half of the time and to be singing all of the time? I don't think so. It's not our job to judge people as they worship. Only God knows a person's heart. In the interest of seeing the church mature in its demonstration of biblical worship, of course we hope to see people kneeling, bowing, raising hands, clapping hands, shouting and dancing. But the worship leader must patiently lead the people, *accepting* them right where they are in their pilgrimage of worship.

Aside from the obvious outward expression of church members, there is the element of spiritual warfare that comes into play. If there is division in the church, the Holy Spirit's activity in worship will sometimes be quenched. This is a problem that is outside of the sphere of the worship leader alone; it must be addressed pastorally.

But what can the worship leader do about a feeling of heaviness during a worship time that might be attributed to some vague form of spiritual warfare? I believe that this kind of warfare is real, because I've experienced it. Certainly we should intercede at times like this. Aside from that, the best advice I can offer is to "overcome evil with good" (Rom 12:21). As ambassadors of God's light, we have the authority to usher in the kingdom and blow away oppression *simply by worshiping God.* As we exalt Christ, his lordship is made manifest. When the going gets tough, we worship as an *act of faith* and trust that God will break through.

A simple rule of thumb in times like these is to use songs that are proven and well-known in your group. If people are struggling to worship, the last thing they need is a brand new song that forces them to read lyrics and learn a new melody.

Another thing I'll do when worship is sluggish is simply to take some time to wait on the Lord and ask him what to do next. This can be done during a song or between songs during a simple instrumental section. Sometimes God will give you a hint to change direction. Most often I continue with the songs I had planned, realizing that making the choice to persevere in worship is the best solution.

When an Idea Comes to You

Sometimes God puts ideas in our minds while we're worshiping. You might ask, "Why didn't he tell us *before* the set began?" I don't know! I guess this is one more way God shows us that h*e* is the boss and we are to be dependent on him.

You have to remember that worship is a vehicle for God to speak prophetically. As we open ourselves to the Spirit's leading, he weaves a prophetic thread through our congregational songs. He leads us before *and* during times of worship. God knows what difficulties and challenges people are experiencing, and he will lead us to sing songs that *speak directly* into those situations. Let us heed Paul's exhortation to not "put out the Spirit's fire;" and to "not treat prophecies with contempt" (1 Thess 5:19-20).

Prayers, Scripture Readings and Words of Encouragement

Songs are just one vehicle for our worship. Praying aloud, reading Scripture and encouraging the church are also effective tools for the worship leader. Most of my Scripture readings are planned, while most of my prayers are spontaneous. Sometimes I plan to read a certain Scripture or two that tie in directly with the theme of the songs or the sermon. There's nothing like the authority of Scripture to call people to worship. For instance, if you're singing a song that's based on the fifth chapter of Revelation, read part of the chapter between verses of the song.

When I get emotionally and spiritually caught up in a song, sometimes the song doesn't provide adequate language for me to express all that is in my heart. For example, when I'm overwhelmed with God's holiness, I express my response to God's holiness in a prayer. This is effective for several reasons. First, it's a genuine prayer to God. Second, the church agrees with me as I pray. In case people's minds were wandering to the postservice pot roast or football game, their attention is recaptured by praying instead of singing. Finally, beginning worshipers can catch a fuller glimpse the heart of worship when they hear songs *and* prayers.

Teaching New Songs

Singing a new song to the Lord is a biblical concept. I've found that it helps keep the worship alive. Fresh vitality is injected into our worship as we find new ways of thanking God and declaring the wonder of his nature and deeds.

Here is Matt Redman's experience of the value of new songs: "New songs are one of the best ways of unlocking something fresh. It might be that you've sung your current repertoire of songs so often that there's not much revelation going on; everything is biblical and it's all singable, but it's not awakening anything in people's hearts . . . then you find this new song and it lights up the whole worship time—a new song or a new way of doing an old song. The new song can unlock the rest of the worship time."[1]

As we sprinkle new songs into our repertoire, the overall energy of the worship set can go up a notch or two. Here are some suggestions about introducing new songs in your church.

Don't teach too many songs in one service or in one month. This is a tough one for me! I love doing new songs, because they awaken my heart of worship and they keep me from being musically bored. As a musician I have a greater appetite for new songs than the average congregation member. So I have to pull in the reins on myself as I consider all the possibilities of new songs I can teach.

The number of worship songs that are recorded these days is far more than any one church can sing. We obviously have to be very selective or else we'll be overwhelmed with new material. We have to remember that familiarity is important if people are going to be able to relax and focus on God.

Isaac Watts, the seventeenth-century hymn writer who is also known as the "father of the modern hymn," faced the challenge of introducing a whole new style of worship song. Though his hymns would not seem modern to us today, they were revolutionary in his time. Because his hymns were a radical departure of the style of music that preceded him, he had to be cautious in introducing his new hymns, and he was. He had to test the willingness of the churches to adopt his hymns. We have a similar challenge.

At the North Langley Vineyard we introduce a maximum of two songs per month. Occasionally we teach even more songs for a few months straight. Though this might seem like a lot, we can do this because our church has *learned to learn songs*.

Repeat the songs several times. Each Sunday, 20 to 35 percent of people might be absent from church. So if you introduce a song, some of them will miss it. Make sure you reinforce it several times in a two- to three-month period. They won't own the song until they've sung it several times.

If there is more than one worship leader, work as a team. When two or more worship leaders alternate leading the same weekly service, it's best to take a team approach to the teaching of new songs. All worship leaders will have their own repertoire, but each leader shouldn't be teaching different songs at the same time!

Not all of the songs we teach become regulars in the repertoire. Some songs are better than others, and these have more longevity. A new song might never be repeated if I don't feel that it's right for our church. I will usually give a new song a second or third chance before determining that it isn't working. One of the signs of a great song is that people catch on quickly. You know you have a winner if people are singing enthusiastically the first time you do a song.

It's easy to overload people with too many new songs. People need repetition. They need lots of familiar songs in order to open their hearts and worship. Tony Campolo, in an interview with *Worship Leader Magazine,* cautions against too much novelty in worship: "I believe that there is far too much novelty in worship these days. Every time I turn around it seems as though some singer has written 10 new songs and, in most instances, they all sound the same."[2]

C. S. Lewis, a man of a different era, also warns us against the use of too much novelty in our worship services:

> Novelty, simply as such, can have only an entertainment value. And [believers] don't go to church to be entertained. They go to use the service, or, if you prefer, to enact it. Every service is a structure of acts and words through which we receive a sacrament, or repent, or supplicate,

or adore. And it enables us to do these things best—if you like, it works best—when, through long familiarity, we don't have to think about it. As long as you notice, and have to count the steps, you are not yet dancing but only learning to dance. A good shoe is a shoe you don't notice. Good reading becomes possible when you need not consciously think about eyes, or light, or print, or spelling. The perfect church service would be one we were almost unaware of; our attention would have been only on God.

But every novelty prevents this. It fixes our attention on the service itself; and thinking about worship is a different thing from worshipping. . . . A still worse thing may happen. Novelty may fix our attention not even on the service but on the celebrant [worship leader]. . . . It lays one's devotion [to] waste.[3]

This is good food for thought in a contemporary worship music culture that is always churning out CDs packed with new worship songs. Don't overdo it with new material.

Vocal Embellishing and Spontaneous Singing

Improvisation by a lead vocalist is common in popular music. Historically the church adopts secular musical forms for worship, and the art of improvisation is no exception. But improvisational worship singing is not just a twentieth-century phenomenon.

Barry Liesch notes that the early Christians improvised much of their worship chant. In his book *The New Worship*,[4] Liesch quotes the *New Grove Dictionary of Music and Musicians:* "The church fathers gave a surprising amount of attention, in music and worship, to improvisation and charismatic utterance . . . [and] spontaneity in prayer."[5]

The early church father Tertullian wrote:

Anyone who can, either from holy Scripture or from his own heart, is called into the middle to sing to God." This refers to a small group of believers standing in a circle and worshiping together.

Musicologists believe that the New Testament term "spiritual songs" (Eph 5:19; Col 3:16) relates to the development of improvised songs on a single word like *alleluia*. The Greek phrase for spiritual songs is *odaes pneumaticae* or "pneumatic odes"—"songs upon the breath." Improvising on a single word like *alleluia* was common practice in the Near East cultures during the time of Christ and later became formalized in the jubilus of the Catholic mass. The final syllable ("ah") of the word *alleluia* was prolonged in a kind of wordless improvisation.[6]

Today worship leaders improvise by singing words and countermelodies that aren't actually part of the song. This happens while the congregation continues to sing the standard published version of the song. Extra words can be sung extemporaneously where there are a few beats of empty space.

Another example is the free singing that a worship leader may interject during a repetitive instrumental section that comes after the chorus of a song and precedes the next verse. A song like "Refiner's Fire" lends itself to this. After the chorus there is a four chord progression: A-E/G#-F#m-E. As this progression is played two or more times, the worship leader can sing a spontaneous song that expands on the theme of the song. Sometimes these songs can have a rich prophetic anointing that strongly evokes congregational worship.

Singing spontaneously requires courage—you are taking a risk because you don't know how the song will unfold until you sing it. It helps to practice singing improvisationally, either by yourself or in a small group of singers. This way it doesn't matter how you sound. Have someone repeat a simple chord progression on the guitar or piano and practice creating melodies. In this context there's no pressure to sing prophetically. Your faith, boldness and musicality will increase as you take one step at a time.

Is the addition of extra words or more complicated melodic phrases helpful or distracting? Does it enhance or detract from the worship experience? What is the congregation supposed to do during these times?

Many years ago I was adamantly opposed to this kind of individualistic expression during corporate worship times. I thought that the only effect this could have was to draw attention to the worship leader and hence steal glory from God. I still see that as a valid danger, and I occasionally see worship leaders who cross over the line into a performance mentality instead of a worship orientation. At that point people are pulled away from God, not drawn toward him.

However, I really appreciate the added intensity and energy that can be released with this kind of spontaneous singing. On many occasions, I have watched as worship leaders are swept up by the Spirit into spontaneous bursts of praise. When it's done at the *right time* and with the *right spirit* and *motivation,* it has the effect of stimulating and stirring the church to greater heights of worship. As the leader interjects a few extra words, the church continues worshiping. If this model is used regularly, people grow accustomed to it and aren't distracted by it.

There are several factors that determine whether or not vocal embellishment is helpful in leading the people in worship. One of the biggest factors is *the spirit in which the leader is singing.* I believe that it's possible to discern the spirit of people by listening to them speak or sing. If they are singing for the purpose of impressing people with their ability, it is obvious, and the spirit of worship is quenched. But if they are genuinely pouring their heart out to God, it's much easier to be caught up in the spirit of worship as they sing.

What guidelines do I use for spontaneous singing? My favorite kind of worship is spontaneous singing. But I don't do a lot of it in the average worship set. First of all, I try to place myself in constant submission to the Holy Spirit during the whole worship time. The Spirit serves as an umpire in my heart, checking me if I get off track. If I slip into a spirit of bravado instead of worship, he lets me know, and I change direction.

If I am filled to overflowing with the spirit and emotion of praise, I will occasionally express my love for God extemporaneously. I don't do this in a contrived or forced manner, but I let it come out whenever it bubbles up. Spontaneous singing is not a *technique* that I use to stir people up, it is a genuine expression of my heart to God. The *secondary* effect is the stirring up of people's hearts.

I find that there is a direct correlation between the level of anointing and congregational participation and the amount of vocal embellishment that is appropriate. If there is a low level of anointing and enthusiasm in the congregation, I don't have much to sing other than the written words of the song. To do so would be mere human striving. But if there is a strong anointing of the Holy Spirit and a strong response from the people, I will be a little more free and expressive. This comes naturally as I am inspired by the Spirit.

If there is a very strong anointing, I sometimes go a little crazy. But if people are going crazy in worship along with me, that's the time to go for it. In case you're wondering if this slips into *emotionalism* rather than valid worship, just take a look at Psalms. The model of worship portrayed in Psalms has a lot more emotion than is shown in most churches in the Western world today.

I've observed that the majority of the congregation is usually experiencing the same amount of spiritual freedom that I personally have while leading. For instance, when we've had a great worship time, usually the whole worship team and some members of the congregation will comment on it. The Spirit of God is in the room, and everyone can drink of him. At times like this, I will be more emotive than usual. Usually the church is not distracted by my energized state; in fact people are encouraged by it. As I lead by example, people are *stimulated* to worship, not manipulated.

One word of caution: Leaders can't use their own experience as the only barometer for what's happening in the whole group. Because worship leaders have the job of leading, they are always more engaged in worship than the average congregational member. So if you're having a great time of worship, do an occasional check to see whether the congregation is following you. What you see may influence the way you continue to lead.

Even with a pure heart, there can be too much of a good thing when it comes to vocal embellishment. Worship leaders should take their cues from their pastors and leaders to help determine where to draw the line regarding this issue. They will help establish how much extemporaneous praise is helpful and how much is *too much*.

Find out how spontaneous praise fits into your church's philosophy of worship. If your church affirms the use of long interludes of spontaneous song, there should be teaching on that subject to support your philosophy. Then the church will understand what it is expected to do—either wait quietly on the Lord or sing its own spontaneous song.

But if your church is not accustomed to longer spontaneous solos, too much of this kind of singing will leave the congregation in the dust. You might be marching on in a blaze of glory while the congregation is left far behind, not knowing what to do. At this point, the congregation becomes spectators, not worshipers. I love to get lost in worship through spontaneous songs, but I do a lot more of it by myself when I don't have to concentrate on leading and including others.

Each church has its own tradition and heritage of worship. As church members worship year after year according to certain patterns and forms, they know what to expect from the platform, and they know how to respond to the different cues given by the leader. It's essential that we respect the traditions of our local churches and lead in such a way that the people can easily follow. If we don't, we're not doing a good job of facilitating congregational worship. To exhibit a pastor's heart in our worship leading, we have to meet them where they are and lead them one step at a time.

When the Set Is Done

Powerful congregational worship times comprise some of the highest peak experiences of my life. When God shows up, I'm often overwhelmed with his goodness and love. After these kinds of worship times, I feel incredibly privileged to have the job of leading worship, and my love for him is deeply stirred.

There's one big problem, however. Worship times aren't always powerful and glorious. Sometimes it feels like I never quite find the handle. The momentum never builds and swells into a crescendo, and every time I start another song it feels like I'm starting from ground zero. So, the feelings I have after a worship set range from ecstasy to depression. Here's what I've learned about managing my postworship thoughts and emotions.

It's about him, not us. If my purpose in leading worship is to glorify God and assist his people, then my success doesn't depend on how good I look as I'm leading. If I'm musically and spiritually prepared, and I do my best as a leader, then I have been successful. If everyone is crying and bowing and kneeling and shouting because the worship is so great, all the glory goes to him. And if everyone is yawning, staring into space and struggling to sing, the glory still goes to God!

Avoid introspection. Musicians tend to be reflective and sometimes overly introspective. We can second-guess our planning for worship and find all kinds of reasons why we blew it. This kind of self-pity provides an open door for the enemy to add his words of discouragement. He's quick to give us reasons why we're really lousy worship leaders and pretty mediocre Christians.

Don't let this happen! Remember, your performance is not *who you are*. Give your offering to the Lord and let go of it. Don't find your identity in your performance. Think about the Lord, not so much about yourself. Early on in my worship-leading journey I came to the conclusion that selfish pride was one of my primary motivations for critically analyzing my worship sets. My depression stemmed more from my desire to look good than from a jealousy for God's glory. So I repented.

Realize that worship leading is an intense experience. Focused worship leading requires a lot of mental and emotional energy. It begins with having high hopes and expectations for meeting with God and leading your group. It continues with planning and forethought. It reaches its climax as you launch into your set. If you're giving it all you have, you're spending energy on every level—emotional, mental and spiritual. As you physically exert yourself, your adrenaline peaks.

When you're finished, you'll be tired! The laws of physiology and psychology aren't suspended for the worship leader. After you exert yourself, there will be a letdown of adrenaline, energy and positive emotion. Fatigue makes you more susceptible to depression. From what I've seen, creative people are inclined to fall into depression, especially after a big event. Preachers can struggle with these same issues.

In view of these human frailties, use wisdom in guarding yourself against intense mood swings. If you feel terrible after worship, realize that a big part of what you're feeling is simply physiological. Don't overanalyze. Involve yourself in positive thoughts and activities instead of plummeting into an abyss of self-pity and depression. At times like this, make the choice to be thankful to God. Thank him for every blessing he has ever given you. After all, *that* is worship.

13

LEADING a WORSHIP TEAM

Rehearsal & Presentation

Teach me the odes of Thy truth,
That I may produce fruits in Thee
And open to me the harp of Thy Holy Spirit,
So that with every note I may praise Thee, O Lord.
THE ODES OF SOLOMON

N O ONE EVER TAUGHT me anything about leading a worship band. In those early days, I had *no idea* what I was doing, and I felt very unsure of myself. How do you tell a drummer what to do when you don't even know the names of his drums? Since I did most of my childhood guitar playing alone in my bedroom, I didn't make the leap to the stage quickly or smoothly. Playing with a band is a different world with all kinds of challenges hitting you at once. Learning to work with a PA system is a challenge all in itself.

At the start, I leaned heavily on the skill of the musicians working with me. Thank God that I had some people around me who knew a lot more than I did. They understood the importance of the bass and drums laying a foundation for the rest of the band by locking into a groove together. They had a basic understanding of what each instrument does in various pop music styles.

Starting from Scratch

What do you do if you have no experienced musicians to learn from? Today there are many training resources available. A book like this isn't the best medium for communicating arrangment principles. A video or a live seminar is much better. You have to *hear it* and *see it*, not just read about it. A helpful resource that I highly recommend to give you some of the basics of arranging for a worship team is the video-tape *Worship Team Dynamics* by Randy and Terry Butler, which is available from Vineyard Music Group. I wish this video had been available when I was learning to lead a band.

The only way to benefit from a training resource like this is to spend time working with other musicians. You learn by doing, and the earliest steps are sometimes slow and awkward. You'll never get anywhere unless you jump in and get both feet wet. Gradually I learned what kinds of parts each instrument should play and how everything fits together. Over the years my arranging abilities have slowly matured through mistakes, patience and perseverance.

Getting Arrangement Ideas from CDs

I still copy a lot of arrangements from worship CDs, using what I like, throwing out what I don't like and the things my band isn't equipped to do. Then I add my own ideas. If you're willing to take the time to listen carefully to each instrument on one cut from a CD, you can learn a lot about the specific roles of each player. Playing and replaying small portions of a song until you can figure out exactly what's happening can be tedious.

There are several things to listen for on a CD. When do the drums stop playing? When is there one vocalist as opposed to three people singing full harmonies? What pattern is the bass player playing in the verse? How does the feel of the drums and bass change when you move from the verse to the chorus? You don't have to be able to play the bass to hear a simple bass line that's repeated over and over again. By listening and learning, you can then communicate with the bass player about the feel you're looking for.

Slowly but surely, you develop a language to give expression to what you're hearing. You learn when the snare needs to be on "two and four" and when it should only be on "four." You figure out when the high-hat should be playing quarter notes and when it should be playing eighth notes. You know the difference between a ride cymbal and a high-hat, and when you want to hear them. You know when the drums should stop altogether, and when you need a fill to set up a chorus or to create tension before the end of a chorus. You also figure out when to let the drummer create the groove and shape the arrangement while you shut up and play your instrument. You know when the piano should be played and when the organ should be played. You figure out when the electric guitarist should do a solo and when he or she shouldn't play a single note in an entire song.

Music Notation
It's handy to learn basic music notation. It doesn't take a huge number of hours to learn this extremely beneficial tool. Either through a book from your local music store or by taking a basic music class, you can learn how to write the notes in a treble clef with sharps and flats for several different keys. For the most part, the only keys I play in are A, C, D, E, F and G, and their relative minor keys. Since keyboardists and horn players are more likely to learn the "flat keys," you should learn to transpose from one key to another. If you learn music notation, you have a great tool to communicate exactly what you want your musicians to play or sing. In some cases, your musicians won't be able to read the notes, but at least you will have a way of remembering what you wanted them to do. Then you can play or sing the part for them in rehearsal.

Only a small percentage of the parts I want the band to play are actually written down on a piece of paper. Most of the solos are left up to the individual instrumentalist. Some of the hook lines—melodic lines that are repeated several times during a song—are committed to memory. Examples of this would be the hook lines in "The River is Here" (played on piccolo) and "Light the Fire Again" (played on electric guitar). Both of these songs have catchy melodies that are repeated many times during the song. If your line is in writing, you can hand it to two musicians so they can play it together. It saves time in a rehearsal if they can see the part on paper.

Experimentation in Rehearsals

I often experiment with different ideas on the same song in a rehearsal. There's always a need for trial and error. In many cases, I don't know what's going to sound best until I try different options. Often I tell the band, "I don't really know what I'm looking for here, so let's try a few different things and we'll see where it goes." After some experimentation, I'll give some input. Fresh ideas come to me spontaneously as I hear the combination of instruments playing.

You can accomplish a lot in preplanning arrangements by yourself, but there are some ideas that only come through the synergy of people playing together. The drummer plays a certain rhythm that sparks a new idea, or the electric guitar plays a part that sends the arrangement in a different direction than you had imagined. The best way to figure out when an instrumental solo is needed is when the whole band is assembled and you can actually play a song to see how the dynamics build through the first and second verses and choruses. Where is the instrumental break needed? When is a change of dynamics necessary? Together as a single unit, the band can feel the changes in momentum, taking cues from the leader to crescendo and decrescendo.

At times, take a free-for-all approach to encourage instrumentalists to really stretch the limits. I asked Matt Redman how he encourages young musicians to grow in their creativity. At certain times in his rehearsals, he encourages his players to play any idea that comes to them: "Most of the time the ideas might not fit, but one out of ten times they'll come up with something that takes the song to a whole new level."[1] Musicians will come up with new ideas only if you gave them the permission to experiment. Capitalize on the fresh ideas of your band members.

After listening to popular Christian and secular music, you will develop an instinct for what sounds right. I learned a lot by listening to all kinds of bands and artists as a kid. I still learn all the time, just by buying new CDs and listening to the radio. In listening to records in my youth, I wasn't consciously trying to develop an understanding of arranging, but the feel of music got in me.

In a rehearsal you sometimes know what a song is supposed to feel like, but you don't know how to explain it to the band members. As you try a few options, and they finally play something close to your target, you say, "That's it!" Remember what the instruments are doing at that moment. Hopefully the band will remember their parts when it's time for worship! Often they don't, but that's all part of the fun and frustration of playing in a band. Blessed are the flexible for they shall not be broken.

Don't Be Intimidated

Most church musicians are not professionals who can play all styles with great skill. We get into trouble when we compare ourselves with those who have more skill and training. Resist the temptation to be discouraged because there's a church down the street that has a great band and you don't have the players to match their quality. Be content with what God has given you and with the people he has put around you in music ministry. God grants differing amounts of gifts and talents; he distributes gifts as *he* chooses (1 Cor 12:7). We can't change our background and level of giftedness, but we can invest every talent we have and have the satisfaction of knowing we've done our best. Make the most of the resources available to you.

Be Courageous

Don't be ruled by the fear of failure. Instead, attempt things that you know you could never do without God's help. If you've never ventured out into uncharted waters, you've never really had to trust God. We only have to trust him when we're doing things we *can't* do in our own strength. Step out and take some risks.

When I recorded my first album as a twenty-year-old, I had no idea what I was doing. I just jumped in with both feet. I had no clue about multitracking, overdubbing or mixing. I'm sure the studio owner was amazed at how little I knew about recording. Listening to that recording today gives me a good laugh.

Don't be paralyzed by the fear of making mistakes—you *will* make mistakes. I've made tons of them! Mistakes are simply part of the learning process. As a popular saying goes, "Courage isn't the absence of fear, it's moving ahead *in spite* of fear." If I never took the risk of experimenting as a musician, I never would have gotten anywhere. Play with all your heart, and stay in it for the long haul. Then you'll see some good results.

Professional Attitude and Professional Ability

At the various churches and meetings where I've led worship, I've played with all levels of musicians—from inexperienced players to great players who have done lots of recordings. I really don't mind undeveloped ability as long as the *attitude* is professional, in the Christian sense of the term. What do I mean by *professional attitude*? I mean people who show up on time, take seriously their responsibility, don't pretend to know everything, pay attention during rehearsal and want to fit into the big picture.

If members of the team consistently show up late without an apology for their tardiness, I'm not impressed. If a beginner or intermediate bass player takes no time to rehearse privately, the message I get is that the person is not very interested in making a musical contribution to the worship ministry. But if people show up ready to serve in whatever way they can, they have the right attitude toward the job.

Performance, according to *Webster's Dictionary,* is "to fulfill; to carry; accomplish."[2] But Barry Liesch gives a helpful definition of performance for the worship musician: "To perform is to do something complicated or difficult with skill in public with a view toward serving and ministering."[3]

King David's musicians were servants: "Now these are the men whom David put in charge of the *service* of song. . . . They *ministered* with song" (1 Chron 6:31-32 NRSV). People just starting out on a worship team can still make a great contribution regardless of their performance level, if they are willing to serve.

For some of us, raising the quality of our performance may mean simply providing lead sheets for the musicians so everyone has a road map in the rehearsal. For others it may mean analyzing the parts of each instrument on a worship tape and taking time to emulate the basic sounds and rhythm patterns. For others it may mean taking vocal lessons or having separate rehearsals for the vocalists. And there is no substitute for private rehearsal.

Some people think that musical preparation is unnecessary and that it's better to flow with the Spirit. I think you can do both at the same time. I think it's *easier* to respond to the Spirit's direction if you are musically prepared. It's pretty discouraging when the band doesn't know the right chords or words to a song. If all I ever did was flow in worship without planning and preparing, there would be a lot of musical mistakes that would detract from worship—both for the band and the church.

Matt Redman explains the value of preparing the band and yourself for the unexpected:

> It's good to rehearse being spontaneous—getting them prepared to flow from one song to another so that when you're doing it [in a worship set] they'll be with you.[4]

Perform at a place where you can flow with God's anointing. That might mean learning enough chords on the guitar or having a vocabulary of fifty different worship songs. It may also mean teaching yourself to play by ear so that you can launch into a song even if you don't know it very well.

Practice, Practice, Practice

We marvel at an athlete like Tiger Woods who wins tournament after tournament. Granted, he has an extraordinary athletic gift, but he climbed to the top through lots and lots of hard work. Can we expect to become good musicians with very little personal practice time? Absolutely not.

Though this example brings competition into the picture, our goal isn't to have victory over other worship musicians and to take home more prize money. The point is that you can't bring much to the table musically if you haven't invested a significant amount of time and sweat into musical training.

My good friend Bruce Babad has played saxophone and other wind instruments on several of my recordings, and he has played with many well-known secular artists. He plays beautifully and loves to worship. He is bursting with musical talent, but he's not a showoff. Here's what he says about practicing his instrument on his own:

> Practicing is a big deal to me. I spent over three years in a row [while I was in school] practicing nine hours a day (without skipping any days) in hopes of reaching a desired level of proficiency. The problem is, the better I became, the higher my expectation was for how I should be playing. There is no limit to how skillful someone can become on an instrument. Even the best players in the world have room for improvement—and they know it! Therefore how could you settle for stagnant mediocrity?
>
> In a worship context God's anointing and sometimes gifting comes upon us and we play better than ever. We are inspired and our sounds become indwelt by the very presence of God. That is way cool. But I must point out God anoints/empowers whatever he has to work with. In other words, if you are playing saxophone for example, and your tone is terrible because you haven't put in the time needed or sought after some good instruction, you'll still sound bad when God's Spirit falls on the worship. It might be anointed and full of his life but without his grace and presence you could be a distraction.

As far as practicing with the team, Bruce comments,

> I'm a studio musician who is skilled enough to do a perfect job the first time through. However, the finished product isn't just me, it's a collective of four to seven other players. We need to learn how *we* fit together. We need to learn how to best support each other. Therefore I show up to the practices and do my part to help make sure we release worship rather than hinder worship.[5]

Worship teams click when people act as team players who can see the whole picture and seek to serve the larger vision rather than playing what they want to. Sensitivity to what other players are doing is a big asset. I've seen Bruce defer to electric guitar players and various other players when there was a musical hole to be filled. He can play with the best bands anywhere, but he likes to let other players contribute what they have.

This attitude is one of the reasons people commented on the unity of our team and the deference we showed to one another. During my years at Anaheim Vineyard, people would occasionally remark on the lack of competition. They could tell the musicians weren't there to prove they were skillful. People noticed that we weren't in competition. The electric guitarist wasn't a showoff, and the singers weren't vying for the limelight. It was evident that we were there to serve one another and the church. As the band sets this kind of tone, worship flourishes.

Bruce also understands the concept that less is more. Overplaying is a common mistake that young musicians make. It's another lesson that can be learned by listening to professional recordings.

The Dynamics of Team Rehearsal

One of my top rules for rehearsals is to *have fun*. I've learned this the hard way. I am very intense about accomplishing goals. When I get focused, I get very serious. In rehearsals, this translates into pressure on the team and me. If I'm uptight, my band can feel it, and they get uptight. Over the years I've loosened up and learned to relax. Part of it is simply trusting God to put the set together.

I want to create a rehearsal environment that people enjoy. If I'm at ease with the band and relaxed about preparing the set, everyone follows suit. Making jokes in the course of conversation helps create a lighter atmosphere. It seems like I've always had one or two jokers in my bands who are ready with some choice one-liners! I don't mind spending a few minutes on this kind of banter because it helps people relax and play more creatively.

Follow the Leader

In the bands I've worked with, there is always a designated leader. If there's no leader, the team lacks direction and unity. The leader can change from week to week, but on any given Sunday, too many cooks spoil the broth. I welcome ideas from band members, but only to help shape the sounds and arrangements, not to determine the overall direction and song selection. Song selection can be done effectively as a team, but that's not the way I've done it.

Working together in unity means taking instructions from the leader, experimenting with new ideas and then reworking the arrangements until they're ready. This may involve tedious repetition of small sections of each song until everyone is together. This kind of rehearsal is hard work—it requires intense focus and a spirit of cooperation. It requires perseverance when things aren't coming together. It requires patience when one band member can't get his or her part and everyone else has to review the section several times for the sake of that person. This is all part of being a team.

In my experience, the two most pressured positions are that of the drummer and the backup vocalists. This is because I spontaneously ask them to play or sing more specific parts and make more changes than I do with the other players. Since our vocal harmony parts aren't written out, they simply sing what they hear. If there are two backup vocalists, they try to work out their parts as the instrumentalists are working out their parts.

If I stop the band in order to highlight one singer's part, the pressure is on even if I treat the person graciously. Everyone is listening, and everyone knows whether the person is getting it or not. This is where the band member can't be insecure or faint of heart. When the leader says, "Try this line instead of that one," the request has to be taken at face value. By looking through a filter of insecurity or a wounded ego, a singer can distort a simple musical suggestion from the leader into "Your singing is terrible." I like working with people who are mature enough not to interpret musical suggestions as personal insults.

This is one example of a character flaw that makes a team member a liability. I shy away from inviting emotionally unstable people to join worship teams. If a team member always has a dark cloud over his or her head, it depresses the mood of the worship rehearsal. The whole team can be dragged down by a depressed, sulking team member. It's one thing if this happens once in a while; it's quite another if it's a consistent problem. The church should be a place where everyone is accepted in spite of their faults. But inclusion on a worship team is another issue altogether. The worship team is a frontline ministry that requires a basic level of spiritual and emotional wholeness and maturity.

Even if we carefully screen worship team applicants, there will be people who have meltdowns under pressure. Sometimes the intensity of a worship team setting brings up insecurities. Sometimes people don't feel appreciated.

Teachable people can recover from a meltdown. They may fall apart emotionally, get angry, withdraw from fellowship and blame it all on someone else. But if they are quick to respond to encouragement and correction, they can overcome mistakes with flying colors. Young, zealous musicians can grow by leaps and bounds if given the chance to mature in a worship team setting. Involving young Christians can be really refreshing for the team and for the church—their zeal is contagious. It also sends a message to the church that you don't have to be one of the "good old boys" to play on the team.

Redirecting Creative Ideas

The bandleader has to take the risk of not always saying yes when leading the band. Sometimes people have creative ideas, but in context with the whole band, their ideas detract from the overall sound. It's not easy to say no to the things people feel inspired to do, yet sometimes it's necessary. If the band members respect and trust the leader's intentions of making the best presentation possible, they'll be willing to lay down their own personal preference for the benefit of the whole.

At the same time, the leader has to allow each musician some room for individual artistic expression. Musicians are on the team because their individual styles are an *asset* to the team, not a liability. You can't expect a country guitar player to play the all the latest pop guitar riffs. If you invite someone to join the team, you have to welcome their musical gift.

Occasionally I find myself in the position of playing a supportive role in a worship team. This is good medicine for me! I'm used to being the leader, so if I'm filling in on bass, I'm reminded of the challenge of serving the leader—of watching closely so I can respond to the next move.

Giving Encouragement

Everyone needs encouragement. When I hear the band playing well, I tell them about it in a specific manner—"You sound great," "It's really coming together!" or "Those harmonies are really happening!" I make a point of telling people they're doing a good job.

After all these years of leading worship, I still need encouragement. It still makes a big difference if *someone else* tells me that God was there during worship and people really connected with God. It's so easy to take for granted the servants that work alongside of us. I work with some great players in my church. I expect them to play great music, and they always do. But I still have to remember to encourage them.

The bandleaders should lead the way in this arena. If the leaders give out the orders on what songs to play and how to play them, they should also be the biggest cheerleaders on the team. We can't pay volunteers with money, but we can at least pay them with our gratitude and appreciation.

Common Mistakes in Leading a Rehearsal

Introducing too many new ideas in one rehearsal or worship set. Band members can only absorb a certain amount of new material at one time. If it's too complex, they will either not be able to remember or play the parts during the set, or they'll have so much crammed into their heads that they'll be anxious throughout the worship time. Higher anxiety makes it hard for musicians to relax and play to their full potential.

In a one-hour rehearsal, I sometimes spend twenty or thirty minutes on one new song. At that point, I have to evaluate and decide how many other new ideas I'm going to introduce in the remaining thirty or forty minutes. I may have to delete a newer song from my list and go with an old familiar one that requires little or no rehearsal.

Building too many introductions and solos into a set. Our prepared arrangements must be held lightly as we see what the chief arranger is going to do during a worship set. It's easy to overproduce a worship set. Too many elaborate introductions and interludes can make a set feel contrived. Remember, our worship is like a conversation with God, mediated by the Holy Spirit. Imagine you have prepared a particular arrangement of a song, but when you arrive at that point in the worship time, the mood of worship is flat—people are not very engaged in worship. At that point, you have to decide whether the song will ignite the people into worship or whether it will come across as a glitzy performance.

A simpler song from the heart might be just the thing that is needed at that juncture. Honesty and simplicity in a worship song do a lot to communicate the spirit of worship to people. People want worship that is real. They know what is real when they see it. If I have to choose passion over polish, I'll choose passion.

You *can* have high-quality sound and still be genuine in your worship. Those two things aren't mutually exclusive. But you have to read the mood that's in the room. What is going to lead people into genuine worship? Sometimes an energetic song with a lot of rhythm and musical backup is just the thing. If the waves of the Spirit combined with the willingness of the people to worship are creating a powerful combination, then go for it.

Instrumental solos are most anointed and inspiring when they embody the heart cry of the people in the church *at that moment.* As the Spirit fills people with a zealous heart-cry, the electric guitar or saxophone can instrumentally express what people are feeling. An instrumental solo can take the worship to a higher level. People are crying out to the Lord, and when the solo is done they can't wait to jump back into singing the next chorus. Often, I can't read the congregation's mood or readiness, so I just jump in and go for it!

Not being sensitive to the Spirit's leading. On one occasion I was lead-ing worship at a pastor's conference. I rehearsed the band and felt we were ready to make a good presentation. After the first song, I thought that I should do something different than what I had planned.

I didn't stop long enough to figure out whether or not that was God talking to me. I was determined to perform the songs I had rehearsed! In that fleeting moment I couldn't imagine that God would want me to abandon my plans, so I didn't take time to let him redirect me. In hindsight, I think it *was* God talking to me, because the pastors weren't very deeply engaged in worship. I think if I had changed course to in-clude older, more familiar songs, they would have entered into wor-ship more easily. This is a great example of elevating the importance of the musical presentation *above* its rightful place.

Having unrealistic expectations of band members. I try hard not to over-whelm my players with musical challenges that are out of their reach. I go through a rehearsal fully aware of each player's musical capabili-ties. It can be embarrassing for a drummer if you keep asking a musi-cian to play rhythms that he or she can't. Sometimes it will take some prodding to see what a musician can hear and play. But if after three tries it's obvious the person isn't getting it, it's time to quickly go to plan B. In a perfect world, everyone should be able to try and fail with-out falling apart in a heap of dejection. But some people are extremely sensitive and are easily bruised. Respecting and treating people with dignity is more important than getting all the riffs just right.

Some people can hear a simple line and reproduce it on the first or second try. Others, for various reasons, will never be able to play or sing it. Music notation might help, and it might not. Get to know your play-ers' abilities, and give them enough challenge to keep them interested and growing, and not so much challenge that they feel like failures.

Don't make a molehill into a mountain. In discussing problems in the church, John Wimber once used the illustration of a ship being hit "above or below the waterline." If a seagoing ship takes a hit below the water line, it will start filling up with water immediately. That's an emergency. If it gets hit above the water line, it's a lower priority problem.

So I try to tune out the musical mistakes that aren't going to sink the ship. If a vocalist is a little off-pitch here or there, the ship will still float. If the keyboardist is overplaying in one song, that's OK. If I confronted everyone on every little thing I don't like, I wouldn't have a happy team. Besides, I figure if I don't demand perfection from everyone else, maybe I'll receive some mercy too!

The Value of Friendship on a Worship Team

Ministry is a lot easier when it's done with friends. Rehearsals are much less stressful when I'm with people I enjoy. At its best, rehearsing is more than practicing music; it's hanging out with friends and having some fun. There are lots of ways to build a sense of team spirit and friendship with band members. Here are some things I've tried.

Attend home group meetings once or twice a month. Home group meetings include worship and prayer for one another, with an occasional Bible teaching. In these meetings I am honest about my needs, struggles and challenges in life. This helps breed an environment where everyone can relax and know they're accepted.

Occasionally gather purely for partying. Have you ever noticed that you can sometimes find out more about a person by playing a competitive board game than you can in ten home group meetings? Playing together lets us see a different side of each other. We can get to know each other on a down-to-earth human level, not just in spiritual terms. Laughter is good medicine for the soul.

Go on a ministry trip. You're together all the time. If you go away for a weekend or longer to minister at another church, or on an overseas trip, you can't help but get closer because you eat together, work together, play together and tackle new challenges together. When you're away from home, you have to stick together, depend on one another and pray for one another. And you share in the joy and satisfaction of a completed ministry task. I've taken teams with me to churches across town, to other states and provinces, and to other countries. One of the best results of these trips is the building of team unity and solidarity. You go a lot deeper into a person's life on a trip than you do in local church meetings.

Go on a worship band retreat. Retreats provide opportunities for extended times of worship and prayer and in-depth sharing of needs. People become more open and vulnerable over a period of a few days than they do in a two-hour weeknight meeting. My wife and I have seen significant breakthroughs and healing in praying for one another in the context of worship band retreats. These times build mutual trust and appreciation. Musicians are less likely to be insecure and competitive if they know that they are fully accepted by their team members.

Avoid too many meetings. I've been to countless meetings in my twenty-seven years of being a Christian. I don't like having meetings for the sake of having meetings; neither do band members. So I'm careful about the type and frequency of meetings that I schedule.

If worship people are building friendships in the natural course of church social life, they might not need extra meetings to strengthen relationships. In my church, I am at ease in the relationships with the core members of the worship team. We enjoy working together, and we see each other in various church contexts. We have an annual church retreat, and some of us go on trips together, so we don't need lots of extra meetings. Many of us have families. So I don't burden the people with unnecessary meetings.

Conclusion

Some of the greatest highlights of my life have been in worshiping with a band. When the band is musically in it together, the Spirit is present and the congregation is fully engaged, there are few experiences that are as powerful and fulfilling. But it's a multifaceted discipline that requires Christlike conduct and perseverance in the not-so-glorious times. For all the mountaintop experiences, we have just as many times of sojourning in the valleys.

But the valleys aren't so bad when we're in them with our friends.

Serving alongside those I love and trust makes the tough times bearable. We work hard at producing a good sound, and if it doesn't end up being one of our best days, we know we've given it our best shot, so we're content. Most of all, we know that God isn't looking for the best players; he's looking for those who will consistently serve him, serve the team and serve the church.

Charles Wesley is remembered as perhaps the most prolific hymn writer of all time. His hymns are still sung around the world in a wide variety of churches. Here is a eulogy written for Charles Wesley by his wife, Sally:

> Tender, indulgent, kind, as a brother, a husband, a father, and master, warmly and unbelievably devoted to his friends, discerning in the character of men, incapable of disguise. . . . His most striking excellence was humility. . . . He not only acknowledged and pointed out, but *delighted* in the superiority of another, and if there ever was a human being who disliked power, avoided pre-eminence and shrank from praise, it was Charles Wesley.[6]

I would rather be remembered for these traits than for being a great songwriter or worship leader.

14

DEVELOPING
WORSHIP LEADERS

*You then, my son, be strong in the grace that is in Christ
Jesus. And the things you have heard me say in the
presence of many witnesses entrust to reliable men who
will also be qualified to teach others.*

2 TIMOTHY 2:1

E VERYONE CAN PLAY is the legacy that John Wimber left
for the church. People who are willing to put their hand to the plow
can be involved in prayer ministry, worship ministry and caring for
the flock. Worship leading isn't just for professionals; it's for the average person. The Holy Spirit is the source of a kaleidoscope of worship
gifts. This swirl of color combines in a mosaic of worship that perme-
ates every corner of the church.

"There are different kinds of gifts, but the same Spirit. There are
different kinds of service, but the same Lord. There are different kinds
of working, but the same God works all of them" (1 Cor 12:4-6). Worship leaders are needed everywhere—in children's groups, youth
groups, women's and men's groups, and seniors' groups. Some will
sing, some will play, and some will operate the sound system or the
video projector. God hands out the gifts, and every part is needed to
get the job done.

It's all part of responding to Jesus' Great Commission to go into all the world and make disciples (see Mt 28:19). To make disciples, churches must be planted. History shows that the best way to evangelize is to plant churches. To plant churches, worship leaders must be developed.

Worship leaders are formed within the community. Parents, teachers, the hard knocks of life, the church—pastors, leaders and other worship leaders—all play a role in developing worship leaders.

I impart worship-leading principles, but I depend on the power of the church to develop people into mature leaders. Worship leaders are first Christians and then musicians. Good training is holistic training that encompasses everything from feeding the poor to setting up PA systems to leading a worship set.

Pastors have much to do with the formation of worship leaders. They communicate a theology of worship, and values and priorities for worship. They walk alongside worship leaders in the daily grind of leading church. They are there over the long haul to envision, stabilize and direct the worship leader. The senior leader plays a role that no one else can play in encouraging worship to thrive and grow.

Worship Leaders as Trainers

Worship leaders themselves develop and train others to be worship leaders. All worship leaders will have a slightly different gift-mix, which will determine their capacity to train others. Some are strong pastors and teachers, others are pure artists. But each one has some mentoring capacity—every disciple can be a discipler.

Don't be intimidated by the idea of training others. You don't have to be a great teacher to train others. I'm not a gifted orator who can consistently stir an audience with great inspirational messages. To be an effective mentor, you don't have to be a great orator.

In 1985 I joined the staff of a church as the worship pastor. I started to take small steps in giving away whatever information and insights I could to the worship leaders in our church. I led by example, taught classes and seminars, gave guitar lessons and answered questions one-on-one.

I've never felt that I was a super-effective trainer, yet I've helped develop lots of worship leaders. I haven't done it by giving lots of great lectures or coming up with any startling new worship-leading concepts. I've done it by sharing what I've learned with anyone who was interested.

If you've been leading worship for six months, you can help people who are in their first month. Don't worry about how much you know. If you've had some success in worship leading, you can help others to do the same. It just takes a willing heart and some time and energy. As long as you're a page ahead of the people you're leading, you have something to say to them.

When I first came to the Anaheim Vineyard in 1992, Larry Hampton was in his mid-twenties and was leading worship for the young adults. He was also meeting with a group of teenagers to give them tips on playing guitar and leading worship. That's an effective way of mentoring—sitting in a circle with a few people, showing them fingering techniques for chords, answering their questions and letting them actually *do it.*

Unselfishly share the platform. This is the simplest yet most important key in developing worship leaders. Unless you have this one figured out, you'll never get past step one. To train others, sometimes you have to give your job away. If there's only one large weekly meeting in your church and you want others to learn how to lead worship, you'll eventually have to share your precious space. Leonard Bernstein was once asked what the most difficult instrument to play was. He quickly replied, "Why, second fiddle, of course. I can get plenty of people to play first chair violin, but it's hard to find someone who will play second violin with as much enthusiasm as they do first."

King Saul's life powerfully illustrates the opposite of this principle. When David, the talented young warrior, gained the favor of the people, Saul was jealous. When the people began to sing, "Saul has slain his thousands, and David his *tens* of thousands" (1 Sam 18:7), Saul felt threatened by David's popularity. He became angry, criticized David, and even tried to kill him. He was deceived because of his jealousy. The book of Proverbs says, "We're blasted by anger and swamped by rage, but who can survive jealousy?" (Prov 27:4 The Message).

I once had a vision of a football team with no numbers on their jerseys. The team scored a touchdown and the crowds went wild. But nobody knew who scored, because the players were nameless and faceless. True humility means rejoicing in the success of others as much as you rejoice in your own success. A big part of my job is handing the football to other players when the time is right. In the church there is only one scorecard. If any player scores points, the whole team benefits.

In 1986 I began to delegate small-group worship-leading opportunities to Brian Doerksen, who was then in his early twenties. At that time he hadn't begun to write songs and make recordings. But he obviously had a heart to serve, an anointing for worship leading and good solid musical skills. By 1988 he was leading some of the Sunday morning worship, and by 1989 he was leading about half the Sunday services. At that time he was only twenty-two years old.

I had to make the choice to share my space. I enjoyed leading worship; it was the peak experience of my weekly ministry schedule. But it didn't belong to me. It was God's. I was in a church that believed in developing leaders and sending them out into the harvest. So I laid down my own ambitions and gave Brian room to grow in his worship-leading skills. Little did I know at that time how far he would eventually go in the field of worship!

Though Brian learned a few things from me, because of his gifts and character he would have skyrocketed as a worship leader no matter who was helping him. But if you're insecure about your place in the church as a worship leader, you might be too afraid to let the young Brians do their thing. Don't make the mistake of Saul, who was threatened by the gifts and talents of David, the young man chosen by God to be king.

Being a team player is essential if you want to reproduce yourself in others. If you struggle with feelings of competition, ask God to change your heart. If you stay with it, he will. If you're like me, you'll have to do some serious repenting along the way, but he *will* give you his heart if you keep asking.

To eradicate possessiveness about your worship-leading position, "overcome evil with good" (Rom 12:21). Act in the spirit that is opposite to the temptation. Do whatever you can to encourage, affirm and speak well of other worship leaders. And if it's within your power, give them opportunities to lead.

Character Qualities and Gifts of the Developing Leader

When it comes to gifts and character, nobody scores a ten out of ten. If we required perfection, none of us would ever make it. But here are some keys for identifying, recruiting and deploying new leaders.

Choose people who are full of zeal to serve. Don't mess around with people who aren't ready to roll up their sleeves and get to work. To illustrate this, I'll use an example from major-league baseball. Charlie Blaney was once the Los Angeles Dodgers' vice president for minor-league operations. He had a great record for recruiting talent.

He describes the five physical tools that scouts look for in prospective players: hitting, hitting with power, fielding, running and throwing. "Scouts can easily look at a player and judge those five physical tools," he says,

> but there's also a sixth tool that isn't physical that's extremely important, and this is a where scouting makes all the difference. That sixth tool is called general makeup. General makeup encompasses habits, desire, drive, attitude and discipline—all those things that a player learns from his family or his coaches in growing up. Makeup, for me is number one.
>
> Quite often we see players who have the physical tools but do not have the makeup. They don't make it. And quite often we see players who have medium physical tools but outstanding makeup, and they can make it. They need to love it. That's the important thing.

I've had the pleasure of working with lots of worship leaders with the right "general makeup." Mark Stokes is a good example. As a young apprentice worship leader in the early nineties, Mark was the model servant. When we were shorthanded, he ran the sound and played in the band all at the same time. He would run back and forth between the soundboard and the stage, until we could find another pair of hands. He was there to help with anything that needed to be done. There was no complaining—just eager, faithful service. Mark is now an assistant pastor in our church.

When people score high in the general-makeup category, their chances of success are much greater. I've seen several worship leaders with all the right musical tools fail because they didn't have the right general makeup—they strayed off the path that leads to mature Christian character.

When developing leaders are full of energy to serve and grow, they have an appetite to learn. They're not picky about the tasks they are given. They come early to meetings and stay late to absorb all they can. Brand new worship leaders can become effective within months if they are gifted and pour lots of time and energy into learning songs and developing their skill.

There are key distinctions between a traditional discipleship model and a mentoring model. In the traditional discipleship model, the teacher sets the agenda and has to maintain the progress of the apprentice. This requires high maintenance for the discipler. In the mentoring model, the onus is on the protégé to progress, with input from the mentor as needed. The best model for training is perhaps a hybrid of these two styles. Both the mentor and apprentice should take initiative toward each other.

I didn't have any mentors in worship leading. I just watched people. I absorbed whatever I could from the example of others. I was eager to learn, and I worked hard at developing my skills. That's not the best learning environment, but it illustrates the possibility of growing if you have a lot of drive and vision.

Choose people who are loyal and willing to follow your leadership. You can't lead people who don't want to follow you. *They* decide who their leader is. Attitude is everything. The apprentice must be willing and eager to learn from the mentor. The most fruitful mentoring relationships I've had are those in which both parties have a mutual desire to cooperate as coworkers.

As a worship pastor, if I see a young leader with leadership potential, a pure heart and musical skill, then I'll have faith to invest in him or her. If the young leader is eager to learn from the mentor, this mutual attraction leads to an impartation of faith, confidence, anointing, ability, sensitivity and overall effectiveness.

I had this kind of relationship with Mark Stokes. He trusted me, was loyal to me, and was willing to do anything to serve as an apprentice under me. Aside from having the right gifts for the job, Mark was committed to me as a friend and a leader. We enjoyed hanging out together. Relationships like these have lots of potential.

Once in a while a close relationship forms between mentor and mentoree. This creates the best possible environment for discipleship. However, the majority of my discipling relationships haven't been like this. Most of the people I've trained have known me from a distance. A smaller number have spent time individually with me, and a much smaller number have spent *a lot* of time with me. It's the same with those that have trained me. There have only been a few close personal friends who have discipled me in twenty-seven years of being a Christian. The good news is that you can carry on the training process in either casual or deep relationships.

Whether you're looking for a mentor or for someone to disciple, be careful about getting your expectations too high for any one individual. I've made this mistake before—letting my hopes for a close relationship escalate too high. It leads to disappointment. Don't put too much pressure on yourself or on others to perform. Trust God to bring you the friends and mentors you need.

Here's another reason why it's essential for a worship leader (especially one with high visibility) to share the senior leader's vision: without commitment to the leader, the chances for divisiveness and misuse of power are much higher. If the worship leaders are not relationally connected to you, there's a danger they'll undermine the leadership.

I found this out the hard way as a senior pastor. I didn't stay close enough to some of the small-group leaders, and a faction formed that led the way in a church split. There wasn't enough relational contact between the leaders and me to build the mutual trust that is so essential for working together as a team.

Choose people who have a well-rounded lifestyle of worship. Within a year after the Langley Vineyard began, Brian Doerksen joined the church. He was about nineteen years old and fresh out of Youth With A Mission. I can remember seeing Brian at a weekend conference in the fall of 1985, shortly after he had started coming to the Vineyard. On the closing night of the conference, he was dancing to the Lord with abandon. He seemed totally uninhibited in his worship, oblivious to the people around him.

I soon found out that he was also a lifestyle worshiper. Before he was twenty years old, he had done short-term missions work in England and Haiti. In his hometown he cared for needy, underprivileged people. These are the kind of people I want to raise up into leadership—people whose lives are devoted to Christ, his church and his cause in the world.

Worship leaders have more authority to lead when their lives match their songs. Furthermore, when church members see someone who is going for it in God's kingdom, they are much more willing to follow that person in worship.

My pastor, Gary Best, has played a key role in developing many worship leaders who have led, written and produced many worship songs that have become standards in many countries and denominations. I asked Gary what he saw to be the essential issue in raising up worship leaders. At the top of Gary's list was the issue of *authority*. Calling worship leaders to live *under* God's authority is key for them to lead *with* authority.

To be effective in the micro, or musical, expression of worship, leaders must be genuine macro worshipers. Gary sees a strong connection between our fruitfulness in musical worship and our attempts do the works of Jesus—healing the sick, helping the poor and reaching the lost. Instead of allowing musicians to become so specialized in music that they became isolated from the church, Gary calls them to a well-rounded life of discipleship. He calls worship leaders to be dissatisfied with a deficit in either category of worship—music or daily life.

Choose people who are gifted in leading worship. Here's a basic principle of leadership from the book of Proverbs: "The mark of a good leader is loyal followers; leadership is nothing without a following" (Prov 14:28 The Message).

The gift of leading worship is a combination of spiritual and musical gifts. Skilled musicianship is one thing; anointed leadership is another thing. Sometimes they coexist in one person.

A basic level of musical skill is obviously required. But this standard will vary widely depending on the size of the church and the availability of other musicians. When John and Eleanor Mumford planted the South West London Vineyard in England, Eleanor was the first worship leader. She was the only musician available. Since John couldn't carry a tune, Ellie was the obvious choice! She led worship on something called an omnichord. It was like an autoharp—you strum the strings and press a button to produce the right chord. She wasn't a great musician, but she could sing on pitch and she loved to worship Jesus. That's all you need to get started.

What is the evidence of God's gifting in a worship leader? People are drawn into worship. They give themselves to God. They respond by saying yes to him. People sense God's authority; they become aware that he is present in the room. The Holy Spirit impacts people, sometimes subtly, sometimes strongly.

Learning to lead with confidence and sensitivity to the Holy Spirit takes time. Potential leaders won't shine brightly every time they lead. Everyone has a learning curve. Even after gaining experience, no one hits a home run every time. But gifted worship leaders gradually develop a track record of being able to engage people in worship consistently.

Choose people who have the potential to lead people as well as music. Musical gifts are obviously essential to worship leading. Vocal and instrumental skills play a huge factor in determining the scope of a leader's ministry. But there are other areas that are equally important, especially at higher levels of responsibility.

When I left the Langley Vineyard in 1989, Brian Doerksen excelled not only because of his musical gifts but because he was a good all-around leader. He was a good communicator, had a pastor's heart and learned how to identify, recruit, train and oversee people. He wasn't just a good worship bandleader, he was a good small-group leader. He ministered effectively to people one-on-one.

The best worship bandleaders are good pastors and leaders. Worship team members need to be cared for, not just deployed as musicians. Sometimes it will be appropriate to appoint worship bandleaders who are inexperienced pastorally. But if young leaders have a compassionate heart, they can come alongside other musicians with a shepherd's heart. Together with other pastoral leaders, the person can get the job done. Maybe you're in a church filled with teenagers. You might have to settle for a person with a good heart and no leadership experience!

Don't just look for the bright and shining stars with dazzling personalities. Look for the sleepers—the quality leaders who at first don't appear to be leaders. They aren't necessarily articulate, gregarious, life-of-the-party types. They are soft-spoken and self-effacing, but faithful, trustworthy and dependable.

Casey Corum, the worship leader at the Vineyard in Boise, Idaho, is a great example of the quiet, artistic personality type. Because of his strong musical gifting and his value for multiplying ministry through other people, he has borne much fruit.

When Casey was only eighteen years old, he joined a team of people from his church in Lancaster, California, to plant a new work in Boise. That was in 1989. Because of his consistent training of new leaders and his unselfishness in sharing the platform, in 2001 there were a total of nine worship bands (adult and youth) in his church, with fifteen leaders. The average Sunday attendance at their church is 1,500. Over the years, Casey has trained between 100 to 150 small-group worship leaders.

I don't think Casey thinks of himself as a super-gifted teacher-trainer. But he has chosen to make a habit of giving away his gifts and wisdom. So his ministry has been multiplied many times over.

Being a Mentor

Paul Stanley and Robert Clinton define mentoring as "a relational process between mentor, who knows or has experienced something and transfers that something (resources, wisdom, information, experience, confidence, insight, relationships, status, etc.) to a mentoree, at an appropriate time and manner, so that it facilitates development or empowerment."[1]

In their book *Connecting,* Stanley and Clinton list several mentoring types, including intensive models (discipler, spiritual guide, coach), occasional models (counselor, teacher) and more passive models.[2] My style of mentoring is largely unstructured and occasional, though I find some structure to be helpful.

Mentoring happens in all kinds of ways: during informal conversations and in formal classroom settings; in structured mentoring groups and in sporadic, spontaneous meetings over coffee; and on road trips. Mentoring happens while working together—during the sweat and strain of setting up a PA system in forty-five minutes, then leading worship for another thirty to forty-five minutes.

Over the past sixteen years I have held staff positions at four different churches in which I have developed worship leaders using all kinds of mentoring techniques. For me, mentoring is more intuitive than a planned course of action. Here are the things I do to raise up worship leaders.

The show-and-tell process. This is the most powerful training tool for worship leaders. It's also known as "the Discipleship Loop" and can be applied to worship leading:[3]

1. Lead worship with someone watching. (Modeling is the most powerful communication tool there is.)
2. Let the person play alongside you while you lead.
3. Let the person lead while you play alongside him or her.
4. Talk about the worship time when it's finished.
5. Let the person lead worship alone.

It is said that Spirit-inspired activities such as worship are "more easily caught than taught."[4] Therefore, if you want your church to learn about worship, take them to a worship conference where lots of zealous worshipers will be diving into worship. A picture is worth a thousand words. It's much easier to get caught up in the heart of worship when a few hundred people around you are doing it.

It's the same with worship leading. There is only so much that can be learned by sitting in a lecture. Worship leading is an intuitive art. There are lots of intangibles that are done by feel rather than by the book.

By playing on a team, an apprentice worship leader catches all kinds of insight, both tangible and intangible. Working with a sound system, running a rehearsal, knowing when to change your set list and being sensitive to the congregation's mood as an aid in leading them are all learned by *watching* and *doing*. Studies on education show that people are most likely to remember what they are taught if they actively apply what they are learning.

The best way to raise up small-group worship leaders is to invite novices to play alongside of the leader. They don't have to lead—all they have to do is play along. When they are ready, they can lead one or two songs in a set of seven. The primary leader will be there to keep the musical momentum going in case the novices falter. After a few positive experiences, they will gain confidence. Then they may be ready to lead an entire set by themselves. By jointly planning a worship set, the apprentices learn the principles of planning for worship.

Another byproduct of playing along with an established leader is an increase of credibility for the apprentice. A group of people will more readily trust a new leader if they know that person has been appointed by their primary leader. The ministry of the new person is validated by the first leader.

In a band situation, an apprentice can play or sing along without being turned up on the sound system. That's not an insult; it's a way of gradually introducing a new player into an intimidating new challenge. Having your voice and instrument amplified is a shocking experience at first! Every little mistake is heard. You can't hide your pitch problems and wrong notes when the volume is turned up!

Even though they're not making a big musical contribution, the apprentices benefit from seeing every nuance of the worship time from the vantage point of a band member. I recently took my son Zachary to a conference where he played percussion and acoustic guitar in the band. At times, his percussion parts were heard by the congregation; most of the time they were buried by the rest of the instruments. But he wasn't disappointed about not being heard—he was thankful for the chance to be in the band, and he learned a lot.

For the mentor/worship leader, coleading can be a lot more work than leading solo. When I colead, I have limited freedom to really develop a theme. I sometimes feel hemmed in with very little room to maneuver and make spontaneous changes. Sometimes the ideas of two chefs are incompatible in one recipe for a worship set. So you go back to the drawing board and start over. Coleaders have to be ready to change their list in order to harmoniously blend with the other person's songs.

That's where the leader has to defer to a team process in order to accomplish the task of training. I must limit my personal freedom as a leader for the greater goal of seeing others reach their leadership potential—it's well worth the sacrifice to raise up new leaders.

On the positive side, there is much less pressure on leaders when they aren't carrying the whole load of a worship set. When I get into a challenging worship-leading situation—like leading a new group of people who come from a different worship background than myself—I can breathe easier when I have a coleader who is sharing the load.

A final word on coleading: it is much more than a training tool. When two or three leaders are on the same page with musical arrangements, a repertoire of songs and a style of doing worship, their team leading can be a wonderfully rich gift for the church.

When I was in the Philippines in 2001, there were several worship leaders playing in the band. On the closing evening of the worship conference, five or six different vocalists led songs. It wasn't contrived or forced; it was seamless. Each song flowed naturally into the next. Each of the leaders had a different voice and personality that came through, and together each of these colorful textures blended into a beautiful tapestry of worship.

This was unusual for me; it's the only time I can remember so many singers leading during one set. (It was a one-hour set, so there was more time for diversity.) Aside from being musically compatible, we enjoyed great camaraderie through several days of worshiping together.

Personal meetings. When I see people I believe in because of their character, gifts and heart after God, I will take the initiative to impart something to the person. Rather than following a set curriculum, mentoring is a unique process for each individual, driven by the needs, questions and goals of the trainee, insofar as they intersect the goals of servant leadership. Personal meetings create a context for getting to the crux of issues that are important right now.

Whether it's having a meal or coffee together or going on a trip together, casual time can be productive. In these settings, you have an opportunity to encourage the apprentice concerning whatever issues are most pressing—worship leading, plans for the future or family conflict. The trainee can ask questions on anything that's relevant. Even if you don't have all the answers, showing your concern goes a long way in building equity in relationships.

When worship leaders hit a wall, they are full of questions. When the PA goes berserk, or there's conflict on the worship team, or they don't feel inspired while leading worship, leaders are ready to learn. Adult learning is life-centered and work-centered, not merely theoretical.

Discipleship regarding the overall issues of life should go hand in hand with development as a musical worship leader. I don't like confrontation, but I don't know anybody who does. Don't let the problem issues slip by because it's uncomfortable to bring them up. I've already seen too many leaders' marriages dissolve, so I'm not going to sweep conflict under the carpet.

Time spent in nonministry settings does a lot to establish friendship between leaders. Don't just talk business. Be a friend, not just an overseer. The bond of friendship makes the rigors of ministry much easier to endure together. A few simple words of encouragement from an established leader can go a *long way* in a young leader's life. I tend to be very task oriented, so sometimes I can neglect people in the process. I have to constantly remind myself that I'm in the people business. The process of relating to people while reaching goals is *everything.*

To get valuable one-on-one time with trainees, I try to take people with me whenever I go on a ministry trip. They watch what I do, and they're always learning. Whether I'm teaching a song to a band that I've never worked with, or dealing with a cantankerous sound technician or managing my anger when my luggage gets lost, they're always learning something. (Sometimes they learn that I'm a long way from being perfect!)

Giving feedback after a worship set. This is the fourth step of the discipleship loop. You have to *see* people leading, and provide specific feedback, or else they won't know what they are doing wrong and right. Be as specific as you can—if the person strays from the mike and can't be heard well enough at times, say so.

It takes sensitivity to know the right time and way to address areas of weakness. I look for the teachable moment. When people ask how they did, the door is opened for your input. Give as much constructive input as you can without being discouraging. If a leader makes three mistakes, I'll sometimes only address one issue because I don't want to weigh the person down with too much negative input. If a problem persists over time, you need to address it even though the teachable moment may never seem to arrive.

Gradually release people into positions of responsibility. I've made the mistake of giving people too much responsibility too quickly. I've seen worship leaders flounder musically because they weren't ready for a larger responsibility. A few times I've seen God's gifting and calling on a person and reacted too hastily, not waiting long enough to determine how to act on those nudges from God.

The safest route is to begin by giving people a little responsibility.

Ask them to lead worship one time. Don't give them a permanent or even semipermanent position at first. If they are called to a greater scope of ministry, they will first be faithful with little things. Even if God speaks to you powerfully about a person's calling, you can't predict exactly how and when God will raise that person up. Let the person's track record confirm what God has shown you before you offer a permanent position.

On the other hand, there will be times when you'll want to give an assignment that overwhelms people. If they have never led a Sunday worship time, the first time will probably stress them out bigtime! If they have never gone on a ministry trip to teach or lead worship, they will feel pressure the first time. But without occasional stretching experiences like this, leaders never grow into their full potential. I've seen people make a quantum leap in their hunger to minister after going on a ministry trip to another city or country. As they take new risks in ministry and see God's faithfulness, they come home with great zeal to do kingdom work.

Information, not just inspiration. Everybody needs to be informed as well as inspired. Information—whether biblical theology or church history or devotional topics—can be communicated in a lecture, through books, or over the Internet. Prospective worship leaders can be exposed to the basics of worship and worship leading in a short course. It's good to repeat basic courses like basic guitar, intermediate guitar and small-group worship leading once a year in your local church.

I find that people enjoy interactive classroom settings more than lectures. One model I've tried is a worship leaders' forum for about six worship band leaders from churches in our city. We held the meeting in my home once every six weeks or so. Keeping in mind the issues they were grappling with, I set the topic of discussion for the evening. Everyone shared insights, experiences and frustrations relative to worship leading and learned from one another. I facilitated the discussion and gave input, but the synergy of the small group was the primary learning tool.

In my experience, worship leaders generally aren't motivated to get training unless they have the responsibility of leading. When they have to lead, they find out what they *don't know*! Then they're more teachable. So don't despair if you can't get people to come to all kinds of classes on worship. If they are leading effectively in small groups, they may not feel a need for more training. If they have busy lives, as most church leaders do, there are a lot of things competing for their time. Choose wisely what classes you will offer, when you offer them and who will speak or facilitate.

Nobody I've trained has learned everything they know from me. With the huge amount of resources available nowadays, we have ample opportunity to put our people in touch with wonderful resources. There is a plethora of teachers and seminars on worship. For those that have a hard time attending training events, there are books, videos and tapes.

Looking Toward the Next Generations

To reach the upcoming generations, young worship leaders must be constantly trained and developed. To reach the youth, we need young worship leaders.

Leadership is all about influence. In week-to-week church life, worship leaders are highly visible; therefore, they are highly influential. Youth are influenced by their peers. Because music styles change with every generation, the church must continue to embrace new styles.

"Often we play it safe in the church," says Matt Redman. He encourages fostering an environment where you don't always have to play it safe. He feels that innovation in worship "might spark some curiosity in people who don't go to church."[5] Sounds like a good idea if we want to see the unchurched come to church.

Looking ahead, there are lots of new trends in the arts that will impact worship in the coming generations. We have rap and electronic music to add to all the different forms of rock and traditional church music. Producing videos for worship is becoming easier all the time as digital technology becomes more and more advanced and user-friendly. The visual arts can be employed as a powerful tool to trigger the imagination and inspire the spirit. Few churches I know of are tapping into this incredible resource. The forward-looking leader will encourage experimentation with these art forms in worship.

To capture the hearts of the upcoming generations, all kinds of art forms can be used. Older people like me have to open up to new artistic expressions, even if at first they feel uncomfortable. I know of a church in southern California that is experiencing renewal in worship, especially among the youth. Most of the older generation in this church have really grasped the importance of using music that will be a bridge to these kids. But inevitably there will be an occasional complaint. When someone bemoans the style or volume of the music, the mature folks remind their peers that it's not for them—it's for the youth.

In a multigenerational church that is evangelistically minded, the music might not keep everyone happy all of the time. I would rather take the risk of offending a few church members than lose the chance of reaching a few teenagers who are seeking the truth.

This isn't to say that youth won't follow an older worship leader. Musical styles aren't specific to any one age group. For example, classic rock or retro styles of rock music are now popular with teens and young adults. They are listening to the same acoustic and electric sounds that I enjoyed in the 1970s.

There will always be a place for older leaders. The church is a multi-generational organism. Youth respond not just to young people; they respond to older people who are genuine, honest and secure. But one of the primary tasks of mature leaders is to teach and train.

To Keep Giving, You Have to Keep Growing

A person learns to teach and mentor by being a good student. I'm continually seeking out new books, songs and experiences that will inform and inspire me. I know that I'll continue to teach the basics, but unless I have fresh input, I get stale. To be a good discipler, I have to be a good disciple. That means continuing to learn for the rest of my life.

15

THE GIFT & CRAFT
OF SONGWRITING

The songwriters are the secular prophets of our day.
EDDIE GIBBS, PROFESSOR OF CHURCH GROWTH,
FULLER THEOLOGICAL SEMINARY

ADDRESSING A GROUP OF Vineyard songwriters in February 2001, Eddie Gibbs stated, "You have far more ability to impact people than preachers or authors." That's an arresting thought for worship songwriters! We're doing far more than singing simple songs in the church.

As worship leaders, we teach. As songwriters, our impact is even broader. We fashion words that shape people's views of themselves, God and the world. Through our songs, we shape culture. While rap artists are selling millions of records promoting violence and misogyny and while chart-topping artists sell millions of records that celebrate an immoral, self-absorbed lifestyle, we can give people a Christian alternative. The tunes and lyrics we sing in church will also be sung in homes, cars and the marketplace. As they are sung, they weave their way into the heart. Songs that stick in people's heads serve as constant reminders of the absolute reality of Jesus.

Because our culture is increasingly biblically illiterate, we desperately need songs rooted in biblical truth. In our postmodern culture, anything goes. The rule of the day is to create your own philosophy and to do whatever works for you. Therefore, in our songwriting we have the challenge of responding to biblical illiteracy by giving people truth.

In the early 1990s, Gordon Fee, a professor at Regent College in Vancouver, British Columbia, spoke at a conference at the Langley Vineyard. He commented on the power of hymnology to form people's thinking: "Show me a church's songs and I'll show you their theology."

Music is the most accessible form of communication. You can get it on the radio, on your computer, in your car and in your home. It's art, but it contains a message. For God-seekers young and old, songs are far more digestible than sermons. The medium of music is an amazing opportunity to influence people, and the most amazing thing is that you don't have to be a seminary-trained theologian (or even a trained songwriter) to have an impact. Given this wide open door of influence, what are we going to give people? Mediocre music and watered-down theology? Therein lies the challenge.

In this chapter I paint a broad picture of some of the most important principles for worship songwriters. Songwriting isn't an exact science. It's a combination of gift and craft. I won't address specifics on the craft of songwriting, but I will share some examples of how the seed of inspiration is planted and begins to grow. I give some guidelines for cultivating the craft. This endnote lists a few helpful books that provide practical guidelines for songwriting.[1]

But let's start at the beginning. What is the most important foundational principle for worship writers? Knowing God's love and being gripped by his vision and mission.

A Passion for Jesus—the Fount of Worship Songs

I never set out to be a songwriter. When I was seventeen God captured my heart with his love. Though I was raised in the church, a whole new world of knowing God opened up to me during my freshman year at university. I was immersed in prayer, the Bible and vital Christian fellowship. I wrote music out of this newfound love for God.

Though I had taken music lessons from an early age, I had never written music before my conversion experience. When I met Christ, I finally had something to write about! I wrote out of my passion for Jesus. This has to be the starting point and guiding principle for writing worship songs.

As a seventeen-year-old I never imagined that my songs would go around the world. In my first ten years of songwriting, I wrote somewhere between three hundred to five hundred songs. Some of them I sang in church and in concerts; some I never sang at all. My music ministry was still limited to a local church context, with an occasional engagement in another church. As far as I could tell, things would never be any different. I was using the gift God gave me, and his blessing was on it for my local church.

I went through a phase in the late 1970s when I sent my songs to record companies. I had been doing concerts around Southern California and was looking for my big break. My songs were a combination of worship and concert music. After a few years of trying to get published, I gave up and focused on the sphere of ministry God had given me—the local church. This is a good rule of thumb for budding songwriters: use your gifts in your local church. Songwriting is first of all about sharing your gifts, not about getting published.

As the years went by, I found that I couldn't stop writing songs. Songs kept coming out of me. That's how spiritual gifting works. When you are called and gifted to do something, it comes naturally. At the same time, there's a lot of hard work as you walk out your calling. There is a practical and technical side of songwriting that takes lots of hard work and years of perseverance. But if you're called by God to do it, it will be hard to stop doing it. God will continue to give you ideas for songs and the desire to write.

For Martin Luther, music was a gift from God that had to be expressed. Luther believed that "he who believes in this salvation by Christ cannot help but . . . sing and tell about it. . . . It is not so much a question of whether he can, but that he must; just as the artist *must* express his feelings in colors or tones."[2]

The writer of the *Odes of Solomon* writes out of his union with God:

> I poured out praise to the Lord,
> Because I am his own.
> And I will recite his holy ode,
> Because my heart is with him
> For his harp is in my hand,
> And the odes of his rest shall not be silent.[3]

A few years after I stopped trying to make it in the Christian music industry, Vineyard Music began to take an interest in my music. So I gave them some cassettes, and they began to record my songs. That's when the challenge to write from pure motives really began! As soon as you get a little visibility, you'll be tested. Once I started gaining some visibility as a songwriter/recording artist, I've had to surrender it over and over and over again. Keeping a pure heart is a battle.

Charles Wesley, the great hymnwriter, was a practicing minister before he ever had deep assurance of his salvation. Even after leaving his homeland of England to go a missions trip to America, he said, "I now have peace, but cannot say of a surety that my sins are forgiven."[4] He was seeking a deep assurance of God's pardon.

In May of 1738, after a missions trip to America, he was critically ill with pleurisy. This forced him to stop ministering and be confined to his bed. On May 21, he records, "I waked in hope and expectation of His coming." Frederick Gill relates the events of that day:

> That day the house in Little Britain was full of Christ; a strange sense of his presence pervaded its dark corners and filled every hour. And Charles, taking his Bible, opened it at words singularly prophetic: "He hath put a new song in my mouth, even a thanksgiving unto our God. Many shall see it, and fear, and shall put their trust in the Lord." God had vanished Charles' unbelief, and that night he recorded in his journal: "I now found myself at peace with God, and rejoiced in hope of loving Christ. . . . I saw that by faith I stood; by the continual support of faith, which kept me from falling, though of myself I am ever sinking into sin . . . yet confident of Christ's protection."[5]

It is estimated that Charles Wesley wrote between six thousand and eight thousand hymns in his lifetime. His songs were a driving force in reviving the church and bringing thousands to Christ. But before this flood of hymns began, God transformed his life. His life illustrates this critical truth: *songs* of devotion spring from a *life* of devotion. Wesley's writing flowed out of his personal knowledge of God. When God is breathing upon us, we can write God-breathed songs.

Towering figures of the Reformation, such as Charles and John Wesley, Martin Luther and Isaac Watts, are among some of the most prolific hymn writers in history, but most of them were not *primarily* songwriters. First and foremost, they were teachers, preachers, theologians and pastors who were zealous to follow the Lord. Out of this zeal came a desire to build up the church. Hymns were one of many tools they used to communicate.

To make church music relevant to his culture, Martin Luther "adapted the finest old melodies and folk songs, and created hymns which have never failed to move the hearts of believers."[6] In 1524 he began to recruit songwriters and poets "to follow the example of the prophets and church fathers and to compose German songs for the German people so that God's word may resound in the singing of the people."[7]

The writers whose hymns have lived for centuries were gripped by an urgent sense of mission. They had a passion to see lost souls saved. They ministered to the needy. Their writing was a product of their lives of service.

Every generation needs a fresh restating of the ancient truths of Scripture, phrased in a musical genre that will catch their attention.

Gift and Craft

So much for the great hymn writers of church history. What about the modern local church songwriter/worship leader?

Songwriting is a combination of *gift* and *craft*. First of all, songwriting is a gift. Even secular songwriters recognize that songs come from "somewhere else." The singer-songwriter Sting comments, "If someone asks me how I write songs, I have to say I really don't know. A melody is always a gift from somewhere else: you just pray that you will be blessed again."[8]

After finishing a recent recording project, Paul Simon said, "When I finish a project I feel depleted, I don't have anything more to say and I have no more ideas—I have nothing. I always wonder, 'Will I ever get another idea?' When I do, if I do, I'm really grateful."

Looking back on the genesis of my best songs, it's obvious that God was giving a gift. But if I look *way back* to my earliest songs, I laugh. I have a few copies of my first album, but I hide them in the basement!

Despite the immaturity of my first few hundred songs, I was using a genuine songwriting gift in its raw, undeveloped form. I recently listened to a recording of my wedding ceremony. For this special occasion, I wrote several songs that were sung by a choir and a few that I sang to Linda. There are good ideas in the songs, but twenty years later, I hear them with an editor's perspective—nice melody, stupid lyric; too much repetition; good idea here, cut this, cut that, rewrite, delete.

Just as a teacher has to learn to teach, so a songwriter must learn to write. But even unrefined songs can inspire people to worship. Your church can benefit from your songs even if you have a gift-under-construction.

Even the great composer Johann Sebastian Bach had to study in order to write music well: "Bach's first attempts at composition, like all early efforts, were unsatisfactory. Lacking special instruction to direct him toward his goal, . . . he realized that . . . the young composer's first, need is a model to instruct his efforts."[9]

Inspiration

There are no real answers when it comes to songwriting; it's a mysterious, spiritual and often ambiguous pursuit.
—PAUL ZOLLO

Most of my songs have begun with God's serendipitous inspiration. These leadings from God are often subtle. Just as in praying for the sick or doing any Spirit-inspired activity, God gives us his insight by quietly whispering his thoughts to us. It's easy to dismiss these words from God as merely our own ideas. It takes faith to step out and write a song when you're not sure if God is in it. I've provided several song-stories that illustrate the inspirational phase and the first few steps in writing a song.

Scripture. My songs "One Thing I Ask," based on Psalm 27, and "Spirit of the Sovereign Lord," based on Isaiah 61, both arose out of first going to a passage of Scripture. Whenever I feel the urge to write a song from a Bible passage, I start asking the Lord, "Which verses?" "What key?" "What tempo?" And then I start experimenting.

Every passage of Scripture is packed with lots of words and ideas—enough for several songs. In writing *one* song with *one* central theme, you have to narrow down your content to a few key ideas and rephrase scriptural language to fit your song. Occasionally you can put entire unchanged lines of Scripture into a song, but that's unusual. Remember, the musical genre of the ancient Near East *and* the original languages of the Bible—Hebrew, Aramaic and Greek—are different from ours!

Often I fumble around with lots of ideas, trying to get a handle on what to do. I may change keys, tempos and rhythm patterns until something feels right. At times I may feel like it's going nowhere, that it's just a vain attempt at writing. Then I stumble on an idea that really works. Conversely some songs never get past the brainstorming stage. Here's a word of encouragement: It's typical for professional songwriters to write dozens or even hundreds of songs to get one great song.

A mental picture. This is how "The River Is Here" came to me. Over a period of several days I kept seeing a picture of a mountain with a river running down it. I didn't know what it meant, so I did a Bible study on key words like *mountain* and *river* to see what themes, imagery and application I could find. I wrote the song while on a brief retreat. I was happy with the way the lyrics fit together, but I didn't think it was a great song at the time I wrote it. I just thought the song was fun and had a different feel from most of the songs I write. So don't be afraid to write in a variety of musical styles.

God's voice. If you hear God telling you to write a song, humble yourself before God by waiting on him. You may feel silly; you may wonder if this is your idea, not God's. You may think you're just striving in your own strength. That's OK; it will become clear in time if God is blessing the song. Remember that the purpose of the new song is to *bless the church with something from God.* If you're a servant-songwriter, you'll write even if you don't feel like it, because you desire to build up the church.

An example of this is my song "Just Like a Child." After attending a songwriters' retreat in Southern California, I spent the night at my parents' house in Woodland Hills, California. I woke up early the next morning and heard God say, "It's time to write." The lyrics were a direct result of God's work in me at the retreat. He was softening my heart, calling me back to simple worship and devotion to Christ. I didn't want my heart to be polluted and tainted by my success as a songwriter. This song is a cry for childlike faith and innocence.

This is a great example of the writer's need to be a Christian who is integrally joined to other Christians. When I wrote "Just Like a Child," I was full of inspiration that came through fellowship with friends and hearing God's Word. Unless I am challenged by the incarnate Word of God through the local church, how can I be a vital Christian, much less a productive songwriter? Songwriting for worship is a byproduct of intimate fellowship with God and other Christians, not a career pursuit for the isolated Christian.

A fresh melodic idea. Sometimes a melodic idea comes to you that's fresh and alive with God's blessing. Then you take the next step and ask God if he wants you to develop this melodic motif into a song.

I wrote the song "How Priceless" after attending a concert by Chris Lizotte, a singer-songwriter who specializes in the musical style known as 'the blues.' I love this style of music and I occasionally I write a blues tune. After Chris's concert I went home to write something in this style. I wouldn't say that God told me to do it; I simply felt inspired, so I began to play and write.

A spontaneous song. An example in this category is "Let It Rain." At a conference in Eureka, California, I began to ask for God's rain, his kingdom, to fall on his people. It was a cry for refreshment and renewal from the Holy Spirit. The song was amazingly pregnant with God's Spirit at that moment. But the next week, I couldn't remember the melody, only the theme of the song. So I started over and wrote an entirely different melody with the same lyrical content.

A sermon message. Johann Sebastian Bach was inspired to write cantatas by listening to Sunday sermons: "Having properly performed my official duties on Sundays in the church, I attempted to transform the most significant thoughts that were treated in the sermon into poetic language for my private devotional use. . . . Thus these cantatas came to birth."[10]

Several years ago I was preparing worship for a Sunday morning service. I knew that the pastor was about to begin a series on God's grace. As I sought the Lord for direction, the song "Precious Child" came to me—a song about God's unconditional love. This song deeply touched me, bringing the Father's measureless love home to my heart. The next morning, I sang the song in church, giving away what I had first received myself.

A transitional event. In 1772 John Fawcett was the pastor of a small church in rural England. That year he was called to become the pastor of a famous Baptist church in London. "He accepted the call, preached his farewell sermon, and had already placed his household goods upon wagons when the love and the tears of his people gathered around him prevailed, and he found it impossible to leave them."[11] Within a week, he wrote the famous hymn "Blest Be the Tie That Binds."

> Blest be the tie that binds
> Our hearts in Christian love
> The fellowship of kindred minds
> Is like to that above.
> When we asunder part
> It gives us inward pain
> But we shall still be joined in heart,
> And hope to meet again. (stanzas 1 & 4)

Though his position at this small church gave him a salary of less than two hundred dollars (U.S.) a year, and though he received other invitations to fields that were more attractive from a worldly point of view, he accepted none of them. He was living out the reality of his song.

Joe and Charmaine Kelder formed a team to plant a church in Vancouver in 1989. Their first Sunday service was to take place on Easter. On Palm Sunday morning, we formally commissioned them with prayer and words of encouragement. I sang a song that I had written specifically for this occasion. It was from Isaiah 27, which is about a fruitful vineyard that God protects and nurtures. Charmaine recalls that the song hit the church-planting team "with a whallop" because God had already been speaking to them through this same Scripture passage. The image of Leviathan, the serpent (Is. 27:1), was a picture that Joe saw as he prayed for their embryonic church. God was telling him that he would protect them from the enemy.

Any church-planting team feels a healthy sense of desperation before God as they leave the mother church to establish a new work. God comforted Joe and Charmaine's team through this Scripture-song, saying that it was *his vineyard* and he would watch over it and tend it. To this day, Isaiah 27:2-3 appears on Vancouver Eastside Vineyard's Sunday bulletin: "Sing about a fruitful Vineyard: I, the Lord, watch over it."

Songs born out of struggle and suffering. The fires of trial are a productive forge for songs of worship. When we feel most dependent on God, most needy and desperate, we pray the most. God draws near with comfort and also with inspiration.

During their evangelistic campaigns, John and Charles Wesley experienced brutal hostility. In one instance, John was dragged by the hair from the steps of his preaching platform, and Charles was violently attacked. Leading outdoor meetings made them vulnerable to all kinds of attack—people argued with them and threw stones at them, and on one occasion, a police constable threatened John with a sword.[12]

It was times like these that God used to inspire Charles's *Hymns for Times of Trouble and Persecution*, which he published in 1744. The well-known hymn "Ye Servants of God, Your Master Proclaim" was one of these.

> The waves of the sea have lifted up their voice,
> Sore trouble that we in Jesus rejoice;
> The floods they are roaring, but Jesus is here,
> While we are adoring, He always is near.

Martin Luther's hymn "A Mighty Fortress Is Our God" arose out of persecution he suffered in fighting for the reformation of the church. His friend Leonhard Keyser was a Bavarian priest who was tried, found guilty of heresy and executed. "Brutal tyranny of the anti-Protestant princes, assassinations, and a serious decline in morals were the order of the day. . . . Luther was near desperation, being tempted and attacked by Satan in many ways."[13] In this fiery trial, Luther penned this great song that is still sung today:

> A mighty fortress is our God; a bulwark never failing
> Our helper he, amid the flood of mortal ills prevailing
> For still our ancient foe doth seek to work us woe
> His craft and power are great, and armed with cruel hate
> On earth is not his equal.

I've never suffered the kind of persecution that Luther and the Wesleys did. But as the senior pastor of the Surrey Vineyard, I went through a difficult time in 1991. No one was throwing stones or threatening my life, but the bitter words that were flung at me felt as painful as real stones. Many people left the church, and some were openly critical of my leadership.

After going through this long, dark tunnel of difficulty, I wrote the song "Yahweh." When the trial was over, I looked back and saw that God was faithful to keep his promises even though at times everything looked bleak. Because I personally suffered and then saw God change the circumstances, this song came straight from my heart. When I sing that song, I can still taste the sweetness of God's faithfulness to me in

the midst of the hard times. A song is *your* song when it testifies to a
real experience you've been through.

> Yahweh, Yahweh, faithful one, you have shown us the way
> Through the years, through all our lives
> You have shown you are faithful to the end.[14]

In 1992, while in England on a ministry trip, I had a night off.
While playing the guitar, I saw in my mind's eye a picture of a mother
in distress over some calamity in the life of her child. That scene provided the fuel for me to write a lament called "Yet I Will Praise." It's a
song of praise especially for people in the midst of great difficulty.

> I will praise you, Lord my God
> Even in my brokenness, I will praise you Lord
> I will praise you, Lord my God
> Even in my desperation, I will praise you Lord
> I can't understand all that you allow
> I just can't see the reason
> But my life is in your hands
> And though I can't see you, I choose to trust you.
>
> Even when my heart is torn
> I will praise you Lord
> Even when I feel deserted, I will praise you Lord
> Even in the darkest valley, I will praise you Lord
> And even when my world is shattered
> And it seems all hope is gone
> Yet I will praise you Lord.
>
> I will trust you, Lord my God, even in my loneliness,
> I will trust you Lord;
> I will trust you, Lord my God
> Even when I cannot hear you, I will trust you Lord
> And I will not forget that you hung on a cross
> Lord, you bled and died for me, and if I have to suffer,
> I know that you've been there,
> And I know that you're here now.[15]

Cultivating the Ground for Songwriting

The discipline of writing. It has been said that songwriting is 10 percent inspiration and 90 percent perspiration. When Bach was asked about the secret of his mastery of composing, he would answer, "I was made to work; if you are equally industrious you will be equally successful." His biographer notes that this is "a remark which made no allowance for his own exceptional genius."[16]

Despite the need for discipline and hard work, once in a while a song falls in your lap. That has happened to me several times. "One Thing I Ask" was written in twenty to thirty minutes. But the vast majority of songs I've written have been the product of hard work. For example, I have twenty-five pages of scribbling that chronicle the development of the song "Multiply Your Love." Over a period of three months, I produced lots of melodic and lyric ideas, and rewrites of that song. Finally, with the encouragement of a fellow writer, I came up with the final version. Few projects in life get finished without some hard work. Finishing songs requires perseverance. It can be a tedious, frustrating process, but it's worth the effort.

Isaac Watts didn't write thousands of great hymns except through long hours of labor. David Fountain describes Watts's commitment to the task of writing:

> He pruned his own sermons as ruthlessly as he did his hymns, that they might be direct, simple in structure, and understood by the ordinary worshipper. . . . His poems appeared in a number of editions and each time, he fashioned, discarded and refashioned his material until he had produced the modern English hymns for popular use. The term "genius" has been defined as "an infinite capacity for taking pains."[17]

Many of the songs I have recorded would be better if I had taken more time to rewrite and get input from other writers. You can get a lot of input on your songs by meeting with one or two other writers and asking for very honest feedback. Cowriting is also a great way to go. A high percentage of popular secular songs are cowritten. On the other hand, writing is a very personal thing—the song is your baby. The writer has to be comfortable with the final edit, regardless of who has suggested the changes.

A regular schedule? Over the years I haven't used any one pattern of scheduled writing time. I write in spurts. If I have a song I want to finish, I may spend fifteen to thirty minutes a day working on it for a several weeks. Often I have two or three songs that have potential, but for a season they lie dormant in my files. Some of my songs have taken years to complete. I wrote the first version of "We Exalt Your Name," but wasn't happy with the chorus. So I put the song aside for a year, then wrote a different chorus. The song finally felt finished.

My writing happens both intentionally and unintentionally. It usually begins during a focused time of worshiping or playing an instrument. More ideas come in relaxed moments—while going on a walk or a drive or taking a shower.

In choosing songs for a recording project in 2000, I had almost given up on finishing the song "Night and Day." I just couldn't finish it. Then I was walking around the soccer field where my son Benjamin was practicing with his team. In this relaxed frame of mind, new ideas for lyrics came to me, and the song was finished. It became the title track for the recording.

Occasionally I have gone on short retreats to write, pray and read. Usually these retreats only last a day or two, but one day of uninterrupted time can be very productive.

Without retreating to a quiet place, Isaac Watts would not likely have been so prolific. Watts was invited by Sir Thomas Abney to spend a week on his estate near Cheshunt, Hertfordshire. At one time this had been one of the finest estates in England, with summer houses, lakes, canals, bridges and fountains. When the week of retreat was over, his host insisted that Watts stay longer. He stayed almost forty years! In that time, he had a wonderful setting in which to read, meditate and write. His life wasn't "a walk in the park," however, as he suffered much physical and emotional sickness for many years. The point is this: retreating to a relaxing place can be very productive for songwriting.

Worship with your song. I can't write a worship song without worshiping. If it doesn't pull worship out of me, it won't be any good for the church. What sets apart a good worship song from a well-crafted song is the spirit of worship. That's an elusive and mysterious thing; it's hard to quantify and define. I reserve judgment on a song's ability to invite God's anointing until I hear the response of other people. If others tell me they can really connect with God during a song, I'm much more likely to use it in church.

For Matt Redman, writing a worship song must *begin* as an act of worship: "Usually, anything that seems to *end up* as worship needs to *start* as worship . . . it starts off as an explosion of worship in my own heart."[18]

Some of my best times of personal worship have been while writing a song. With "Blessed Be the Name" and "Let It Rain," I was lost in an ocean of worship as I wrote. The writing process was inseparable from the act of worship. This is worship songwriting at its best. I wish that songwriting was always as easy as floating down a river of praise, getting lost in the eddies of the Spirit. But often it feels like paddling upstream!

In the early stages of writing, I try to suspend the self-critic. I let a stream of ideas come, untamed by rules and restrictions. Later on comes the critical-analytical phase of writing.

Fill your mind with truth. Fanny Crosby, born in 1820, was one of the world's greatest hymn writers. "Blessed Assurance" and "To God Be the Glory" are among the more than three thousand hymns that she wrote that are full of biblical truth. Though she was blind, when she was a mere child she committed to memory the four Gospels and the first four books of the Old Testament. What we read comes out in our writing. If our minds are saturated with truth about God, our minds will be renewed and our lives transformed to be more like Jesus. There's no substitute for the basics—reading the Bible, praying and reading other inspirational books.

I wrote the song "Multiply Your Love" after reading a book called *Discipling the Nations,* by Darrow Miller.[19] This song kindled new zeal for one of my favorite themes—taking the gospel to the nations. My very first album, recorded in 1980, contained several songs with a missions theme. Miller's book stirred me up to write a song of intercession on the theme of asking God to multiply his love through our simple acts of obedience and service:

Multiply Your Love
Multiply your love through us to the lost and the least
Let us be your healing hands
Your instruments of peace
May our single purpose be to imitate your life
Through our simple words and deeds
Let love be multiplied

Multiply your love through me to someone in need
Help me Lord to freely give
This grace that I've received
Let my single purpose be to imitate your life
Through my simple words and deeds
Let love be multiplied

(Bridge)
Let us see your kingdom come
To the poor and broken ones
Let us see a mighty flood
Of justice and mercy
Oh Jesus, let love be multiplied

Multiply your church through us
To the ends of the earth
Where there's only bareness, let us see new birth
Use as your laborers working side by side
Let us see your harvest come
Let love be multiplied.[20]

The Craft of Songwriting

Prime the pump. I've talked a lot about divine inspiration. Let's focus on developing the *craft* of songwriting. Few composers in history are as well respected as Wolfgang Amadeus Mozart. I ran across a comical quote from this colorful personality: *"I write as a sow piddles."* What did he mean by that? For one thing, a sow piddles frequently. Here are three things we can glean from this curious quote.

First, the human vessel is the container for the song. In his imperfect earthy state, Mozart was the conduit for some amazing pieces of worship music. God uses imperfect people.

Second, to write well, we must write a lot. Though we depend on divine inspiration, we learn the craft of songwriting just as we learn to play basketball or play the saxophone—by repetition and trial and error. When an idea comes, put it down even if it's just a phrase or two of lyrics or melody. Writing is part of living. As melodies and lyrics float through the air, grab them and remember them.

Finally, what felt like "piddle" for Mozart, sounds like genius to generations of music lovers. Don't kill your creativity by smashing your song with self-criticism before it ever gets a chance to fly. As you begin to write a song, don't worry about how divine it is. It comes from *you*. It's a human creation. Later in the creative process, evaluate whether God's blessing seems to be on the song. Often I enlist the help of friends to evaluate my songs.

Fear of rejection and false pride. One of the biggest obstacles to writing songs is fear of failure and rejection. The composer Edvard Grieg said, "I am sure my music has the taste of codfish in it."

Sometimes I hear my songs and think, *Yuck! What was I thinking when I wrote that!* I still struggle with being overly critical of my own work and second guessing myself.

False pride can be the underlying force in our reluctance to share our songs. I once heard a friend teach this truth: "Don't be too proud to be thought proud." In other words, don't abort the giving of a song gift because you're afraid people are going to think you're full of pride and arrogance. The gift isn't for *you;* it's for the people who *hear it.* If you have something from God for the church, give it away! Don't withhold a precious gift out of fear. Have the courage to sing your songs.

Perseverance in writing. Here is the story of the well-loved hymn

"America" in the writers' own words: "One *dismal day* in February 1832 about half an hour before sunset, I was turning over the leaves of one of the music books, when my eye rested on the tune which is now known as 'America.' Picking up a scrap of waster paper which lay near me, I wrote at once, probably within half an hour, the hymn 'America' as it is now known everywhere."[21] The whole hymn was written on a piece of scrap paper, five or six inches long and two and half inches wide. Though it was a "dismal day," Samuel Francis Smith stirred himself to action, looked through his music books and wrote some lyrics to an already existing melody. That hymn later became a nationally loved song.

In songwriting, it's easy to give up hope, feel defeated and depleted. You hit a wall in writing and feel like quitting. You lose perspective and feel like everything you're working on belongs in the garbage bin.

Those emotions are typical for creative people and are perhaps typical for everyone. There are lots of drastic emotional swings in the creative process. In those times I put aside my work and move on to something else. If a song is destined to be completed, I can finish it later.

Matt Redman compares the writing process to making a cup of tea: "Sometimes you find several verses from the Bible and use them straightaway in a song. Other times it feels like making a cup of tea. It has to brew awhile. If you pour the water out right away, the tea is weak. If you let it brew, the theme floods out with much greater strength."[22]

My creedal song "I Believe" took over two years to finish. It began as a gift from heaven. I was at Hang Fook camp in Hong Kong, which for many years was the main base for St. Stephen's Ministry. I woke up, sat up on my bed and sang the first few lines of "I Believe." I wasn't thinking about God, the creed, or writing a song. I wasn't thinking about *anything*. I was just waking up.

The song began in a flourish of inspiration, and the verses were pretty easy to write. Then, just as suddenly as it began, it came to a screeching halt. I experimented with lots of different ideas for the chorus of the song, none of which felt right. The choruses I made up sounded like they belonged in a different song. Finally, over two years later, on the day before my thirty-ninth birthday, the Lord said, "I'm giving you a birthday present." It was the chorus of the song.

Write for every occasion, every person. Along with worship songs that are universal in their application, explore some of the important occasions where an original song can be like "apples of gold in settings of silver." This is one place where the local-church songwriter can write songs—for friends, family and church.

I have written songs for my sister's wedding, funerals of small children, installation services for new leaders and church-planting teams being sent out. When I've taken the time to create a song especially for one person, couple, family or team, people really appreciate it. It's a wonderful way of saying, "I love you and God loves you."

In the larger context of contemporary Christian hymnology, we are currently tapping only a small percentage of potential relevant topics. What about all the great Bible stories that we never sing about? What about all the challenges of life that could specifically be addressed through song?

Again I turn to Charles Wesley as an example of using songs to teach and encourage people in all kinds of situations. Charles wrote collections of all kinds of hymns for everyone and for every occasion.

In 1780 the Wesleys published a hymnbook that was a compilation of the best works of their lives. Many of the songs were very specific in their application. The book included songs "for mourners convinced of sin, for persons convinced of backsliding, for backsliders recovered, for believers rejoicing, fighting, praying, watching, working, suffering, seeking for full redemption, interceding for the world."[23]

As a local-church worship leader, you know the needs of your congregation better than any other worship leader. If you are in touch with the week-to-week developments in the life of the church, you can speak to those situations through your songwriting.

In 1986 I was the worship leader at the Langley Vineyard in Canada. For the first few years after the church was planted, we met in rented facilities. Then God gave us a building. We were excited to move into this facility, but wary of becoming attached to a building. We didn't want to become inward and focused solely on our own needs. We wanted our resources and new facility to be a means of bringing God's love to the community.

Right before we moved in, I wrote a song called "We Are Your Church," which speaks of our calling to be the salt and light of the earth. On that special Sunday, the song helped us declare our choice to commit to God the property he had so generously given us. I specifically remember that I didn't feel like writing a song for that occasion, but I felt God nudging me to do it. It was a way of giving language for the church at a transitional point in the church's pilgrimage.

What to Do with Your Finished Songs
Writing songs is much like any other spiritual gift. The only way to test the waters is to get out of the boat and take a step. If God has gifted you to write songs, in time the fruit will be obvious, and the authenticity of the gift will be confirmed by others.

What if you write songs primarily for your own personal use? Then you don't have to worry so much about following songwriting rules. If your songs enable you to genuinely commune with God, they have served a wonderful purpose. But there is a distinct difference between the personal worship value of a song versus the usability of that song for the local church.

If you think your song might work in a small prayer group or Bible study, try leading it there. See if the people catch on and can sing it easily. Are they drawn into worship? See if the Lord draws you into his presence when you sing it. See if people encourage you to keep writing. If all these things are happening, you might try the song in a larger context if you have the opportunity.

Trust God for the effect and distribution of your songs. If he wants to use a song widely, then people will ask you for copies of the song. They'll begin to sing it in their churches without any urging from you.

I heard John Wimber tell the story of the lightning-fast distribution of his song "Isn't He." Within a week or two of writing the song in Southern California, he traveled around the world to South Africa. They were *already* singing the song when he arrived! The song hadn't been recorded; it spread because of its reputation as a great song.

There's certainly nothing wrong with sending your song to a recording company; just make sure you trust God and leave it in his hands. Minister in the place God has put you; if he wants to expand your sphere of influence, he can.

Appendix 1

THE BIRTH
OF A WORSHIP
MOVEMENT

THE RISE OF A NEW kind of worship music in recent decades has stirred much debate and controversy. Many churches still eschew modern worship songs in favor of traditional hymns. Indeed, traditional hymns still can be contemporary and a primary pillar in our worship vocabulary. It would be foolish to throw out such a powerful and theologically rich treasury of hymns.

But history shows us that when a new worship form is vehemently opposed by some, it often becomes the standard form of worship in the following generations. For instance, the style of worship songs that Martin Luther introduced was radical for his day. Luther made use of melodies from popular folk songs, which were seen as irreverent by established church authorities. Generations later, they are considered a traditional, standardized form of conservative evangelical worship.

Just as Luther's worship was a product of cultural and religious factors specific to his day, there is a distinct set of spiritual, cultural and musical factors that have given rise to the kind of worship my generation espouses.

Part of my purpose here is to show that worship forms were evolving long before the time of Christ. So it's only natural for a continued evolution to meet the needs of modern culture, not just to meet peoples' needs, but to provide artistic models, symbols and language that will enable them to express devotion to God and be formed by his Word.

I am one of thousands of baby boomers (post-World War II babies born between 1946 and 1964) who found Christ during the Jesus movement of the 1960s and 1970s. My generation of California youth was baptized into vibrant Christianity through a form of worship specific to our unique cultural context.

Baby boomers are also called the "rock generation." Weaned on pop and rock music of the 1960s, 1970s and 1980s, baby boomers speak the language of rock. Pop and rock have dominated the radio airwaves for three generations. Yet as recently as a month ago, I found myself in a conversation with a sincere Christian woman who viewed anything with a rock beat as "of the devil." There are many musical cultures within contemporary Christianity.

Before I delve into the genesis of Vineyard-style worship, I will take a step back into history to show that worship forms have always been changing and evolving.

Worship—a Culturally Specific Activity

A study of church history shows that worship is a culturally specific activity. Throughout history, God's people have adopted models and practices of the surrounding culture and reinterpreted them as a means of worshiping him.

Even the earliest worshipers in the Old Testament borrowed customs from their contemporaries. In the time of Jacob, the building of altars after a divine encounter was a common practice. Following the example of his culture, he built a pillar of stones to memorialize God's visitation (Gen 28:10-22). In the culture of David and Solomon, kings built temples to their deities. Hence, the building of a temple to Yahweh, though divinely inspired, was also a borrowed expression of worship.

Early Christian liturgies were deeply rooted in the ritual patterns of first-century Judaism. The Passover meal was reinterpreted from a memorial of the Exodus to the Christian Eucharist.

As converts from Greco-Roman culture filled the church, customs and rituals were adapted from cultic rituals to Christian conversion. In the *Apostolic Tradition* of Hippolytus, newly baptized converts were given a drink of milk and honey after receiving the Eucharist for the first time. "Hippolytus explains the sign as 'the fulfillment of the promise God would give them a land flowing with milk and honey.' Yet this type of drink would not have been unfamiliar to a Christian neophyte, since it was an ancient Roman custom to give a similar drink to newborns as a sign of welcome into the family and to ward off evil spirits."[1]

I appreciate Paul Bradshaw's argument for a plurality of worship styles as presented in *The Renewal of Sunday Worship,* volume three of The Complete Library of Christian Worship. He points out that Christian worship patterns have been varied since the very beginning: "What we do know [about worship in the early church] suggests less the existence of a single, standardized liturgical practice and more a pluriform and variegated style of worship within different communities that only very slowly and belatedly accepted some measure of conformity under the pressures caused by the need to define orthodoxy over heresy in the fourth century."[2]

As the church grew from an underground movement in the first century to a religion endorsed by the emperor Constantine in the fourth century, worship moved from small living rooms to large church buildings. Worship evolved from very informal gatherings in the first century where each member was invited to share a psalm, hymn or spiritual song, to a highly structured church service in the fourth century with a formal liturgy and a priesthood that was elevated in spiritual privilege above the common person.

Jumping ahead to the Reformation of the sixteenth century, we see a radically different strain of worship develop as the Protestant church was born. The Reformers created a new liturgy using the *lingua franca* of the day instead of Latin, which was unintelligible to the majority of people. The Reformers emphasized the availability of the Word of God to all the hearers. Contemporary polyphonic musical forms were introduced that were a radical departure from the chants of the historic church.

Musical forms were borrowed from popular culture and used for worship. In the era of John and Charles Wesley's outdoor preaching and worship meetings, the crowds of unconverted and newly converted were eager to sing Charles's hymns "to the catchiest tunes of the day."[3]

In the last five hundred years, thousands of permutations of worship styles and liturgies have proliferated throughout the earth. Without doing a thorough study of every phase of change in the history of Christian worship, it is easy to see a repeating pattern. The two major influences in the evolution of worship forms are secular culture and specific church cultures that develop through tradition passed down from the preceding generations.

From generation to generation, and between countries, regions and church affiliations, worship forms vary. Though we learn from the worship practices in the early church and the succeeding generations, they shouldn't limit the evolution of worship forms. I agree with Paul Bradshaw—there is no "universal yardstick" against which all worship styles are measured. "Liturgies can only be judged . . . in their context, and not in an absolute sense."[4] One worship pattern wouldn't work for everyone.

I want to emphasize that my style of worship is only one of many viable models in the church today. Despite my commitment to worshiping the way I do, I don't think it is necessarily *the best* form of worship in the world. I think the right question to ask is not "What is the best kind of worship?" but "What is the best kind of worship for a particular subculture or church culture?"

The Cultural and Spiritual Elements Shaping the Birth of Vineyard Worship

As with all new church movements, the Vineyard has a specific history that shaped its style of worship. Several major factors that influenced and gave rise to the style of worship that characterizes the Vineyard movement.

During the late 1960s, the charismatic movement reached its peak and impacted thousands of people from mainline denominations. The distinctives of this movement were the filling of the Holy Spirit, speaking in tongues, ministering in many of the gifts of the Holy Spirit and worshiping expressively through folk music. The immanent presence of the Holy Spirit was a contentious issue in many evangelical churches in those days, but through the 1970s and 1980s it was gradually being accepted as a biblical phenomenon valid for contemporary times.

The Jesus People movement of the 1960s and 1970s was centered in Southern California. Many of the people who became the leaders of the Vineyard were profoundly impacted by the wave of salvation that rippled through the youth culture in the late sixties and early seventies.

This wasn't just a religious movement; it was intertwined with the youth counterculture that was characterized by rebellion and a quest for independence from the previous generation. It was known as the "rock generation." A rejection of traditional morals and values characterized this generation. This was demonstrated in the wild lifestyles led by college students, the violent demonstrations on university campuses and the unbridled consumption of sex, drugs and rock 'n' roll.

Bill Jackson, in his book *The Quest for the Radical Middle,* describes the generation gap that occurred between baby boomers and the "establishment": "The cultural forms and values of the parents' generation are obsolete for the children who must carve out a new life, new values, new forms, new heroes, new gods, new art and new music."[5]

Into this period of cultural change came a time of revival. Calvary Chapel, the precursor of the Vineyard movement, grew phenomenally in the late 1960s and early 1970s as a result of counterculture hippies and other youths coming to Christ. One friend of mine pastored a church of new converts while he was still in his early twenties. He told me that leading people to Christ during this time was "as easy as the falling of a log."

This new generation of Christians had to find a way to express their newfound love for Christ. In this milieu of radical cultural change and genuine spiritual renewal, it was only natural that a new style of worship would be born. Baby boomers rejected the rigid forms and styles of their parents' generation. For the boomers, rock music was their language of choice.

The first Christian artists to introduce rock 'n' roll to the church were Larry Norman and several artists connected with Maranatha Music, such as Chuck Girard. Maranatha, a recording company still existing today, was at that time a ministry of Calvary Chapel in Costa Mesa, California.

John Wimber's Influence

Before becoming the leader of the Vineyard movement, John Wimber was a pastor at the Friends church, otherwise known as the Quakers. John and Carol were influenced by the Quakers' emphasis on waiting on the Lord and openness to the Holy Spirit.

> The silent meeting for worship is the most visible element of classical Quaker worship. Worshippers assemble without leader or program, stilling their minds and focusing their attention, waiting to sense the presence of the Spirit of God and then to respond as they are moved in their own spirits. The silent meeting for worship is but a means, however, for achieving the essential element of Quaker worship: the response of the soul to the felt presence and the moving of the Spirit of God. "Worship is the adoring response of the heart and mind to the influence of the Spirit of God," says the Richmond Declaration of Faith (1887). "It stands neither in forms nor in the formal disuse of forms; it maybe without words as well as with them, but it must be in spirit and in truth."[6]

John had a deep desire to have genuine communion with God in worship, and he resisted any musical or manipulative techniques that would cheapen the worship experience and make it a fleshly rather than spiritual experience.

God met John and Carol in the essence of Quaker worship as they met in a small group in 1977. This small group later became the Anaheim Vineyard. Carol Wimber describes those early days of worshiping together:

> We began worship with nothing but a sense of calling from the Lord to a deeper relationship with him. Before we started meeting in a small home church setting in 1977, the Holy Spirit had been working in my heart, creating a tremendous hunger for God. One day as I was praying, the word "worship" appeared in my mind like a newspaper headline. I had never though much about that word before.
>
> As an evangelical Christian I had always assumed the entire Sunday morning gathering was "worship"—and, in a sense, I was correct. But in a different sense there were particular elements of the service that were especially devoted to worship and not to teaching, announcements, musical presentations, and all the other activities that are part of a typical Sunday morning gathering. I had to admit that I wasn't sure which part of the service was supposed to be worship.
>
> After we started to meet in our home gathering, we noticed times during the meeting—usually when we sang—in which we experienced God deeply. We sang many songs, but mostly songs about worship or testimonies from one Christian to another. But occasionally we sang a song personally and intimately to Jesus, with lyrics like "Jesus, I love you." Those types of songs both stirred and fed the hunger for God within me.[7]

John's Quaker and early Vineyard experiences taught him to follow Jesus' example of "doing what the Father does" (see Jn 5:19). Jesus couldn't do anything by himself; he could only do what he saw the Father doing. "Whatever the Father does, the Son also does " (John 5:19).

John applied this principle to the task of Spirit-empowered ministry. We can't heal on our own, we can't build churches on our own, and we can't produce anointed worship on our own. So we try to follow the Father's leading in all we do. This applies to leading worship sets. We don't assume to know everything we should do before the service begins. We plan and prepare ourselves, but we welcome whatever spontaneous gifts the Holy Spirit may bring.

John was the most casual church leader I've ever seen. He came to church in Hawaiian flowered shirts and Bermuda shorts. He didn't care if people thought he was being irreverent. It was his way of being naturally supernatural, and he did away with false exterior forms of religiosity as a deliberate choice. His honesty with God was reflected in this casual style of dress.

John figured that we should "come as we are" to worship. One of his strongest values of worship was honesty before God. If we're pretending to be something we're not, God won't accept our worship. If we're putting on our best face in worship, we're missing the point. God accepts those who know they need mercy.

Saved out of Show Biz
Another major factor in the mix of John's nurturing of Vineyard worship was his background in the music business.

Growing up as an only child, John spent long hours alone and learned to play over twenty different musical instruments, his favorite being the saxophone. By the age of fifteen he had become an accomplished musician, and after graduation from high school he began a professional music career. In 1953 he won first prize at the Lighthouse International Jazz Festival. After graduating from junior college in 1954, he began to pursue music with a passion. In 1962 he bought an up-and-coming musical group called The Righteous Brothers and played sax for them. In 1964 they released their hit single "You've Lost That Lovin' Feeling" and were booked to support the Beatles at the start of their American tour in San Francisco.[8]

John's love of music was obvious, but much of what he saw and did in the music business was completely contrary to his philosophy of worship. John passionately called Vineyard worship leaders to "make Jesus famous" instead of promoting their own ministries. John was turned off by anything that smacked of self-promotion or glitzy performance. He grew up in a musical scene where all the players were try-ing to impress one another.

He discouraged musical exhibitions that would steal the church's affection for Jesus by drawing attention to the worship leader or band members. I remember him describing secular jazz musicians who turned inward toward one another on the stage with their backs to the audience. He saw the musicians getting into themselves and playing to one another rather than including the audience. Elitism and exclusiv-ity among musicians was diametrically opposed to the servant heart that he encouraged among leaders.

Simple, pure devotion to Jesus was the outstanding trait of early Vineyard worship. When it came to spiritual gifts, John liked to say, "Everyone can play." It was the same with worship. Worship wasn't re-served for a few talented performers; it was for the whole church. Wor-ship wasn't a concert performance by a special choir or a small group of soloists. It was the bride of Christ gathered together, worshiping be-fore an audience of One. Therefore whatever we did had to be acces-sible for the whole church. We sang songs that were simple enough for the average person to sing, and we didn't do lots of extended in-strumental solos.

The adoption of rock music is a classic example of reinterpreting a contemporary artistic form for use in Christian worship. But we turned the model upside down. Worship leaders aren't heroes; they are ser-vants. Worship leading through rock music isn't about showing my stuff, displaying my talents or doing all my songs.

And that's one of the reasons it's such a powerful vessel for wor-ship. Wimber used to quote Marshall McLuhan's saying, "The me-dium *is* the message." By using rock, we're saying a few different things. One, we want to be relevant to popular culture. Two, our pri-mary goal in using this medium is to exalt Christ, not the musician.

The Love Song
Carol Wimber recalls the early days of learning to sing *to* Jesus, not just *about* him: "We realized that often we would sing about worship yet we

never actually worshipped—except when we accidentally stumbled onto intimate songs like 'I love you, Lord and I lift my voice.' Thus, we began to see a difference between songs *about* Jesus and songs *to* Jesus."[9]

Ever since then, Vineyard worship has placed an emphasis on singing *to* the Lord. It's like having a conversation with someone in the privacy of your own home. Jesus said that he and the Father would come and *make their home* with whoever loves them and obeys them (Jn 14:23). To create space for people to have an extended dialogue with God, we worship for long periods of time (thirty minutes or more) without being interrupted by things like announcements.

Vineyard worship is characterized by simple songs of love and devotion. Many other worship movements in the world today have been influenced by the Vineyard's emphasis on this kind of intimate worship. John felt that God entrusted the Vineyard with a gift of worship that would be imparted to other parts of God's church. Whenever John traveled to teach and attend conferences, he brought worship leaders with him who would model and impart this gift.

I believe that these Christian love songs to God are the church's alternative to the secular love song. Whenever I turn on a secular radio station, about two thirds of the songs I hear are love songs. It's the most universal theme there is.

While the typical love song portrays the romantic relationship as the ultimate answer to the need for personal fulfillment, we know that's a false reality. While God bestows the precious gift of marriage as a means of companionship and intimacy, it isn't the answer to every need. It's amazing how many phrases I hear in secular love songs that should realistically be found only in a worship song—"You are my everything," "I can't live without you."

Here is an example of the church borrowing from an artistic form that pervades our culture and reinterpreting it as a form of worship: "You are the air I breathe. . . . I'm desperate for you"[10] and "Now that I am here with You there's no place I'd rather be, now that I have felt your touch, make your home in me."[11] Of course, the feelings side of worship isn't all there is. Christ is the focal point of our worship. In him we find a God with whom we can be personal and intimate.

Rock Music—the International Language

In 1978 the Lord spoke to John Wimber in a vision. The vision was of many garage bands playing worship music, all simultaneously. He could not only see the bands; he could *hear* them. The sound of one garage band was bad enough, but hearing a bunch of them all playing at the same time was awful!

This vision foretold the multiplication of worship in the form of contemporary rock bands. This was the style that God would use to capture the hearts of thousands of baby boomers and the generations that followed. We are now into our third generation of worshipers who love rock 'n' roll.

As a teenager I was captivated by bands and singers like the Beatles, James Taylor, and Crosby, Stills, Nash and Young. It was only natural for me to be drawn to Jesus through a similar genre of music. It was a relevant sound and was accessible for me as a young guitar player. So I began a journey of learning to play with bands.

Wherever I go in the world, rock music rules. The almost worldwide acceptance of this musical form has created an amazing bridge for the gospel through music. These days there are dozens of types of rock music that appeal to different ages and subcultures.

Different Strokes for Different Folks

Despite the fervor of many converted teenagers and young adults, the introduction of rock music was a very slow process in many churches, and is still inching its way into churches around the world. Even today, in many denominations, the kind of beat used in rock is believed to be evil. But rock music gradually became adopted as a standard genre for many Christian denominations and renewed churches.

Alongside the churches that have adopted this rock model as their primary worship model, many churches prefer a model of blended worship—combining traditional hymns and liturgies with contemporary rock worship. There will always be a large portion of the church that stays exclusively with a more traditional model of classic hymns and liturgical forms.

Communion with God can happen through all kinds of musical and liturgical styles. An eighteen-year-old might meet with God through alternative rock, while an eighty-year-old finds the Lord through old-time gospel hymns played on the piano and organ. The issue is much more than age—lots of sixty-year-old Vineyard worshipers love rock, while lots of thirty-year-olds prefer the traditional organ and hymns of the Anglican church. I guess that's one reason we have so many different kinds of churches—different strokes for different folks.

I see some weaknesses in my free style of worship compared to a structured liturgy. First, it opens the door to a lack of theological richness and diversity in the selection of songs and hymns. Second, there is too much turnover in the songs we sing. Familiarity in liturgy (songs) is important and can get pushed aside in favor of the latest popular tunes. Finally, it gives rise to a failure to fully appreciate the most important events in the Christian year (namely Advent and Christmas, Lent and Easter) through deliberate planning of worship services to reflect on those events.

None of these potential pitfalls are insurmountable, but the free style of our worship opens the door for weakness in these areas. Every worship style has its weaknesses, and every church has to take measures to compensate for those weaknesses.

John Wimber's Description of the Worship Experience

In the final section of this appendix I present John Wimber's description of the worship experience. This section consists almost entirely of quotations from John's articles "The Worship Experience"[12] and "Worship: Intimacy with God."[13]

In order to plan for the musical presentation of a worship set, it's essential to understand the responses of the heart that may occur as the set progresses. I am quoting extensively from John's articles because his description provides a clear window into the core values and genesis of Vineyard worship.

Lest we think that the phases of worship John describes are "gospel" and should define and limit our worship times, he is careful to note that "this discussion is *descriptive* and not *prescriptive*, an *observation* and not a guiding *structure*. . . . The responses between God and his people should be dynamic, natural, and spontaneous" (emphasis added). You can't legislate the dance of love between God and his people, nor the spiritual and emotional ebb and flow during a worship time. Near the conclusion of "The Worship Experience" article, John notes, "The only law governing worship is the law of love."

The Call to Worship

The invitation. "The first phase is the call to worship, which is a message directed toward the people. It is an invitation to worship. The underlying thought of the call to worship is 'Let's do it, let's worship now.' Song selection for the call to worship is quite important, for this sets the tone for the gathering and directs people to God. Is it the first night of a conference when many people may be unfamiliar with the songs and with others in attendance? Or is it the last night, after momentum has been building all week? If this is a Sunday morning worship time, has the church been doing the works of God all week? Or has the church been in the doldrums? If the church has been doing well, Sunday worship rides on the crest of a wave. All these thoughts are reflected in the call to worship. The ideal is that the appropriate tone be set in the call to worship."

"The call to worship is a message to God inviting Him to visit us. Often it comes as a prayer of invocation. Sometimes a Scripture reading or a general word of encouragement is included."

"Remember that each person will be at a different place in terms of his or her readiness to worship. Some will come with many problems on their minds and enter worship slowly. Others will have spent the previous hour meeting with God and will be primed, ready to enter worship quickly. Encourage and remind people to come prepared, expecting God to come!"

"It is important for the worship leader to be sensitive to how quickly the group moves into intimacy, choosing songs according to the people's readiness. This is a fine line to ride: leading people into worship, yet not getting too far ahead. Worship leaders not only need to be aware of who the group is, and where God is taking them, but also what they need to do to get the people there."

Engaging in worship. "When we connect with God, worship can take a variety of courses. God is the conductor, and we are the orchestra. There are many parts being played simultaneously: love, adoration, praise, prayer, tongues, celebration, intercession. Thanksgiving, petition, stirrings of prophecy, words of knowledge. . . . Much of worship is prayer, for both are intimate communication."

In this phase we experience "the electrifying dynamic of connection to God and to each other. An individual may have moments like these in his or her private worship at home, but when the church comes together the manifest presence of God is magnified and multiplied."

The expression of intimacy. "As we move further in the engagement phase, we move more and more into loving and intimate language. Being in God's presence excites our hearts and minds and we want to praise him for the deeds he has done, for how he has moved in history for his character and attributes. Jubilation is that heart swell within us in which we want to exalt him."

"The heart of worship is to be united with our Creator and with the church universal and historic. Remember, worship is going on all the time in heaven, and when we worship we are joining that which is already happening, what has been called the communion of the saints. Thus there is a powerful corporate dynamic."

In this phase, "we become more personal, speaking to Him tenderly, quietly, and gently. Often we talk of issues which we may never share with anyone else. Meeting with our Father like this causes our hearts to pound because we know the exchange is one of unconditional love, a love which we will never receive from anyone else. This is our bread of life."

"We recall the vows and covenants we have made with Him and He has made with us. God might call to our mind disharmony or failure in our life, thus confession of sin is involved. Tears may flow as we see our disharmony but his harmony; our limitations but his unlimited possibilities. We confess our sin, asking for forgiveness and healing. Intimacy helps us recognize our incompleteness. In response we turn more toward Him, asking for help."

"We lay ourselves before Him in humility. We express our desire to serve Him and obey His every command. We tell him we want to be like him."

"Physical and emotional expression in worship can result in dance and body movement. This is an appropriate response to God if the church is on the crest. It is inappropriate if it is whipped up or if the focal point is on the dance rather than on true jubilation in the Lord."

God's visitation. "Expression then moves to a zenith, a climactic point, not unlike physical lovemaking (doesn't Solomon use the same analogy in the Song of Songs?). We have expressed what is in our hearts and minds and bodies, and now it is time to wait for God to respond. Stop talking and wait for him to speak, to move."

God speaks to us in a variety of ways. "If we are speaking intimately to God, he responds intimately to us. God may change course by giving us an exhortation (calling us to change) or joy (calling us into celebration). On the other hand, we may come out of an extended period of celebration only to have God bring us into intense intimacy."

"Often God responds with a move of the Spirit. People will fall, shake, experience mass deliverances, healings, salvation, forgiveness, anointing, intercession, etc. Prophecy is another common response. God will express his heart back to the assembly through the mouth of one or more worshippers. Coupled with prophecy is another common response: a message in tongues."

"At times, God will give various individuals Scripture readings. These texts generally carry a prophetic interpretation with them which suits the context."

The expression of ecstasy. "At this stage, worshipers are taken into the heights of joy and celebration in their experience with God. They are engulfed in God's presence. In the Vineyard, we visit this place only occasionally, usually in conference settings after three to five days of seeing God move in great power. The experience is more rare at home because of our caution lest we find ourselves in a frenzied, counterfeit experience.

"This phase of worship is commonly termed 'celebration'. Many of the models for celebration found among the different churches of our day are unattractive to us because they seem artificial or "worked up." However, in our efforts to avoid such excess, we often miss out on one of the most beautiful and fulfilling experiences available to us. To reach this stage, we must take the risk of looking and sounding foolish before God and men. As we move into such worship, there is a learning process just as when we learn to heal or prophesy.

"Celebration is an expression of the totality of the results of God's work. It is a full response to the wonder of God's hand. This revitalization, this surge of energy, all cry out for expression. The release during such worship is staggering as people are swept up into the awesomeness of God. A heart swell occurs inside and causes a (flagrant, loud, physical) exultation of the Creator of the heavens and the earth."

After a time of celebration, "It is difficult to generalize or predict what may happen. We simply need to be open to whatever God wishes to do. . . . After God has responded, the group may return to one of the earlier stages I have already described. They will continue to commune with God, moving in and out of the various stages of worship in a variety of ways. Alternatively, the meeting could end. The only law governing worship is the law of love. Because worship is dynamic, it has life and needs room to breath in order to be properly expressed."

John completes this article by discussing the continuation of worship through the giving of one's financial resources and service in all arenas of life.

Appendix 2

LEADING WORSHIP IN A SMALL GROUP

MOST OF THE PRINCIPLES of worship I've discussed throughout the book apply to small-group worship leading. But leading in a small group has its own unique set of challenges. Ironically, leading a small group can be much harder than leading a large group of people. With a larger group, there is built-in momentum because of the number of people worshiping together.

But if you're leading a group of eight people, sometimes it can be hard to get the engine running. Two of those eight people might be too afraid to sing out; two more might be visitors, so they don't know the songs, and of the four core members of your group, only one person besides you has a strong singing voice. I don't want to paint a bleak picture, but let's be realistic. Leading in a small group can be a major challenge. It can be really intimidating for the beginning worship leader. I have included some suggestions to pave the way for strong participation in smaller settings.

Choose Accessible, Easy-to-Sing Songs

Choose lots of "can't miss" songs. If you do songs people know well, they'll be more confident and willing to take the risk of singing out strongly. Don't use the small group as a place to try all of newest trendy songs. With limited instrumentation, there are a lot of songs that are hard to play. (To expand your repertoire, use a capo on your guitar so you can play songs in difficult keys just by sliding the capo to whatever fret you want.)

Another way to lower the hurdle for people is to give them song sheets. If you want people to participate, put the words in front of them.

Be Assertive

Being too loud is better than being too quiet. It takes a lot more volume to lead in a group than it does to sing by yourself in your bedroom. High intensity can compensate for a lack of skill and musical polish.

Your example of bold singing will stimulate others to do the same. If you are tentative, they'll be tentative along with you. If they can barely hear you, they'll be worried about whether or not you'll make it through the set. They might be praying for you instead of worshiping.

At times you might want to invite the people to stand up. Singers don't usually perform while sitting down—that's because a lot more volume can be generated while standing. Getting people off the couch can give them a boost toward expressiveness, especially at the end of a long day when people are tired.

Percussion Instruments

To create more momentum, recruit people to play percussion instruments. Shakers and hand drums can add a lot of energy in a living-room worship time. Many of these instruments are easy to play and very inexpensive. People who have a good sense of rhythm can learn to play percussion instruments very quickly.

If there are other guitar or keyboard players, invite them to play along. If they are just beginning, they can start by playing along with one or two songs. If you give them chord sheets, they can gradually learn more songs.

Give People Time to Get Comfortable with One Another

Sitting in a small circle of people and facing each other can be threatening, especially as people are just getting acquainted. Freedom of worship is tied to the freedom and security of personal relationships in the group. When people grow in openness and mutual trust, they become more open and vulnerable to God in worship. Give them time to loosen up.

Come to Serve the People

When there's not much momentum in worship, worship leading can be hard work. At those times you realize you're there to serve the people. You're there to give a gift to God, and you don't always get an immediate payoff. It takes a lot of perseverance. You have to decide to worship even if it feels like no one else is going there with you. In those moments, remember that success is defined by obedience. If you give freely of yourself, you have been successful.

Prepare for the Long Haul

If you're a beginning guitarist or pianist, you can lead a lot of songs with only a basic working knowledge of your instrument. But if you want to grow musically, take some private lessons. It's worth the investment of time and money to gain skill and confidence. Another option is to find some courses that can be self-taught through an instruction book and accompanying CD.

Appendix 3

INDEX
OF SONGS

Song Title	Composer	Publisher	CD Title
All Creation	Brian Doerksen/ Steve Mitchinson	Vineyard Songs UK/Eire, 1999	*Hungry*
All Hail the Power of Jesus' Name	Edward Perronet/ William Shrubsole	Traditional	*Vineyard Hymns & Choruses*
All Who Are Thirsty	Brenton Brown/ Glenn Robertson	Vineyard Songs UK/Eire, 1998	*Winds of Worship #12*
All Your Promises	Andrew Smith	Mercy Vineyard, 1996	*I Will Lift My Hands*
Amen Hallelujah	Graham Ord	Vineyard Songs Canada, 2001	*All I Need*
Amazing Love	Graham Kendrick	Make Way Music, 1989	*Make Way for the Cross*
Be the Centre	Michael Frye	Vineyard Songs UK/Eire, 1999	*Hungry*
Better Is One Day	Matt Redman	Thankyou Music, 1995	*The Friendship and the Fear*
Blessed Be the Name	Andy Park	Mercy/Vineyard, 1995	*Blessed Be the Name*
Breathe	Marie Barnett	Mercy/Vineyard, 1995	*Hungry*
Change My Heart, O God	Eddie Espinosa	Mercy/Vineyard, 1982	*Change My Heart, O God*
Did You Feel the Mountains Tremble?	Martin Smith	Curious? Music UK, 1994	*Cutting Edge (Delirious)*

Song Title	Composer	Publisher	CD Title
Draw Me Close	Kelly Carpenter	Mercy/Vineyard, 1994	*The River Is Here*
Eternity	Brian Doerksen	Mercy/Vineyard, 1991	*Eternity, We Are One*
Exalt the Lord	Cindy Rethmeier	Mercy/Vineyard, 1991	*Best of Acoustic Worship; Winds of Worship #11*
Faithful One	Brian Doerksen	Mercy/Vineyard, 1989	*Winds of Worship #15*
Father I Want You to Hold Me	Brian Doerksen	Mercy/Vineyard, 1989	*Why We Worship— Father; Why We Worship— Healing*
Father of Lights	John Barnett	Mercy/Vineyard, 1991	*Why We Worship— Father*
Give Thanks	Henry Smith	Integrity's Hosanna Music, 1978	*WOW Worship 1999*
Glorify	Linda Barnhill	Mercy/Vineyard, 1992	*Songs of the Vine- yard #4 Song- book*
Great Is Thy Faithfulness	William Runyan/ Thomas Chisholm	Hope Publishing, 1951	*Vineyard Café— Shelter*
The Happy Song	Martin Smith	Curious? Music UK, 1994	*Cutting Edge (Delirious)*
His Love	David Ruis	Mercy/Vineyard, 1992	*Glory and Honor, Acoustic Worship—Glory*
Hold Me Lord	Danny Daniels	Mercy/Vineyard, 1982	*Songs of the Vine- yard #1 Song book*
Holy and Anointed One	John Barnett	Mercy/Vineyard, 1988	*Change My Heart, O God; Eternity*
Holy, Holy, Holy	John Dykes/ Reginald Heber	Traditional	*Vineyard Hymns and Choruses*
Holy Is the Lord	Kelly Green	Mercy/Vineyard, 1983	*Winds of Worship #12*
Holy Love	Andy Park	Mercy/Vineyard, 1992	*Before You Now; Winds of Worship #7*
How Great Thou Art	Karl Boberg	Stuart K. Hine, 1953	

Song Title	Composer	Publisher	CD Title
How Priceless	Andy Park	Mercy/Vineyard, 1994	*Winds of Worship #7 Café—Mercy, More Love, More Power*
Humble King	Brenton Brown	Vineyard Songs UK/Eire, 1999	*Hungry*
Hungry	Kathryn Scott	Vineyard Songs UK/Eire, 1999	*Hungry*
I Believe	Graham Ord	Vineyard Songs Canada, 2000	*Believe*
I Could Sing of Your Love Forever	Martin Smith	Curious? Music UK, 1994	*Cutting Edge* (Delirious)
I Give Thanks	Brian Thiessen	Mercy/Vineyard Music, 1991	*Winds of Worship #15*
I See the Lord	Andy Park	Mercy/Vineyard Music, 1995	*The Very Best of the Winds of Worship*
I Surrender All		Words c. HarperCollins, Religious, lyrics- public domain, 1896	
I Worship You	Carl Tuttle	Mercy/Vineyard Music, 1982	*Acoustic Worship: You Are the Mighty King*
In the Secret	Andy Park	Mercy/Vineyard, 1995	*Blessed Be the Name*
Isn't He	John Wimber	Mercy/Vineyard, 1980	*Winds of Worship #9*
Jesus, Lead On	Brent Helming	Mercy/Vineyard, 1996	*Jesus, Lead On; Café: Mercy*
Jude Doxology	Terry Butler/ Randy Butler	Mercy/Vineyard, 1991	*Acoustic Worship: Eternity*
Just Like a Child	Andy Park	Mercy/Vineyard, 1999	*Night and Day*
Keep Me	Andy Park	Vineyard Songs Canada, 2002	
Kingdom Celebration	Andrew Smith	Mercy/Vineyard, 1996	*Winds of Worship #15*
Let It Rain	Andy Park	Mercy/Vineyard, 1996	*Jesus, Lead On; Winds of Worship #9*
Let Your Glory Fall	David Ruis	Mercy/Vineyard, 1992	*The Very Best of the Winds of Worship*
Light the Fire Again	Brian Doerksen	Mercy/Vineyard, 1994	*Revival*

Song Title	Composer	Publisher	CD Title
Lord I Lift Your Name on High	Rick Founds	Maranatha Music, 1989	
Make Your Home in Me	Michael Frye/ Helen Frye	Vineyard Songs UK/Eire, 1999	*Hungry*
Merciful God	Terry Butler/ Randy Butler	Mercy/Vineyard, 1992	*Why We Worship: Father*
More Love, More Power	Jude Del Hierro	Mercy/Vineyard, 1987	*Winds of Worship #11*
More Precious Than Silver	Lynn DeShazo	Integrity's Hosanna Music, 1982	
Multiply Your Love	Andy Park	Vineyard Songs Canada, 2000	*All I Need*
Name Above All	Brian Thiessen	Mercy/Vineyard, 1999	*Name Above All*
Night and Day	Andy Park	Vineyard Songs Canada, 1999	*Night and Day*
Nothing Is As Wonderful	Scott Underwood	Mercy/Vineyard, 1996	*The Very Best of the Winds of Worship*
On Christ the Solid Rock	Edward Mote/ W. B. Bradbury	Traditional	*The Source Hymn Book, U.K.*
Once Again	Matt Redman	Thankyou Music, 1995	*The Friendship and the Fear*
One Thing I Ask	Andy Park	Mercy/Vineyard, 1987	*Winds of Worship #7*
Only You	Andy Park	Mercy/Vineyard, 1988	*We Are One*
Precious Child	Andy Park	Mercy/Vineyard, 1989	*Songs of the Vineyard #2 Songbook*
Refiner's Fire	Brian Doerksen	Mercy/Vineyard, 1990	*Best of Acoustic Worship*
Shout to the Lord	Darlene Zschech	Hillsongs, 1993	*Shout to the Lord*
Show Your Power	Kevin Prosch	Mercy/Vineyard, 1991	*Winds of Worship #1*
Spirit of the Sovereign Lord	Andy Park	Mercy/Vineyard, 1994	*Winds of Worship #5: Spirit*
Still Small Voice	Brian Doerksen	Mercy/Vineyard, 1990	*Café: Freedom*
Take My Life	Scott Underwood	Mercy/Vineyard, 1995	*Hallelujah Glory; Holiness*
Thank You, Lord	Andy Park	Mercy/Vineyard, 1996	*Winds of Worship #15*
The Heart of Worship	Matt Redman	Thankyou Music, 1999	*The Heart of Worship*

Permissions

Portions of chapters four, seven, eleven, twelve and fifteen appeared in "Worship Update," published by Vineyard Music Group, Anaheim, California. All reprinted material used by permission.

John Wimber is quoted at length in appendix one. All quoted material is used by permission of SeanWimber@doin-the-stuff.com. A variety of John's resources can be found at <www.doin-the-stuff.com>.

All Vineyard song lyrics quoted are used by permission of Vineyard Music Group, USA, Vineyard Music U.K. and Vineyard Music Canada.

Resources for worship, including the magazine *Inside Worship,* teaching videos, cassettes, CDs, songbooks and other products, can be found by calling Vineyard Music Group (800-852-VINE) or through the Vineyard Music website, <www.vineyardmusic.com>. All Vineyard Music songs listed in appendix three may be found on the Vineyard Music website.

Notes

Chapter 1: Diving into Worship Ministry
[1]See appendix one for more on the history of worship in the Vineyard movement.
[2]Andy Park, "God Be Gracious unto Us," published by Andy Park, 1980. Used by permission.
[3]Andy Park, "I Am His," published by Andy Park, 1980. Used by permission.
[4]Matt Redman, conversation with author, Vancouver, BC, June 22, 2001.
[5]David Peterson, *Engaging with God* (Grand Rapids, Mich.: Eerdmans, 1992), p. 64.
[6]Brennan Manning, *Ragamuffin Gospel* (Portland, Ore.: Multnomah Press, 2000), p. 47.
[7]Kelly Carpenter, "Draw Me Close" (Anaheim, Calif.: Mercy/Vineyard, 1994).

Chapter 2: The Door to Intimacy
[1]David Peterson, *Engaging with God* (Grand Rapids, Mich.: Eerdmans, 1993), p. 57.
[2]*The Book of Common Prayer* (New York: Seabury, 1977), p. 323.
[3]Eddie Espinosa, "Change My Heart O God" (Anaheim, Calif.: Mercy/Vineyard, 1982).
[4]Kathryn Scott, "Hungry" (Hull, U.K.: Vineyard Songs UK/Eire, 1992).
[5]A. W. Tozer, *Worship—the Missing Jewel of the Evangelical Church* (Camp Hill, Penn.: Christian Publications, 1961), p. 9.
[6]Randy and Terry Butler, "Merciful God" (Anaheim, Calif.: Mercy/Vineyard, 1992).
[7]Kelly Carpenter, "Draw Me Close" (Anaheim, Calif.: Mercy/Vineyard, 1994).
[8]Andy Park, "In The Secret" (Anaheim, Calif.: Mercy/Vineyard, 1995).

Chapter 3: The Fruit of Intimacy
[1]A. W. Tozer, *The Knowledge of the Holy* (San Francisco: Harper & Row, 1978), p. 3.
[2]Philip Yancey, *What's So Amazing About Grace?* (Grand Rapids, Mich.: Zondervan, 1997), p. 70.
[3]Martin Luther, quoted in Karen Armstrong, *A History of God* (New York: Alfred A. Knopf, 1974), p. 276.
[4]David Seamands, quoted in Yancey, *What's So Amazing About Grace?* p. 15.
[5]Andy Park, "Precious Child" (Anaheim, Calif.: Mercy/Vineyard, 1989).
[6]An exercise of creative imagination from Stephen R. Covey, *First Things First* (New York: Simon & Schuster, 1994), pp. 107-9.
[7]James Burtschaell, *Philemon's Problem: The Daily Dilemna of the Christian* (Chicago: Acta Foundation, 1973), p. 21.
[8]Brennan Manning, *Lion and Lamb* (Old Tappan, N.J.: Revell, 1986), p. 21.
[9]Ibid.
[10]*The Odes of Solomon*, ed. and trans. James H. Charlesworth, Society of Biblical Literature (Missoula, Mont.: Scholars Press, 1977), p. 35.

[11]Donald E. Miller, *Reinventing American Protestantism: Christianity in the New Millennium* (Berkeley: University of California Press, 1997), survey respondent #192.

Chapter 4: The Lifestyle Produces the Language
[1]Terry Butler and Mike Young, "This Is Love" (Anaheim, Calif.: Mercy/Vineyard, 1998).
[2]Eddie Espinosa, "Change My Heart, O God" (Anaheim, Calif.: Mercy/Vineyard, 1982).
[3]Brian Doerksen, "Faithful One" (Anaheim, Calif.: Mercy/Vineyard, 1989).
[4]Brenton Brown, "Humble King" (Hull, U.K.: Vineyard Songs UK/Eire, 1999).
[5]Kathryn Scott, "Hungry" (Hull, U.K.: Vineyard Songs UK/Eire, 1992).
[6]Brent Helming, "Jesus Lead On" (Anaheim, Calif.: Mercy/Vineyard, 1996).
[7]Andy Park, "One Thing I Ask" (Anaheim, Calif.: Mercy/Vineyard, 1987).
[8]Andy Park, "Only You" (Anaheim, Calif.: Mercy/Vineyard, 1988).
[9]Andy Park, "In The Secret" (Anaheim, Calif.: Mercy/Vineyard, 1995).
[10]Matt Redman, conversation with author, Vancouver, BC, June 22, 2001.
[11]David Ruis, "Let Your Glory Fall" (Anaheim, Calif.: Mercy/Vineyard, 1992).
[12]Scott Underwood, "Take My Life" (Anaheim, Calif.: Mercy/Vineyard, 1995).

Chapter 5: The Ministries of Priest, Prophecy & Healing
[1]Amos R. Wells, *A Treasure of Hymns* (Boston: W. A. Wilde, 1945), pp. 16-17.
[2]Donald E. Miller, *Reinventing American Protestantism Christianity in the New Millennium* (Berkeley: University of California Press, 1997), survey respondent #333.
[3]See John 16:7-11, esp. "The Holy Spirit comes to convict the world of guilt."
[4]Andy Park, "Keep Me" (Fort Langley, BC: Vineyard Songs Canada, 2002).
[5]David M. Mazie, "Music's Surprising Power to Heal," *Reader's Digest* (August 1992). Reprinted with permission from the *Reader's Digest*, August 1992. Copyright © 1992 by The Reader's Digest Assn., Inc.
[6]Miller, *Reinventing American Protestantism,* survey respondent #1148.
[7]Andy Park, "Holy Love" (Anaheim, Calif.: Mercy/Vineyard, 1992).
[8]Katherine Cryer, conversation with author, Langley, BC, March 2001.
[9]Miller, *Reinventing American Protestantism.*
[10]Music for the Mind, homepage (April 22, 2002) <members.tripod.com/~donlevi/index.html>.
[11]Paul Nettl, *Luther and Music* (New York: Russell & Russell, 1967), p. 17.
[12]Ibid., pp. 21-25.
[13]Ibid.
[14]Philip Yancey, *What's So Amazing About Grace?* (Grand Rapids, Mich.: Zondervan, 1997), p. 41.
[15]Mark Stibbe, *From Orphans to Heirs* (Oxford: Bible Reading Fellowship, 1999), pp. 84-85.
[16]Brenton Brown and Brian Robertson, "All Who Are Thirsty" (Hull, U.K.: Vineyard Songs UK/Eire, 1998).

[17]Andy Park, "Yet I Will Praise" (Fort Langley, BC: Vineyard Songs Canada, 1999).

[18]*The Odes of Solomon*, ed. and trans. James H. Charlesworth, Society of Biblical Literature (Missoula, Mont.: Scholars Press, 1977), p. 29, emphasis added.

[19]Ibid., p. 7.

[20]Sting, in a graduation address given at Berklee College of Music in Boston.

Chapter 6: The Ministries of Teaching & Evangelism

[1]Terry Butler and Randy Butler, "Jude Doxology" (Anaheim, Calif.: Mercy/Vineyard, 1991).

[2]Robert Webber, "Worship in the Early Church," in *The Ministries of Christian Worship*, The Complete Library of Christian Worship (Peabody, Mass.: Hendrickson, 1994), 3:323.

[3]Inga and Ronal Freyer Nicholas, "Story, Structure, Style," *The Renewal of Sunday Worship*, The Complete Library of Christian Worship (Nashville: Star Song Publishing, 1994), 3:209.

[4]Webber, "Worship in the Early Church," pp. 324, 325.

[5]Jack Hayford, *Worship His Majesty* (Waco, Tex.: Word, 1987), p. 54.

[6]Ibid., p. 58.

[7]F. Forrester and Terrence J. Mulry, eds., *The Macmillan Book of Earliest Christian Hymns*, (New York: Macmillan, 1988), pp. 180-81.

[8]Paul Nettl, *Luther and Music* (New York: Russell & Russell, 1967), p. 49.

[9]Tony Campolo, interview by Samuel D. Perriccioli, *Worship Leader* (November/December 2000): 24, emphasis added.

[10]*Contemporary Christian Communications* (New York: Thomas Nelson, 1979), p. 79.

[11]Walter Heidenreich, personal letter to the author, May 2001.

Chapter 7: The Worship Team

[1]Matt Redman, conversation with author, Vancouver, B.C., June 22, 2001.

Chapter 8: Working Together

[1]Interview with author, Vancouver, B.C., May 2001.

[2]Ibid.

[3]All information on Christian Church of Clarendon Hills taken from an interview with Robert Locklear, January 2002.

[4]Robert Jourdain, *Music, the Brain and Ecstasy* (New York: Avon, n.d.), p. 191.

[5]Frederick C. Gill, *Charles Wesley, the First Methodist* (London: Ebenezer Baylis & Son, 1964), pp. 231-32.

[6]David G. Fountain, *Isaac Watts Remembered* (Herts, U.K.: Gospel Standard Baptist Trust, 1974), p. 51.

[7]Robert Bellah, *Habits of the Heart* (Berkeley: University of California Press, 1985), p. 228, quoted in Charles Colson, *Against the Night* (Ann Arbor, Mich.: Servant, 1989), p. 31.

[8]Barna Research Online, study on relationships, 2001 <www.barna.org>.

[9]Cyprian, *On the Unity of the Church*, quoted in Robert Webber, *Ancient-Future Faith*

(Grand Rapids, Mich.: Baker, 1999).

[10] Rodney Clapp, *A Peculiar People: The Church as Culture in a Post-Christian Society* (Downers Grove, Ill.: InterVarsity Press, 1996).

[11] John Piper, sermon given in Parksville, British Columbia, spring 2000.

Chapter 9: The Ups & Downs of Worship Leading

[1] F. Forrester and Terrence J. Mulry, eds., *The Macmillan Book of Earliest Christian Hymns* (New York: Macmillan, 1988), pp. 148, 150.

[2] Frederick C. Gill, *Charles Wesley, the First Methodist* (London: Ebenezer Baylis & Son, 1964), pp. 73-74.

[3] Ibid.

[4] Ibid., pp. 89-90.

[5] Edward Mote and W. B. Bradbury, "On Christ the Solid Rock."

Chapter 10: Encouraging Expression in Worship

[1] Frederick C. Gill, *Charles Wesley, the First Methodist* (London: Ebenezer Baylis & Son, 1964), p. 98.

[2] Brian Doerksen, "Refiner's Fire" (Anaheim, Calif.: Mercy/Vineyard, 1990).

[3] See also Ps 150:4; 1 Sam 18:6; 21:11; and Ps 30:11. Some Hebrew and Greek words connote the idea of dancing but can also be translated "rejoice." For example, the word *rejoice* (the Greek word *agalliaō*) in Lk 1:14, 44, 47; 10:21; Mt 5:12; Jn 5:35; 8:56; Acts 2:26, 46; 16:34; 1 Pet 1:6, 8; 4:13; Heb 1:9; Jude 24; and Rev 19:7 can also be translated "jump for joy."

[4] James Strong, *Strong's Exhaustive Concordance of the Bible* (Iowa Falls, Iowa: World Bible, 1984), p. 33.

[5] Ibid., p. 126.

[6] Ibid., p. 107.

[7] Tony Campolo, interview by Samuel D. Perriccioli, *Worship Leader* (November/December 2000): 25.

[8] David Di Sabatino, "The Power of Music: What to Keep in Mind While Under Its Influence," *Worship Leader* (May/June 1999): 21.

[9] Jonathan Edwards, *Religious Affections* (Portland: Multnomah Press, 1984), pp. 95-96, emphasis added.

Chapter 11: Preparing a Worship Set

[1] Matt Redman, conversation with author, Vancouver, B.C., June 22, 2001.

[2] Ibid.

[3] Ibid.

[4] Ibid.

[5] Ibid.

Chapter 12: Delivering a Worship Set

[1] Matt Redman, conversation with author, Vancouver, B.C., June 22, 2001.

[2]Tony Campolo, interview by Samuel D. Perriccioli, *Worship Leader* (November/December 2000).

[3]C. S. Lewis, *Letters to Malcolm: Chiefly on Prayer* (London: Fontana, 1966), p. 6.

[4]Barry Liesch, *The New Worship* (Grand Rapids, Mich.: Baker, 1996), p. 35.

[5]John S. Andrews, "Music in the Early Church," *The New Grove Dictionary of Music and Musicians,* ed. Stanley Sadie (Washington, D.C.: Grove's Dictionaries of Music, 1980), 4:363-64.

[6]Egon Wellesz, "Early Christian Music," *The New Oxford History of Music* (London: Oxford University Press, 1954), 2:2.

Chapter 13: Leading a Worship Team

[1]Matt Redman, conversation with author, Vancouver, B.C., June 22, 2001.

[2]*The New Merriam-Webster Dictionary,* ed. Frederick C. Mish (Springfield, Mass.: Merriam Webster, 1989), p. 541.

[3]Barry Liesch, *The New Worship* (Grand Rapids, Mich.: Baker, 1996), p. 143.

[4]Matt Redman, conversation, June 22, 2001.

[5]Bruce Babad, interview with author, 2000.

[6]Frederick C. Gill, *Charles Wesley, the First Methodist* (London: Ebenezer Baylis & Son, 1964), p. 230.

Chapter 14: Developing Worship Leaders

[1]Paul D. Stanley and J. Robert Clinton, *Connecting* (Colorado Springs: NavPress), p. 40.

[2]Ibid.

[3]John Wimber used this model widely to train people to pray for the sick and to train teachers and pastors.

[4]John Wimber often used this phrase in his teaching.

[5]Matt Redman, conversation with author, Vancouver, B.C., June 22, 2001.

Chapter 15: The Gift & Craft of Songwriting

[1]Pat & Pete Luboff, *88 Songwriting Wrongs and How to Right Them* (Cincinnati, Ohio: Writer's Digest Books, 1992); Sheila Davis, *The Craft of Lyric Writing* (Cincinnati, Ohio: Writer's Digest Books, 1985); John Braheny, *The Craft and Business of Songwriting* (Cincinnati, Ohio: Writer's Digest Books, 2001); Paul Zollo, *Beginning Songwriter's Answer Book* (Cincinnati, Ohio: Writer's Digest Books, 1993).

[2]Paul Nettl, *Luther and Music* (New York: Russell & Russell, 1967).

[3]*The Odes of Solomon,* ed. and trans. James H. Charlesworth (Missoula, Mont.: Scholars Press, 1977), ode 24.

[4]Frederick C. Gill, *Charles Wesley, the First Methodist* (London Ebenezer Baylis & Sons, 1964), p. 230.

[5]Ibid.

[6]Nettl, *Luther and Music,* p. 33.

[7]Ibid., p. 39.

[8]Sting, in a graduation address given at Berklee College of Music in Boston, Massachusetts.

[9]Johann Nikolaus Forkel, *Johann Sebastian Bach* (New York: Da Capo, 1970), pp. 69-71.

[10]Leo Schrade, *Bach—the Conflict Between the Sacred and the Secular* (New York: Da Capo, 1973), p. 60.

[11]Amos Russell Wells, *A Treasure of Hymns* (Boston: W. A. Wilde, 1945), p. 112.

[12]Gill, *Charles Wesley*, p. 108.

[13]Nettl, *Luther and Music*, p. 27.

[14]Andy Park, "Yahweh" (Anaheim, Calif.: Mercy/Vineyard, 1994).

[15]Andy Park, "Yet I Will Praise" (Fort Langley, B.C.: Vineyard Songs Canada, 2001).

[16]Johann Nikolaus Forkel, *Johann Sebastian Bach* (New York: Da Capo, 1970), p. 106.

[17]David G. Fountain, *Isaac Watts Remembered* (Herts., U.K.: Gospel Standard Baptist Trust, 1974).

[18]Matt Redman, conversation with author, Vancouver, B.C., June 22, 2001.

[19]Darrow Miller, *Discipling the Nations* (Seattle, Wash.: YWAM Publishing, n.d.).

[20]Andy Park, "Multiply Your Love" (Fort Langley, B.C.: Vineyard Songs Canada, 2001).

[21]Cecilia Margaret Rudin, *Hymns We Love* (Grand Rapids, Mich.: Singspiration, n.d.), pp. 32-33.

[22]Matt Redman, conversation, June 22, 2001.

[23]Gill, *Charles Wesley*, pp. 207-8.

Appendix 1: The Birth of a Worship Movement

[1]Anscar Chupungco, *Cultural Adaptation of the Liturgy* (New York: Paulist, 1982), p. 16.

[2]Paul Bradshaw, *The Renewal of Sunday Worship*, The Complete Library of Christian Worship (Nashville: Star Song Publishing Group, 1993), 3:208.

[3]Frederick C. Gill, *Charles Wesley, the First Methodist* (London: Ebenezer Baylis & Sons, 1964).

[4]Bradshaw, *Renewal of Sunday Worship*, 3:208.

[5]Bill Jackson, *The Quest for the Radical Middle* (Kenilworth, South Africa: Vineyard International, 1999), p. 29.

[6]Warren Ediger, "Friends (Quakers) Worship Renewal Among the Contemporary Churches," in *The Renewal of Sunday Worship*, The Complete Library of Christian Worship (Nashville: Star Song Publishing, 1993), 3:50.

[7]Carol Wimber, quoted in John Wimber, "Worship: Intimacy with God," in *Worship Conference Resource Material Handbook* (Anaheim, Calif: Mercy Publishing, 1989), p. 5.

[8]Dave Roberts, "Worshipper and Musician," *Christianity and Renewal*, quoted in Bill Jackson, *The Quest for the Radical Middle* (Kenilworth, South Africa: Vineyard International, 1999), p. 45.

[9]Carol Wimber, in Wimber, "Worship: Intimacy with God," p. 5.

[10]Marie Barnett, "Breathe" (Anaheim, Calif.: Mercy/Vineyard, 1995).

[11]Michael and Helen Frye, "Make Your Home in Me" (Hull, U.K.: Vineyard Songs UK/Eire, 1999).

[12]John Wimber, "The Worship Experience," in *Worship Leaders Training Manual* (Anaheim, Calif.: Vineyard Ministries International, 1987), pp. 171-83.

[13]John Wimber, "Worship: Intimacy with God," in *Worship Conference Articles* (Anaheim, Calif.: Mercy Publishing, 1989), pp. 7-8.